YESTERDAY WAS MINE TOMORROW WILL BE YOURS

I made my choices, sure I made my mistakes, but I lived my life with no regrets.

Chris Farmery

ISBN number 978-0-9931237-0-2

I am not aware of any infringement of copyright in respect of the material used in this book but if in any circumstance it has been overlooked I offer my apologies and this will be acknowledged in any further edition.

A donation of 50p will be made to Cancer Research for every book sold.

Published by Peanut 51 Publications
PO Box 1281
Billinghay
Lincoln
LN4 4ZA
acepeanut51@aol.com

All rights reserved. No part of this publication may be reproduced, stored in a retrieval system, or transmitted in any form or by any means - electronic, mechanical, photocopying, recording, or otherwise - without prior permission of the copyright holder except for the purpose of comment or review.

ACKNOWLEDGEMENT
My eternal gratitude to my family for the continued belief in me.

Copyright 2014
Chris Farmery

Contents

1. THE BEST IS YET TO COME — page 8

2. I AM WHAT I AM — page 12

3. THE WORLD I WAS BORN INTO — page 32

4. EARLY YEARS — page 41

5. WHAT DO I KNOW? — page 47

6. COUNTRY WOMEN AT HOME — page 61

7. HIGH DAYS AND HOLIDAYS — page 108

8. POOR SUBSTITUTE — page 170

9. CAN I BE OF SERVICE — page 180

10. NO HORSE AND CARRIAGE — page 192

11. LOST — page 218

12. LIFE TOOK ON A WHOLE NEW MEANING — page 231

Dedication
To my adored daughters
You will be loved by many my darlings
But I have had the privilege of loving you first
No one will ever love you more.
You have given me more happiness
Than I knew existed outside of dreams.
Thank-you for so many Golden years.

My life I owe to my beloved Dad, he gave me life, he was my life. My treasured Gran, I have no doubt that she was the backbone of our family unit, the axis round which we revolved, also my adored Aunt Edna a remarkable lady, between them they looked after me, built my character, guided me, gave me strength of mind, comforted me, were always there for me, they upheld the standards Gran set for us all that were adhered to throughout our lives, not only taught but inspired good manners, to mind our P's & Q's, shaped our moral fibre, very wise, shrewd and wonderful advisers. I know what I owe to them.

What has my life been for? My family, I've loved and treasured my wonderful daughters, precious grandchildren and adored great grandchildren from the moment of birth. I nursed them, protected them, guided them. There are no lessons in parenting but I hope I got it right on my uncertain progress, my wish is that you remember me as the one who always had time for you. No matter how outlandish it seemed at the time, I tried to treat your opinions with respect, helping you find your way in an ever changing world. At the end of a difficult day, I tried to remember that things get better. I hung on to the thought that there were others so perfect that I would not want them to end.

We are not indestructible, there is not endless time to say what's in our hearts, so I leave for you a record of my early life a rich but distant memory. A life so totally different to yours, just as my dad's was totally different to mine, and his was totally different to his mum's.
One thing you must never forget; what we have done in our lifetime, however long ago, has helped to make your world what it is today.

Every person born is a story; from womb to grave we live a tale, I see my story as a success story, a story worth telling, however modest. Images flash through my brain, some happy, some disturbing, memories can play tricks with us, but this is my story, told as I remember it, thousands of wonderful days with heartache and sadness along the way.

I am what I think about when alone, not what I pretend to be in public. I have always suffered from being controlled by my birth sign Pisces, pulled in two directions at once. I have never been rich, in fact I have had periods of near poverty, but I have experienced many things, experienced riches beyond mere money.

By reading this you can share the parts of my life you never knew, but though I have shared a large portion of yours there will be your future I will never know.

The only desperately sad and unhappy event to occur in recent years has been the loss of my beloved Dad. When he died the bottom dropped out of my world, nothing can prepare you for the shock.

The pain was excruciating, what was I going to do without him, the grief rocked my whole existence. Dad had been so dearly loved by all of us; the sense of loss still haunts me.

When I was told I dropped the phone, I collapsed screaming hysterically, the floodgates opened. I simply could not believe it was true; part of me died that day. Seeing him laid there was too much to bear I broke down, crying and repeatedly asking him why he'd left me, why now when he'd been so much better, I loved him I did not want him to go, I'd never felt such pain, but the body that remained after his spirit had slipped away was not my dad.

No one could, nothing would, comfort me or bring my precious dad back. Man or children you love have limitations to bring comfort when you so desperately need it.

I'd lost my safe haven; we shared a very special bond, which lasted from my birth to his death. The one person with whom I could be totally myself. Dad dried my tears with his handkerchief through all the trials and tribulations. As a child we shared many hours, I sat on his knee and shared his dinner, we made things together, he taught me things, many days he took me to work with him. Wherever I lived he drove many miles to visit, quite an undertaking for him, further than he had ever driven before or ever would again.

Saving me from myself, when I lost my way. Providing me with a home to return to when my relationships broke down.

I know sometimes I hurt him with my choices, there's an old saying that springs to mind "they (children) break your arms when they are young, and your heart when they are older", but no matter what I did, he never criticised me, his love for me never wavered, when your kids are involved nothing is too much trouble.

For the next six weeks I was a wreck, life was a living nightmare. Then somewhere in the fog, realisation dawned; my children and grandchildren needed me they were grieving too. His death went to the deepest core of our existence. Slowly I grew stronger, but never a day goes by that I do not think of him. Sad as I am, I strongly believe he's there watching over us. His grandchildren, great grandchildren gave him great joy, how much he would have enjoyed the new additions, a constant source of joy, a symbol of the future, his reborn self is ever our's and their companion, his spirit is in all of us.

Dad had a tough childhood but what a sense of achievement he had. A difficult life as a single parent throughout the years he provided me with a stable home, rearing a balanced, well adjusted daughter. From 1958 he made a living by his own resources, strong willed, answerable to no one. To start from scratch, he wrenched gardens from scrubland, built sheds from any available resources (old doors, packing crates, corrugated sheets etc.) fenced in some areas for an animal or two, Making a modest living from his own wits, the forefather of today's gang masters. A canny dealer of anything and everything, he would turn a pound into two (in his own words - "I bought and sold everything except an elephant"), a more gratifying option than mortgaging your wages for twenty five years to own a central heated brick box of a house identical to all those around, and unstamped by an iota of the owners personality. One of life's characters an hard act to follow.

Being his daughter in financial terms poor, but rich in love, each day of my childhood was sheer magic.

There is no headstone marking a grave
No carved image to his memory
His is a tribute, carried in the heart of me,
His grandchildren and great grandchildren
A memorial of LOVE

Although my future is uncertain. I want to walk on the beach, read, write and paint, have time for myself, do what I want when I want. I have devoted my life to my three girls, four grandsons and two granddaughters, loving them all equally and unconditionally. Now in my Autumn years it's my time, I believe you have to live life for today, tomorrow may be to late. I have so much to look forward to, a million and one things I still want to do. We have but one life, with many things that can restrict us - deteriorating body, slower intellect - so I will contentedly sit in the sun enjoying the space, freedom, simplicity, chewing the cud of youth, finding the earliest years come clearest from the mists of time, a time when all the world was new, each day a voyage of discovery.

I'll still be there for them and my new great - grandchildren, just as I've always been, but they have their own families now. There will still be love, fun and laughter, parties; visits will be many and every day a chance of a holiday in the sun.

I have riches beyond measure. I give to them, my greatest gift LOVE.

Given a choice when my time comes, I want to die by candlelight in my own bedroom, holding the hands of those I love, easing my exit from this life, not lying in sterile sheets in a geriatric ward.

I have no wish to be buried in a cold, dark tomb with a slab of marble to recall my passing. Let me go in a ring of fire, I could not settle in life, so scatter my ashes into the wind that I may drift forever. I have always loved books, so perhaps this book will be my memorial instead. If the love I leave behind me isn't memorial enough, then I do not deserve one anyway.

1. THE BEST IS YET TO COME

**I have loved and now I begin to love more than ever.
Today as yesterday the stars are shining.
Avoid as you would the plague,
Those whose heads are bowed in woe.
Live always as if life were just beginning.**

WHAT IS PROGRESS? The only sort that seems to count today is that which can make life easier for people and give them more happiness - *but does it*. The only life, which seems to be considered important today, is this orgy of materialism, the biggest house, the most possessions, the best holidays, designer clothes, trapped on the treadmill, a nation of shopaholics. We are now living in the age of the machine, lightening men's burden at all stages of life.
Take this morning for instance. You awoke in your own bedroom, stepped out of your bed onto a thick piled fitted carpet, in a warm centrally heated house, going to the bathroom to use the flush toilet, with running hot water to the hand basin. Took your power shower, dressed in your crease resistant, latest fashion clothes. Downstairs, taking your ice-cold milk from the fridge to make your porridge in seconds in the microwave. Mum will run you to school in the car. If not at school, with remote control for your own television, you do not even have to get out of bed to watch round the clock programmes. At school you will use your calculator and computer, with your own mobile phone almost glued to your ear. Mum meanwhile will be at work, but still have to find time to put the dirty laundry in the automatic machine to wash and dry in one step, while she hoovers top to bottom in less than 30mins. Whisk the duster around, plump the pillows and shake the dúvet on the beds. After collecting you from the school gates, or your after school clubs, or childminders, a visit to the supermarket will provide everything needed from basic necessities to luxuries, chemist to photography in one stop. With frozen ready meals, packet sauces, just add boiling water custard, boil in bag, instant mash, cup a soup and ready prepared vegetables, no need to preserve or bake. No pans to scrub, the dishwasher will bring everything to a sparkle. No waiting for dad, eat your meal on a tray in front of the television if not visited the takeaway or fast food outlets. In the evening, chose between more television, videos, D.V.D's, computer games, internet.
We have gained much in terms of physical well-being, of medical

care, of opportunities for travel and cultural enrichment.

BUT: What has happened to our country? Today Britain is less British. National sovereignty sacrificed to Europe. Men no longer open car doors for ladies, walk on the outside of pavements *do they even walk,* give up a seat on trains or buses, doff their hat to ladies, *do they refer to women as ladies,* good manners cost nothing. Mass immigration, little moral guidance from the church. Betrayed by comprehensive education, that deepens class divide? The drain on the welfare system. The world is far from safer, not the wars my Grans generation endured, but riots, international terrorism, suicide bombing fanatics, muggings, gun and knife crime, streets not safe to walk. The constant sprawl of housing estates spreading like fungus, new towns over flood plains. Motorways so everyone can get from A-B faster, all carving our beautiful countryside into ever smaller portions, destroying landscapes and some of our wildest scenery, shaped and moulded over thousands of years. Greater need for water means more villages flooded for reservoirs. More nuclear power stations, lurking to blight our lives, in order to supply the ever increasing need for power for our array of gadgets and appliances. What will the future bring, what happens when Britain disappears under concrete or brick?

WILL YOU: really be better off, financially maybe, but at what cost? True progress is far from being a question of money or perfecting machines. A human being is judged by the way he/she conducts himself during their life. Will you hear the birds singing or the wind blowing in the trees, with your ever-present mobile phone and MP3 player permanently attached to your ear.
Will you play in the fields of clover, - will there be any fields left, make daisy chains or pick armfuls of wild flowers - disappearing due to overuse of insecticides, and intensive farming? enjoy the park, bicycle rides with the wind in your hair, a picnic, a bus or train ride? With more opportunities for travel and cultural enrichment, holidays in exotic locations, will you ever go camping? Are you destined to fly to the moon? No visit to the circus for you, you will see the animals in the wild on safaris.
How will you maintain our heritage, what legacy will you leave? Not simply by preservation of the old, nor mindless imitation, nor destruction of all that's old, but a brave new world of inheritance. The future has much to learn from the past, at some stage along the

journey we ceased to be a society.

When you set off in search of your past you look back over the years, it would be easy to contemplate what might have been. I'm a strong advocate that some guiding force controls our destiny, but your own efforts also shape your life. I firmly believe my ancestors laid the foundations of my life, some people shaped me, developed my tastes, but I built on it, I made me the person I am.

Writing a book of your life can be a disturbing experience, but it is a life worth having lived. Some memories I recall easily, some have become vague, I would like to have them arranged in neat compartments, but I find instead some merge into each other, life connects by haphazard events. A look back at the past means long closed doors must be opened and unpleasant 'sleeping dogs' disturbed. Life gives you enormous opportunities and you don't get them without having to endure some pain. Nothing comes easy. My life until now has been about survival, the practical business of getting through the days, one after another. Abandoned by my mother at eighteen months old. An austere childhood, with none of the modern facilities like electricity and bathrooms. A stepmother I hated. Married with a baby by seventeen, always broke, a single parent at twenty-three. A nervous breakdown that nearly destroyed me. An ectopic pregnancy in 1972 that nearly cost me my life. But throughout the difficult times I concentrated on the really important thing, my family. Throughout my life I have strove to be the best daughter, granddaughter, niece, mum, nana.

I was a normal, average, happy child, prone to shyness. I have not been brave, lack of confidence -a curse - has plagued me all my life, deep seated, impossible to shift. Born I suppose from a lack of security. I have not been beautiful, but I would not necessarily have been happier.
Today people would wring their hands, crying at how deprived we were, the truth is I grew up without any sense of deprivation. We did not know any different, this was our life, it was normality to us. Loving in our family was about sticking together and providing for all, defending to the death.
I find it strange that in the 21st century we excuse a lot of the country's problems on the grounds of poverty. We were poor and life was harsh but in my childhood, we were fed, we were clothed,

we got on with it, life was as simple as that. How could I have known life would be so different in my lifetime? My family taught me values with a high moral code. We were taught to tell the truth, it was better to own up than be caught telling a lie. You didn't touch anything that wasn't yours, if you found anything you handed it in. You were encouraged to believe you were as good as the next, there were richer people, but that didn't make them better than you. Listen to your elders, respect them they were wiser, had lived longer, had learnt the hard way. Thrift was a necessity, "take care of the pennies the pounds will take care of themselves" still holds true. To help those less fortunate than us is our duty, no matter how little we had, something was always found for collections of clothes for flood, earthquakes and famine in other countries - thankfully still mainly true, but now they prefer money, which is a corrupting commodity.

In turn I have tried to instill those ethics into my own family who I hope have enjoyed a better quality of life, than most children today. Happiness is not measured by how much is in bank, we knew what it was to be stony-broke. But I was there for them; they were not latch key kids whose mother was always at work in some high-powered job. Life's not about greed and selfishness, who's got the best house, newest car, goes on the best holidays to the most exotic locations. I got there in the end, I got all those things, granted not the newest, not the best, and not the fastest but enjoy them all the more for the struggle, and brought up three well balanced, happy girls. I don't know that all the trappings of modern life necessarily make it a better life.

Like all good stories, I divide my life into beginning, 1945 - 1968; the middle, late 1969 to end of 1977 I'd rather forget; and the end, which was my new beginning. I fully intended to live happily ever after. The pattern of life is changing all the time, and even if nothing in my life had changed, I can honestly say, being a fighter I still would have come out on top. My life has taught me that now lost secret of being happy on little.

When looking back over the years it is the pleasant things I want to remember the most.

Some people believe, that today is just something that has to be put in for the sake of something better tomorrow, I take one day at a time and know what I want from life.

2. I AM WHAT I AM.

I love Lincolnshire
The land of my birth,
The wide open sky's
The rich fertile soil.

Running with rivers
A spirit of place,
Flying with wild geese
In the Fen's high space.

In snug, warm-stoned towns,
In folds of Wolds deep,
In ancient markets
It still does not sleep.

Through corn and cabbages
Potatoes beet,
Racing like foxes
Escaping a meet.

I love this county
sky, roads Where a keen wind blows,
Bending not breaking
The spirit it grows.

Valerie Venables

I am proud to be at least a 6th generation Lincolnshire Yellow belly, the nickname, given to a born and bred Lincolnshire person.
I still believe Lincolnshire, the second largest of the ancient counties in England, is the loveliest county in England, with its variety of coastline and countryside. The North Sea roars and crashes against some of the finest golden sandy beaches, from flat swampy fens a unique landscape, a place of huge horizons and dramatic skies, to the rolling chalk hills rising to over 150m, affording extensive views to Lincoln Cathedral in the west, the sea to the east and the fens to the south.
Ancient woods that may be the last outposts of the great wildwood that covered Britain after the last ice-age. Meadows grazed by Lincoln Red Shorthorn Cattle, shimmering veins of rivers meander across the county with arteries linking towns and villages, patchwork fields, the richest arable county in the land stretching for mile upon

mile, my spirit stays but my body won't rest.

Every man, so people said, was born into a certain place in society. A farm labourer or shopkeeper, a man of property or a king, but whatever he was, he must remain in the same place all his life. Man was not free and never could be free.

In about 1760 James Watt developed a new type of steam engine with the necessary rotary action that enabled the use of steam engines to become widespread throughout English industry

For as long as could be remembered much of England's farming land had been common land in which the farm worker had a share. The big landowners began to introduce bills into parliament, allowing the enclosure of the common lands. Fences went up around what had been the property of all; the farm worker lost his share and the large farmer had large new tracts of land on which his sheep could graze, and sheep were very profitable, the price of wool was high.

There were many who were rich, the great landowners and the factory owners, but there was much poverty and distress in the farming areas nevertheless a life in a village had a value and earthiness it would be hard to find in villages today.

That you may know your family that's gone before us, throughout this chapter the dead will live again, as I try to tell their stories.

On my dad's side the earliest I have been able to trace is John Rudkin born 1791, when George 111 was on the throne and William Pitt was Tory prime minister. He was my 3x great grandfather. I have no knowledge of where this John was born. It has been passed down through the generations that we are descended from Irish blood, but as yet I have not been able to prove this. I can well believe I am descended from Irish travellers. *If not born a Romany, certainly a Romany by choice.* His parents had settled in the village of Carlby Lincolnshire a huddle of hovels, the kind then thought good enough to house a farm labourer's family. Sewage flowed along the gutters, the stench would be unbelievable, the signs of poverty could be seen everywhere, men, women, and child in rags, children struggling with work to hard for them, lives that were nasty, brutish and short.

Jane Francis was baptised in 1789 to Richard and Sarah at Creeton. In 1828 she married John at Carlby, after his first wife Elizabeth died. Life would have been incredibly tough, from 1815 times were difficult for agriculture there was a general post - war depression in trade and industry, farming prices fell to an extremely low level. This John would miss the recovery through the 1860's, which until 1875 led to prosperity on Britain's farms. 'The Golden Years', came to an end due to the cheap American wheat pouring into Britain. He was buried in Carlby in 1844 aged 50years.

So far only two children have been found from this marriage, William baptized 1831 and John baptized 1833 at Carlby

This John, my great, great grandfather was born during William 1V reign.

In June 1837 Princess Victoria became Queen of England, she had the resources, iron, coal and steel, and the manpower to take the next step forward into an unknown world. Railways criss-crossed the country and stations like cathedrals were built. Poverty and human suffering side by side with wealth and prosperity, great new factories sprang up, built close to coalmines. From these factories poured the iron and steel, the cotton and woollen goods, which made England rich. But in the shadow of the factory chimney, in heavy smoke which created the impenetrable smog lived the millions of men, women and children who worked as much as sixteen hours a day at the benches, furnaces and looms, for an average industrial wage of twenty two shillings and ten pence a week. It's most probable from the age of eleven when his dad died, he would have to do a man's work without even the average man's wage, eight shillings and six pence for an agricultural labourer.

While the rich and famous enjoyed the maiden voyage of S.S. Great Britain on 26th July 1845 or a visit to the 1851 Great Exhibition at Crystal Palace, London, John would have tilled and ploughed the land with considerable toil; by means of rudimentary tools through the years when the harvest in England was poor and the effects of the potato crop failure led to the Irish famine. Inventions in his life had not yet gone beyond a halter slipped over the head of their horse. He married Betsy Ann Richardson in 1861. Betsy Ann was born 1835 in Castle Bytham like her parents John and Sarah Richardson, and grandparents Thomas and Mary Richardson before her. John and Betsy Ann lived in Castle Bytham after their marriage, where thirteen children were born, ranging from Mary Jane the first born in 1858 to Edward born in 1881.

My great grandfather John the second child, born in 1861 in Castle Bytham, was born to honest, god-fearing, hardworking folk.

By 1881 the family were living in Little Bytham. In 1884 John was

23yrs old when his mum died at only 49yrs old, leaving the youngest child only 3 years old, with his Father only 52yrs old dying the following year. He was only fourteen years old when his first son John was born in 1875 to Marie Ellen Sharpe. A further two sons and a daughter were born before he made an honest women of their mother, marrying in 1882. In 1885 they were living in Creeton. 1886 he goes to live in Carlby.

In 1890 following Marie's death he married my Great grandmother Fanny Elizabeth Williams at Long Clawson Leicestershire. Great grandmother who was born in 1869 was by all accounts a remarkable, down to earth woman, with a strong old-fashioned sense of duty; she passed on Victorian virtues to their large family. Daughter of Henry and Mary Anne, granddaughter of Robert and Francis, great granddaughter of William and Elizabeth Williams. Fanny Elizabeth was the first of the Williams, all whom where born at Exton then in the county of Rutland, to leave in over a hundred years. Whilst living at Long Clawson, Fanny Elizabeth gives birth to two daughters, a son named John had been born in 1885.

The years had been good for farmers, but years of distress and hardship for labourers on an average 37½ shillings a week.

How I wish I'd known my great grandfather, I am of the opinion a desire to improve their life drove him to move more and further, than any of his previous generations. I believe its from him I've inherited my gypsy lifestyle cravings.

During 1872 - 1900 over two and a half million acres of arable land were turned over to grass and pasture, vast numbers of sheep were fattened, with great wealth from wool, leading to the potential opportunity to thrive better for those willing and able to become shepherds.

Trading his hard graft, and in all probability acquired skills, including the willingness to work long hours that shepherding entailed. Always seeking to improve his living conditions with a better tied house or an extra ½d. I'm sure he would have been one of the 86,000 members who in 1874 joined the newly formed National Agricultural Labourers Union which saw weekly wages rise to 73shillings a week.

An agricultural labourer all his working life, at thirty years of age, he rises to the post of farm bailiff for Mr. Robert Millington Knowles, lord of the manor who lived at Colston Hall, situated within a park of 50 acres, at Colston Basset, one of Nottinghamshire's prettiest villages with a medieval cross. Another girl, two boys followed by another girl are born, but the two little girls die, both only a few months old.

Michaelmas Day, 29th September was the day that contracts ended between masters and workers. With no employment exchanges, 'hiring' fairs were held where many new working agreements were made. No farmer wished to be accused of stealing another's best workers, so there was a reluctance on the part of farmers to offer employment to men from adjoining farms.

Moving to another parish John is back to being a farm labourer. *What went wrong?* Passing through Shelford, described as a delectable village standing at the open end of a great horseshoe bend of the River Trent, where Sarah Margaret is born, followed by my Gran in 1899. The death of Queen Victoria in 1901seemed to many the end of an age, she had become the symbol of the stability of Britain and Empire. Edward V11, with his glamorous wife Queen Alexandra, brought a different atmosphere to the country, loved and cherished by the people, he carried on enhancing the dignity of the British crown it was the golden period that was to vanish forever at the outbreak of war.

Meanwhile John was moving on to Carlton, Nottinghamshire were another daughter was born that year. Next move in 1902 to Southwell brings another son. In 1903 Mrs. Pankhurst founded the women's social and political union, whose aim was to declare war on society until women's rights were conceded. The suffragette's movement however would have had little effect on Fanny Elizabeth. 1905 sees John in another job, in Bothamsall, now a shepherd again with another son born. Then the last daughter 1907, followed by the last three sons 1909, 1911, 1913 whilst living at North Wheatley.

In 1911the General Election returned a Liberal Government, King George V was crowned, the Official Secrets Act was introduced, MPs voted to receive salaries, strikes took place by railway workers, dockers and miners. The most significant events taking place in our family was whilst the youngest children were being born the older ones were getting married.

Shortly after the birth of the last son, John makes an attempt to escape from the long hours of arduous, grafting slog of poor paid farm work by becoming a publican at the Boat Inn, Hayton. I was to frequent this pub regularly in 1974/5, *one of many coincidences* without then knowing, my family's past connection, until one day Dad told me of a story (which was the catalyst of starting my family history research) of his grandfather having a pig in the outbuildings (now holiday-let cottages). When the pig was sold it didn't like it's new surroundings for some reason, swimming home down the Chesterfield canal, which runs alongside the pub. Today it has been considerably extended at both ends, although the bay windows and upstairs windows remained unchanged, the small canopy over the front door has been extended the length of the old front, the old outbuildings converted to holiday cottages. Beside the canal a pleasing beer garden added to watch the passing holiday boats that have replaced the working boats. That once quite village road the domain of the horse and cart, is now frantic with traffic.

The first world war in 1914 began with such euphoria, changed the whole picture, four long years of trench warfare began, soldiers lived and fought in appalling conditions with a generation marching to it's death. In those days Britannia ruled the waves and Britain's naval force saved the realm from starvation. In 1917, with bully beef, jam made from swedes, black pudding and boiled sheep's head on the menu, a time when the only accessible form of recreation for the working population was the public house. With the population of Hayton at around two hundred, perhaps these were a few years when John and Fanny Elizabeth were in comparison to their earlier life, comfortable.

11th November 1918 the armistice was signed, everything had changed, the way people dressed, thought and lived. The world was tired and sad, the war killed four million men, one out of seven of the marriageable men, injuring many, many more. Two of Gran's brothers are commemorated on a plaque in Hayton Church.

Within a few years poverty and unemployment threatened mankind with endless suffering. Did this along with the war deplete numbers to the point were John could no longer keep the pub?

Employment was next found by John at Charnock Hall, Eckington, Derby.

But, slowly, very slowly indeed, the world recovered. Great changes took place new machinery and methods brought prosperity and improved conditions to the agricultural population. The working classes benefited from shorter working hours, the world was changing more rapidly than it had ever done before. The roaring twenties was one long party for bright rich young, confident, independent women. 'Flappers' and their escorts danced the Charleston, drinking cocktails in nightclubs while listening to jazz.

Food had an American influence with double decker sandwiches and potato crisps. The twenties was an exciting time in which to live but not for our John and Fanny Elizabeth.

Whilst John is back to being a farm labourer at probably one of the last great estates, some of his grown-up son's and daughters are also employed at this large self-contained establishment, that had its own ballroom where people now waltz around the aisles of the supermarket, that's taken its place. The girls were employed amongst the many varied maids, house, sewing, linen, laundry, kitchen, paid about £10 a year. The males most likely gardeners, stable and farm workers earning £1 a week.

Fanny Elizabeth having lived on the edge of poverty, with no advantages except those of fresh air and an uncomplicated way of life, died there in 1928, 'old' and 'done' before sixty (59 years old). Worn out no doubt from the harsh life and giving birth to sixteen children, the youngest only fifteen years old. All of whom were born at home, there was no NHS then, an experienced mother would be fetched from nearby. Husbands were never around for the birth. No drugs either, she had to grin and bear it, just as there was no contraception. She'd been a hard worker keeping her large family, clean and healthy against insurmountable odds. No man would do what was termed 'women's work'. Husbands gave no help with the children, scrubbing or the drudgery of washing, lift a dirty plate or mug from the table, not so much as pick up their own dirty clothes from off the floor, nor empty the 'slop bucket' (from the potty under the bed), in all likelihood the contents of which was theirs.

What happened next is family speculation, facts are sketchy, at some point John worked in the coalmines, he manages to get some money together to become a farmer around 1937 at Tuxford. In his last years, he lives a while with son Charles, by now living and farming at Fillingham, then goes to live with his daughter, my Gran.

John sired twenty children, he died at the workhouse, - today the site of Aldi's supermarket- Lea rd Gainsborough Lincolnshire on 19th March 1949. I was 4yrs old when my great grandfather died. I have no recollection of him, but I wish I had. I have been told he had a wicked sense of humour. After 90years of living what stories, he could have told me.

In 1899 with the Marquis of Salisbury, Conservative prime minister, Violet Annie Rudkin, my Gran was born on 10th August at Shelford, near the end of Queen Victoria's reign John and Fanny's ninth child, sixth daughter.

She was to continue the life of house moving, having at least 6 marital homes. Little is known of Gran's early life, or indeed her parents or grandparents, no boxes full of priceless papers, no drawers full of forgotten keepsakes only snippets of their life handed down by word of mouth. Moving house fairly often they cleared up as they went, never imagining their doings would be of interest to me years later, I also regret that Gran never talked much of her youth, based on hindsight I think they thought there wasn't much interest in a hard cruel regime of, poverty, drudgery, with little schooling, harsh employers or alternative unemployment. Conditions sooner forgotten. I also now realize they regarded themselves as private people there were revelations that would have been embarrassing, things they believed would stay locked away forever and go to the grave with them. But of course we rightly, have access to records, but not feelings, to piece together our ancestors past. I do not sit in judgement on the life they had to make the best of, children born out of wedlock when women had no control of birth control, no money of their own, children, the old and infirm taken into workhouses. Great sacrifices were made to care for their own sick and disabled, as well as aged parents in their declining years, responsibility for illegitimate children was accepted without question, all were embraced in the family unit where possible.

New manufacturing processes created new products. White flour, margarine along with tinned condensed milk was cheap and popular. Biscuits, jam, chocolate and cheese also began to be factory made, often cleaner and purer than those previously available, but of less nutritional value. People mostly bought food day-by-day or even meal-by-meal, fuel was expensive. In towns, the first chains of grocery shops, mainly the new Co-operative retail societies opened, but street traders selling food - muffins, pies, whelks - were still a common sight. Many people had small vegetable plots or were paid partly 'in kind'. One third of the population were poor and undernourished, school medical inspections, and free school meals began.

I don't know if Gran went to school before attending North Wheatley between 1906 - 1912, but she would almost certainly have had to help with her siblings in such a large family. On leaving school at thirteen, she was placed as a maid, in service, to Mr. James John Matthews, farmer at Beckingham. She had a room in the attic, shared with other servants, toiled long hours with one afternoon off a month when she walked the six mile round trip home to see her mum. Mothering Sunday would be eagerly looked forward to, it was the time work eased up a little, a day for family reunions a bright and cheerful day, servant girls took trinkets, flowers or a cake home to mother. It received its name from the fact that, on that Sunday, people in little villages went to the 'mother' church of their parish to offer gifts. It was while working here she met her first husband John James Matthews's brother of her employer. They were married - her sister Daisy (Margaret) the following year - in the local church of her then home village Hayton, in 1917. Gran was 17years old and her husband six years older. Her siblings ranged in age from 4 years to 42 years. The only other thing her marriage certificate throws light on is William Alfred her brother, and Hannah Matthews witnessed the event. How many attended the marriage? Did they have a horse and carriage or did they walk the half-mile down the canal towpath? Did her father bring her along when everyone else was assembled, leading her up the aisle? Did the couple, parents, bridesmaids if any, rush to the house for the traditional line up to receive guests? So frustrating, so many questions with no one to provide the answers.

Gran's first year of marriage was spent at Bole with her in-laws. Their first child Mary was born there.

I can only speculate, that James John as the oldest child had inherited the family farm, as was custom then, brothers and sisters having to make their own way in life.

In 1919 John discovered a higher standard of living could be achieved from employment in engineering at Marshalls, Gainsborough as opposed to farm work, so they found a house to rent joined the population of approximately 20,000, in the exodus of labour flooding into Gainsborough. For the first time in her life she found herself living in a town. Being a typical countrywomen, those years of her life, living in Pleasant Place, hundreds of small houses packed together in yards of the old downtown area, now demolished, must have been especially difficult for her, apart from missing the countryside which I know she loved, tragedy came with a capital T.

She gave birth to her second daughter Doris Minnie, in December 1919, but the child died in February 1921 whilst she was carrying a third daughter Violet, born in October of that year. Then their first son John was born on May 11th 1923 and her husband died on the 29th May. She had the unenviable task of registering the birth and death on the same day.

Only married for four years, she had 5yr old and 2yr old daughters, 18days old son and was still only 24yrs old.

When my Dad was born, Gran's fifth child, second boy, in November 1924, George V was the King until 1936, when Edward V111 the uncrowned king abdicated in favour of his brother George V1. He was given the name Tom, although registered by the family name Matthews, he never knew who his father was. I could be descended from Lord Someone or Other and there may be a fortune out there waiting for me to claim. I'll never know but it's nice to fantasize.

Life and work was hard, their possessions were minimal, their expectations low, yet goodwill to others was abundant, she helped at childbirth, and laid out the dead.

Gran had self-reliance, a heritage of those, who had to face the grind, and get on with it. There was no room for sentimentality in life, rent to pay and food to put on the table for hungry mouths, led to a second marriage in June 1926, to her next door neighbour William Wilkinson, a kindly man, a widower, twice her age, with four children, he had helped her look after her husband in the last months of his life. Her new husband had an older brother Tom who led a more prosperous life with a cobblers and tobacconists shop on Trinity Street.

More tragedy followed, in May of that year she gave birth to their first child a daughter Jean, but she was to die at just 7 months old in January 1927.

Gran was tough, she had to be, life was not kind to her. In January 1928, her mum died aged 59years. She had four children of her own, along with four grown-up stepchildren, William, Alice, Tom, and Emily; moreover she herself was still only 29years old.

Two more children were born in Gainsborough, Geoffrey in January 1929, followed by Edna in May 1930.

The first world war had brought home just how dependant Britain was on imported food - and how unfit the nation was. So now British food production was boosted with the help of subsidies and import restrictions. Cheap meat, wheat and butter from abroad encouraged farmers to specialise even more than before in milk, eggs and vegetables, but researchers found less than half the population could afford a diet for good health. Rickets, T.B., anaemia and physical underdevelopment were common among the poor. School milk and infant welfare clinics were introduced to combat these problems. 'Instant' foods came in - custards, jellies, crisps. Midday dinner consisted of meat and potatoes, a pudding with cup of tea. Eating out became popular with the rich, following the introduction of roadhouses, milk bars and Lyons teahouses.

Around this time William became friends with Mr. James Forrest, who lived in an old wooden caravan on iron wheels, - the kind the road menders lived in - (one can be seen at the Museum Of Lincolnshire Life).
In August 1931 the family lived at Ferry House, Walkeringham *another coincidence that only came to light when I myself went to live in Walkeringham* a little house at the end of Station Rd, by the side of the River Trent just where the ferryman crossed to Walkerith. Now demolished, only odd garden flowers amongst the weeds to mark a family who once resided here.
William junior and Tom senior were by now married, Emily and Alice had live in jobs, Mary, thirteen; Violet, ten; John, eight; with Dad, seven; were enrolled at the old Church School in Grinley Rd, which entailed a two mile walk each way, each day often in winter through huge snow drifts, back then those things were normal. Jeff 2yrs and Edna only 1yr were still at home.
Dad recalled the Trent flooding in 1932, the wettest year recorded, which saw the worst floods for ninety years; they were stranded upstairs for the duration.

In 1933 circumstances changed, Gran became house-keeper to James who rented White House Farm, Low street, Beckingham, (currently called Thistle Farm). *Another coincidence, in 1960 my friend, lived here, employed as a maid renamed home-helps, by the family then residing there.* More suited to the large family, with their six children who still lived at home they moved into this large, rambling house with heavy oak beams. William senior was employed around the farm. Outside the appearance has changed little; two doors on the front are gone, along with the iron railings. At that time it had a stackyard, was surrounded by fields, nowadays a house even stands within the yard. Further fields were rented wherein they grazed cows; work was done by shire horses. Three of the oldest girls married at Beckingham. A last son and daughter were born here too, Robert 1934, Annie 1933
Life was tough for the children, a never-ending round of chores

before and after school, girls had to help around the house, feed the chickens and pigs kept for home use, collect the eggs. Dad, only nine years of age, had to fetch large shire horses (no tractors then) up from the grazing fields, leading horses when too small to have proper control over them. The horses had to be harnessed up even before own breakfast, in winter with freezing hands more often than not with itching red chilblains on fingers and toes. In the hot summer days flies were troublesome to man and beast, suffering damage from the hoofs of a fractious horse was a common problem. Farm vehicles were considered to dangerous to ride on, better control was obtained when walking at the horses head. The farm itself was a never-ending round of gruelling work, unlike a tractor you switch off, the horses had to be fed , groomed, stables mucked out, brasses polished, harness oiled. Ditches had to be cleaned and drained, hedges plashed (cut, branches weaved into gaps to aid growth and thickening), cows to fetch from fields for milking, in winter muck carting (removal of dung) from cattle yards. Growth and harvesting of hay for winter feed, the straw for bedding. Potatoes to set, pick, riddle, store, load and deliver when sold. Dad also told of helping James to lay tar on neighbourhood roads being built.

Nobody thought it would happen twice but in 1939, Germany invaded Poland and the Second World War began and nothing was ever going to be the same again. As supplies ran low, and all money was channelled into the war effort, rationing of soap, clothing, petrol, was introduced which lingered on for several years. In the shops meat, butter, lard, margarine, sugar, tea, cheese - the list was endless - all rationed. Housewives battled to produce palatable meals with the available ingredients , powdered eggs, stale bread, whale steaks, with cod liver oil as extra nourishment for children. The average wage was £3.9s.10d. With the average minimum agricultural wage about £1.75 a week. Prices were outrageous, with a lack of everything including, adequate housing, money and prospects. People queued for clothes, buses and food, even air-raid shelters, moaning about the restrictions. Coupons issued by the government dictated how much you could buy legally. Rationing was supposed to be the great leveller, everyone had the same allowance for food - 1s.10d. worth of meat and two eggs per week, with 4ozs of butter, 4ozs bacon or ham, 12ozs sugar, 1oz of cheese and 2ozs of tea.

Life was tough for ordinary folk, but black racketeering was rife. I have been told this household did not go without; the huge cellar came in useful. War made some people enterprising including James, who was big friends with Christopher's of Lincoln, who did a very brisk trade in horse flesh for food. A well known jingle at the time went,

Christopher's for horse flesh
Bob a pound
Nice and juicy all around.

James became quite prosperous, about 1943 renting a larger farm at Wharton. The family were on the move again. The four children from William's first marriage were married, as was Mary and Violet junior. John was in the army, on discharge he whisked my mother (at that time my dad's girlfriend) away to Bristol - or was it she who whisked him away? Dad continued to live at home and work for James until his marriage, Jeff remained employed by James until James death in 1987, Robert after finishing school continued to work for him for many years, until he got his own farm. Edna went into service for a few weeks before coming to look after me. After leaving school Annie worked at the wig factory in Gainsborough. William senior died in 1946.
I have hazy, shadowy images of visiting the house at Wharton. As I recall there was a hefty beautiful polished mahogany banister that rose up the side of the immense staircase, the farmhouse kitchen contained a substantial *(they would need it)* scrubbed topped pine table. In the huge walk-in pantry off to the side was Grans butter churn, for a bit of money to call her own Gran made butter which along with eggs she took to market to sell. The milk went into the separator which delivered the cream from one of the spouts, which was then churned into butter. A slow, and difficult process in summer, Dad recalled long hours turning the wooden paddles in the glass churn. When ready the butter was divided and squared with wooden pats into one pound weights, each was then marked with your own distinctive patterned roller.
Gran stayed at Wharton until 1951, when following a quarrel Gran came to live with Dad and I. To my knowledge Gran never spoke to James again.

Gran worked early morning to late evening, week in week out, year in year out, the pill had not been invented and she bore a large family, She'd scivvied from the age of fourteen, no doubt before that helping her mum, then did all the thousand and one jobs in her own homes, having four step children.

She knew heartache and poverty; life was hard and unbearably cruel. In 1905 when she was six years old she had lost her little sister Lillian Maud, who was only four years old. She lived through two world wars, in the First World War at fifteen years old she lost her uncle John who served in the 1st/8th battalion Sherwood foresters. He was killed in action at Flanders aged just twenty-one years; he's commemorated at Menin Gate Ypes. In the Second World War two of her brothers fought. Edward served in the 3rd Dragoons and Joseph who was taken a prisoner of war, in the 1st Battalion Lincolnshire regiment. Both are commemorated on a plaque in Hayton church.

At twenty four years old she lost her first husband, two children, and later in life lost an adult daughter who died before her. Then aged fifty two taking over her son's household she looked after me for seven years, continued to watch over me for the next ten years, all without any of today's gadgets that make life easier, but I never saw her cry, never saw her afraid, or complain she accepted life for what it was. Did she have fears, dreams, regrets?

My child hood home to me meant grandma, Gran was our strength, like glue she held us altogether.

From Gran I learnt you could have the best of everything that's important, the best family, the best fun, laughter, the best love, the best life, when HAPPINESS COME'S FROM WITHIN.

The only life, which seems to be considered important today, is this orgy of materialism, the biggest house, the most possessions, the best holidays, designer clothes. Trapped on the treadmill, a nation of shopaholics. For the rest of my life through all the ups and downs, I try to lead my life as if she were beside me. I did not do badly in the end. I like to think she would have been pleased I have found happiness and done well, made the best of what life threw at me and achieved a life she could never have imagined. I miss her just as much today as the day she died. There was great emptiness in my life when Gran died in August 1968.

On April 3rd 1944 Miss Edna Caroline May Holgate in long white dress with three quarter length veil, carrying her bouquet of mixed flowers in the midst of trailing fern, its likely she along with her mum and dad walked from the Maltkins Blyton to Blyton Parish Church to be joined in Holy Matrimony by Rev. Davies to Tom

Matthews. The bride was 18yrs old and the groom was 19yrs old. The best man was his brother Jeffery; youngest sister Annie was bridesmaid along with one of Edna's sisters. The marriage was not to last long.

Dad unhappy working for James, got a job with a tied house, a farm labourer for Sam Skinner. So they set up home at Cold Harbour Cottage on the Blyton aerodrome two miles from the village. Then the aerodrome was operational, so I'm not surprised all that remains of the house today is a chimneystack sticking two fingers to the sky defying the odds. I'm told it was quite scary walking along the edge of the runways when an aeroplane was coming in to land, today the runways are still there, rough, jarring, rutted, eroded pot-holes. The nearest shopping entailed a long walk to the village either to the local shop or to catch a bus into the nearest town, Gainsborough.

Until 1963 I did not know I had a Mother, no one had told me anything, as a matter of fact her name had never been mentioned. In 1956, aged eleven, during an essay entitled Myself, I'd wrote, I live with my Grandma and dad because I have no mum. I do not recall it making me sad; it was just the way it was, but then one day in 1958, something during assembly sparked floods of tears, my friends took me out to a quite place, for the first time ever I sobbed "I haven't got a mum, she's dead".

Not until March 1963 was the truth revealed, as a conversation with my aunt Edna went like this.

"Sit down I have something to tell you" pause, *this is serious.*

"You have a mum" *silence, to take it in,*

"She's just left here and wants to meet you".

"Why have I never been told?"

" Your dad had not wanted you to know, therefore his wishes had to be respected. Now you are married you can make up your own mind."

Because mother had not only left dad, but for her husbands brother she was considered the guilty party, therefore was forbidden from seeing me. Gran had kept in touch with John, after all he was her son, she had visited Bristol to stay with them, likewise they came back to Lincolnshire occasionally.

I'd had two sightings of this woman, now told was my Mother. One sighting took place around 1954; this woman I barely noticed, had called to see Aunt Edna at the same time as I was staying, whilst she was living on Bankside. I was so shy I had run into the bathroom to hide. The other occasion was around 1957, Dad had taken me with him to see Aunt Mary but strangely, as we went often, he ask me to remain in the car he would not be long, I am amazed now, why I did not ask why. Not one for questioning something, as a child I accepted things more easily, I waited as told. Looking around I glanced up to the bedroom widows, to see my cousins with a strange women, I waved to them, then turned away. The conversation brought back to mind both long forgotten incidents, although at the time I had no idea who she was.

My first meeting with mother was April 1963. I travelled by bus down to Bristol alone except for my five months old baby daughter. I was much younger for my age than the street-smart seventeen year olds (even 14 ear olds) of today.

ON REFLECTION I THINK THAT'S THE MOMENT I GREW UP, not leaving school, getting my first job, not getting married or having a baby, but AN UNFAMILIAR WORLD I'D JUST ENTERED.

When I arrived at this noisy, massive, draughty bus station I was absolutely terrified, foolishly I'd left the basic rural world I'd lived in for 17yrs, previously having never been further than Bridlington and never alone except shopping in the then small market town, a place where I knew almost everyone. We no longer live in the immediate vicinity and a few weeks ago sitting in a Gainsborough pub on market day, I could not believe apart from our accompanying friends, we never saw another sole we knew, such has Gainsborough changed.

Fifty years ago people seldom moved far from the area where they were raised you either knew people from school, neighbours or family acquaintances, it really was a small world. Its difficult to appreciate just how enormous the country was back then, everywhere was far from everywhere, only about thirty - forty miles away seemed a considerable distance, anything further was almost foreign.

No one was there to meet me. I had expected to be met by my husband who was already living at mothers, remember there were no mobile phones then and few people had telephones at home, letters had made arrangements. I did not know where I was apart from its name Bristol bus station, surrounded by strangers all dashing about confidently. I sat down on a bench, tears rolled down my face, fears coursing through my mind, what was I going to do, I had no money in my purse and stupidly did not even have an address. I had no idea what these people picking me up looked like, not so much as a photo, Thankfully about twenty minutes later a couple that obviously recognised me, came towards me and introduced themselves, explaining that my husband was at work. A mother I never knew existed until that month whisked me away to their home by car.

Capel road. Lawrence Weston, thankfully not in the city centre. I'd never seen houses built like this the road higher than the front doors. Down the steps we entered the hall with the stairs rising in front of us. Taking the door to the right we entered a large oblong living room with a smell not encountered before and one I'd never forget, a paraffin stove burning, (there was a fireplace but I'm told, paraffin was cheaper than coal). The room was full of my mothers other children, my first meeting with Stan fifteen and half years old, an apprentice to the grocery trade; Eddie almost fifteen yrs, leaving school at Easter; Peter thirteen yrs, introduced as the 'rum' lad; Jean, at secondary school, nearly twelve yrs, a big help around the house; Sandra, who was knitting dolls clothes with all the odd bits of wool, ten yrs; William nearly nine yrs, really interested in his school work; Rose five half yrs, a very quiet child; Edna two and half yrs; last but not least my baby brother Jimmy 'an hand full' at only eighteen months old, only thirteen months older than my daughter Jacqueline; eighteen pairs of eyes silently taking me in.

Cups of tea followed the introductions and pleasantries were exchanged, "how was the journey?" "How were my Gran and Dad?"

Next came a tour of the rest of the house. From this room another door was taken into the dining room, continuing into the kitchen and back to the hall and stairs. Upstairs, eye level with the road, were four bedrooms - one of the back bedrooms was to be ours - plus good use had been made of the attic by placing a bed up there. Mother took me into her room and opened the bottom drawer of a large chest of drawers, she took out a bundle of tissue paper and unwrapped a needle case I had made at school, I recognised it immediately, I hadn't realised it had been spirited away by my Gran all those years ago. I never saw it again, when mother was giving personal possessions away to sons and daughters years later, the only thing I wanted was my own handiwork, I ask her about the little needle case, why? after carefully, lovingly treasuring it, all those years had she no idea were it was.

Over the next weeks long conversations took place. Mother made known her side of the story. I was glad and forever grateful Dad had kept me. I would not have liked growing up with my mother, much less living in a city.

A family I did not know existed was made known. I had introductions to grandparents, aunts, uncles and cousins.

Mother was born On 24th April 1925; To Lillian May and Cyril Gernard Holgate and christened Edna Caroline May.

My Great Granddad James Arthur Holgate was born in 1879 believed to have been Derby; he was 19yrs old when he married the 21yrs old Harriet Elizabeth nee Shotter on 2nd June 1897 at St. Marks Church, Woodhouse, Leeds. He was a hairdresser, his father was a tailor; Harriet's father was a painter.

Their son, my granddad Cyril Gernard was born 17th August 1898 in Bloomfield St, Leeds when Cyril was born James was a tram car conductor, when Cyril marries Lillian May Cox in 1922 his father lives at 57 Curzon St, Derby, both father and son were flour millers.

Lillian's father Willis William Cox was born in 1878 in Lower Swainswick Bath, when he died at 41yrs of age in 1919 he was a general labourer living in Salisbury rd Downend nr Bristol. He left a widow Sarah.

When their daughter Lillian May was born 15th October 1902 they were residing at Baugh farm, Downend. Her father was farm labouring.

Gran and granddad Holgate told me a little of their life. Gran went into service at Westbury-on-trim were she met granddad after he returned from serving in Egypt during the First World War. They later moved to Derby and were married there. Then they returned once more to Salisbury Rd, Downend were mother was born.

Over the years I have pieced together a general picture of the lives of the Holgates, but many questions have to remain unanswered. It would appear that Willis and Sarah Cox bought the house in Downend before his death there, or it is probable that the house was inherited, upon the death of his parents, but that house remained in the family until my grandma died in 1986. Granddad had died in 1981 both died at the house where they had returned to live since 1945.

Although her mum and dad were not living there then, Mother was born in that house, the second child, born to Cyril and Lillian, a daughter Margaret had preceded her in 1923, and three more girls followed, Barbara in 1926, Kathleen 1927and Pauline 1930, then a son Cyril 1932. Mother's earliest memories was living at a farm in Shelley in Huddersfield, which they left around 1932 to join her Holgate grandparents now living at Victoria terrace, Kirton-in-Lindsey, working in the Maltkins. At first living on Dunston Hill, then Cross Street were her dad made and sold ice cream. In 1935 my granddad worked the gold-plated figures on Kirton-Lindsey church clock.

In 1937 they rented Pilham Rectory for a short time until going to live in the Maltkins from where mother married, Shortly after they returned to 30 Salisbury rd Downend, granddad worked at the flour mills and later in cattle food manufacture until he retired in 1963, they remained living there until their deaths.

Living at 4 Station Rd Kirton-in Lindsey, in November 1936 my great grandparents lost a son Basil Douglas only 22years old in a motorcycle accident I went to see his grave, a shield upon a stone cross, it was very sad to think of my great uncle left in a village church yard the only sign of a family that once passed through this village on life's journey.

Presumably my Holgate great grandparents could not remain with the unpleasant memories and moved to live in Leicester, where in 1946 Great Gran died in the Royal Infirmary following a fall at home in Fairfax rd.

Until it was too late, I did not know that great granddad had still been alive in 1964, enjoying his second marriage in Grimsby.

Two pieces of gossip fascinate me I have not been able to prove or disprove one was great grandma was related to Winifred Shotter the actress born in 1904, the other has great granddad coming down in the world through utter recklessness, it's said he owned a row of houses and a pub in Derby before drinking and gambling his fortune away, then going religious.

Grandma and granddad had hundreds of certificates and rosettes adorning the living room walls, marking achievements and paying tribute to the Alsatian pets, which they bred and trained since 1961. They were members of the Alsatian club of Bristol and the German shepherd dog club of Bristol. Winning obedience shows all over the Midlands, Wales and the South of England.

Auntie Barbara gave birth to son Basil in 1947 grandma and granddad adopted him in 1949.

Auntie Margaret unfortunately I was never able to meet she died in March 1949 in Omagh, Ireland where she was living; she left a husband and four children.

Auntie Kathleen married, had six children, then emigrated to Australia shortly after our reunion.

My difficult relationship with my mother was painful to me, we never became that close, we did enjoy some good times, but the missing years could not be repaired. Wasted opportunities to build a mother/daughter relationship, so many things I will never know. If and where did they have a reception after their wedding? How did the war effect it, even, what was the weather like? Was I a good baby? Did you want a boy or a girl, who chose my name and why? Mother's moods could be unpredictable, I often wish at times I could have been a fly on the wall to overhear what my mother truly thought of me. I do not think she ever truly loved me; I have often thought she used me to get back at Dad. Through-out the years John, who was after all my uncle, was my saviour, he showed me more love than my mother ever could. Biologically I inherited some of her traits, but my upbringing meant we were nothing like each other. How things would have been different, if she had raised me.

In a telephone call to my daughter in 2003, Mother made it known that she did not want anything more to do with me. I never really understood what I was supposed to have said or done to cause offence, I would never knowingly hurt anyone. I felt she owed me an explanation, but she refused to speak to me, I was desolate. She gave me up when I was a toddler, choosing love for her brother-in-law, over her child, now she'd turned her back on me again. Sadly mother died in 2006, I found it impossible to go to her funeral, a mother's double rejection is a difficult thing to live with, it had left me with a deep and abiding grief a feeling of being unloved and unwanted by her, when all I ever wanted was a mum.

3. THE WORLD I WAS BORN INTO

Gainsborough 1945
I stood on Thonock's mound that Sabbath morn,
When silver moon and golden haze did blend
To make Trent Vale a scene like Heaven's dawn
Though hunnish bomb and gun did blaze and rend
Me thought the angels wings with music fraught
Did whisper "fear not who this evil wrought"
To kill and maim your kindly English folk
Shall 'ere the year be spent
The Lord of nations comes to this fair land
Lift up your hearts and guides you with his hand
To see beyond the bounteous realm of space
Where yon blue dazzling stars speak to the race
His changeless purpose justice, love and peace -
That pagan hatred lost and crime may cease.
Rev. E. T. Barton. East Stockwith

On 30th August 1944, finding she was pregnant Edna booked into the Gainsborough Maternity Home ready for the birth of their first child. This cost 5 shillings in respect of charges for treatment.

I arrived, one of 372,023 girls and 394,838 boys born that year in the U.K., at 9.10pm on Thursday - child has far to go - 15th March 1945, blue eyes, dark hair, weighing in at eight pounds. A world very different from anything you've known, utterly unrecognisable from the Britain of today. No supermarkets, no central heating but fewer allergies., no lager, no home computers, no vinyl, no CDs or iphones, nor text speak. With corner shops, leaf tea, red telephone boxes, quaint Austin Sevens, Ford Eights, words in full, correct grammar, the first artificial kidney machines, no global warming or global terrorism.
It was also a Britain of smog in the cities, chilblains for children clustering around coal fires, with new fears about the emerging Soviet Union , the atomic bomb, Woodbines (cigarettes) and beers.
My parents and grandparents could not have visualized the massive changes in wealth and material compensation to take place in the next sixty years to revolutionize the land utterly. Was it for the better, did we loose something along the way? I'll leave you to judge.

Britain was looking forward to a return to normal, although it took a decade for prosperity to return.

It is difficult to grasp, how badly Britain had emerged from the horrors of the Second World War, bombed out, shattered, and bankrupt. Public Buildings and private housing a disgrace. Filthy, pitted with shrapnel, windows peeling, cracking, unwashed, steps unswept, gardens untended. Peacetime was difficult to adjust to. Proud men who had engaged in battle for their country returned to living in squalid lets or forced to lodge with in-laws. Demobbed service men were pushed to back of the queue for boring civilian jobs. For a while there was more house-breaking, vandalism and lack of control among boys who grew up without the presence of their fathers, furthermore the returning stranger was resented by children along with wives used to coping alone.

Thankfully the vast majority 'made do and mend' long suffering families struggled on making the best of their circumstances. Suffering the loss of comrades, loved one's, the hardships of war, military discipline, all had made them resilient, resigned, more accepting of their lot in the face of harsh conditions.

Shortages became the norm when the U.S. withdrew aid which hit general supplies. Waiting became something the nation was good at, orderly queues formed for everything. Manners prevailed, Men were 'Mr.' young girls 'Miss'. Gentlemen raised their hats to ladies, walked on the outside edge of pavements, gave up their seats on crowded buses.

On this momentous day in 1909 Gordon Selfridges opened a big shop in Oxford Street, the first blood bank was set up in America in 1937, in 1943 Christopher Columbus returned convinced he had been to India and clothes rationing in Britain came to an end in 1949.

King George VI was the reigning monarch, Clement Attlee the prime minister, with Winston Churchill opposition leader.

The most popular, film 'The Lost Week End', starring Ray Miland; singer 'Perry Como'; song 'Don't Fence Me In'; musical 'Carousel'.

The ballpoint pen went on sale for the first time in Gimbels department store in New York, costing $12.50.

Demob suits for the men, utility clothes for the women to wear, poorly made, loose fitting in scratchy, cheap fabrics. Over in Paris, the fashion trend at Christian Dior had shaped, luxuriant dresses with sloped shoulders.

The heavyweight-boxing champion was Joe Louis, but there was no Grand National, Cricket, Wimbledon, or Rugby winners; British Open Golf, or World Snooker champions; no FA Cup; all cancelled due to war. Eric Lidell, the Scottish Olympian, portrayed in Chariots of Fire, died from a brain tumour in an internment camp in China where he had been a missionary.

A 3 bed roomed house could be bought for £1,320; the average car cost £360, a gallon of petrol 2s; a newspaper 2d, loaf of bread 4 1/2d, with pint of beer 11d.

The average yearly wages £329 with inflation at 8.2%. A 1945-pound is worth just eleven pence today.

The local paper for that week makes fascinating reading. Informing mum and dad a really good assortment of baby clothes, lovely fabrics in pretty pastel colours could be purchased from Elsie Gascoigne in Lord Street. Whilst Wildbores claims to be best for baby. Bombers had everything for baby. In the small ads a nearly new black and cream utility pram cost £6. Whilst a special offer at Harrison's, bought you a utility pram reduced to £7-17-6.

Pinkettes, the liver pill you need, small in size, effective in action at all chemists 1s 5d inc. tax. 'Here's the pain, where's the Sloans' a ligament to kill pain. For the relief of blotchy skin Cubicula Ointment, or Kolynos Denture Powder. For 3s 1 1/2p bottle of Parmint Concentrated Essence could be bought from your local chemist, made up, it claims it brought relief to influenza, coughs, head noises, catarrhal deafness.

Jar of savuree *(what's this?)* was delious on toast or sandwiches the Gainsborough Ind. Co-operative Society Limited, Gainsborough largest grocery and provision services, states 'size isn't everything' …… 'but in some directions it has definite advantages' explaining it enables the wholesale buyer to purchase in larger quantities in turn means larger choices, quicker turnover with consequently, freshness, that's why you should shop at the CO-OP.

Recipes for steamed puddings could be found.

Russell and Russell in Lord St were offering quality utility furniture in pleasing design at board of trade prices with speedy delivery. 4ft oak bedstead with wire mattress £12. 0s. 0d. Choose between kitchen tables with metal top £2. 9s. 1d, or for the wealthy, dark oak dining set £52. 14s. 5p. Goods value £10 needed a deposit of £1.5s with monthly repayments of 10/-. (*How many?*) Chappell pianos in walnut cases (overstrung) bought for £67. 3s. 0d. *(how many of those are still out there?)*

F. E. Fox a registered footwear repairer, urged you to get those boot repairs done for Easter. Coneys the Costumiers were prepared to take as circumstances permit a limited number of alterations; While W. Mannifield repaired any make of cycle speedily, reasonably and with lasting efficiency. Urging you to know the joys of cycling with this little ditty,

'if you take your bike to Mannifield your worries then are ended.

He specially caters for your needs.

You'll ride away contented'.

G.W.Belton was advertised as 'the pen corner', with items for sale from leather goods - toast racks, hair brushes - bibles, and why not 'join our lending library'. Best selection in Gainsborough of sweets, chocolates and confectionery. Open daily <u>and</u> Sunday mornings

Markets reported brisk trade with millable wheat 14s.6p. Cwt; newly calved third calf cows to £52.10s; butter 1s. 5d lb. Wholesale, 1s. 8d lb. Retail, grade A and B eggs 2s. Doz. Retail; potatoes grade A 7s. 3d cwt., carrots 9s. Cwt. wholesale. Stennett, Son and Stevenson at Mart Yard were selling matured pullets 22s. 6d each, Aylesbury drakes 14s. Pigeons 2. 6d, goose eggs 2s each live rabbits to 10s each.

In the small ads everything from Philco radiogram to pure American bronze turkey could be bought. In wanted, we have highest cash paid on the spot for all furniture, carpets etc, you no longer have use for.

Or the more unusual, wanted 10,000 dozen rabbit and hare skins, also buyers of waste rags, brass, copper, lead, scrap iron, horse hair, motor and cycle tubes.

Savings could be deposited at York County Trustee Savings Bank at 8 Beaumont St or another rhyme urged you to buy national savings certificates. Because every 15/- earns you 5/6 in 10years time, savings help to win the war.

'Old King Cole was a wise old soul,

deep in his pocket he dug,

to save more money week by week,

and diddle the Squander Bug.

But for the less wealthy loans could be arranged by M. Goldman, established 38 years or from F. S. Richards, from £2 to £300 without security.

(crime was low) Magistrates imposed a total fine of £5 with five guineas (five pounds five shillings) advocates fee on a Gainsborough man who 'committed a very serious offence' made a false claim of losing his ration book
A Kirton Lindsey man was fined for the theft of sweet coupons.

(everyone did their bit to help others) Thanks to the generosity of the people a substantial amount was raised to provide more aid for prisoners of war.
1s. 3d would admit you to a 'sale of work' being held in the assembly rooms on March 24th organised by the Red Cross
St. Dunstan were organising a house to house collection, for men and women blinded on war service
Letters to the editor page, Lily Boys, county organiser of the W.V.S. reported on knitting for the children in liberated countries, how Dutch parents had been in tears at the relief of seeing their children warmly clad once more, appealing for knitters to continue the good deeds.
The emergency Blood Transfusion Service will be visiting the Technical College, urgently needing volunteers. Anxious that Gainsborough should not fail in this very important task, so that the lives of our men who are wounded on the battlefields of Europe may be saved.
Following a raid on a north midland town a few nights ago, one residential district got a nasty packet of anti-personnel bombs. Within a few minutes the local Salvation Army was busy ministering to the needs of others, rendering splendid assistance. Wherever there is work to do you will find the Salvation Army.
Gainsborough took part in the 'get-you -home service' whereby; volunteers delivered those whose homes are in the villages around Gainsborough and as far afield as Lincoln and Brigg after Rotarians met Servicemen arriving at Retford Station.

The first two pages were dominated by auction sales.
Drewery and Wheeldon (*appear to be the largest auctioneers*) on behalf of Mr.. L. Fenwick, were selling on the premises, Padmoor Lane farm, Upton, live and dead farming stock. 'Duke' black gelding; 'Punch' brown gelding; 83 beasts; 25 pigs; implements; gearing for two horses; wheat straw; the cattle are chiefly Lincoln reds.
At the assembly rooms Gainsborough, a choice of two. Low Wood

farm, Fillingham, what was described as a compact farm. Farmhouse, comprising sitting room, kitchen, back kitchen with copper, pantry, coalhouse. Farm buildings, and an area of 147 acres, 2 roods and 4 perches; or if you wanted a larger home, Gravel Pit farm Kirton Lindsey, a very attractive small farm with 76 acres of rich fertile land of good colour and 37 acres of excellent grazing pasture. The brick and tile dwelling house contains 2 front rooms, front kitchen, back kitchen, pantry, 5 bedrooms, box room. The ample range of buildings provided stable, cowhouse, chaff and chop houses, boiling house, piggery, 4 bay cart shed all in good state of repair.

Also at the forthcoming Gainsborough fair, sale of store cattle and sheep on April 4th, 389 beasts were already entered; meanwhile the four annual sale of pure large black pigs would take place at Manor farm Wharton, for Mr.. J. A. Forrest. *(where my Gran was living).* Looking ahead to May 2nd store cattle and sheep could be bid for at the cattle market.

Rivals, Stennett, Son and Stevenson were instructed by Mr. J. F. and Miss D. W. Gibson to sell by auction on the premises Britannia Mills, Kexby a highly important unreserved dispersal sale of 550 head of utility poultry, housing equipment and appliances, effects of an up-to-date poultry farm, followed by household effects.

Over at Misterton, Mr. R. K. Grice was favoured by Mr. B. Gagg to sell 2 good working horses, 37 home-bred beast, 2 pigs, implements, 20 tons of wheat straw and 200 tons of manure *(how much did that fetch).* At Haxey the following sale was fixed, the modern freehold bungalow known as 'Woodbine' Misterton, modern household furniture and effects being the contents of the residence.

Nottinghamshire War Agricultural Executive Committee were giving a film show and talk 'the chemical control of weeds and insect pests meanwhile Lindsey War Agricultural Executive Committee were holding a lecture by W. S. Mansfield, Esq. Titled 'Old saws and adages in the light of modern knowledge'.

Gainsborough Allotment Holders Association with a membership of nearly 2,000, have again received a consignment of 'a gift of (free) seeds from the British War Relief Society of the United States of America', consisting of peas, beans, beet, carrot, cabbage, lettuce, parsnip, radish, turnip and onions. Distribution is on the basis of membership. *(everyone was encouraged to grow-your-own)*

Public and legal notices stated the onus for the destruction of rats

during threshing of ricks rested with the occupier of the land warning failure to comply would result in a heavy fine, imprisonment or both. *(how many went to prison)?*
Farmers were urged to make every effort to obtain good seed potato at the earliest possible moment, whilst an advert contained a memo to plant potatoes early, 'every farm a better farm'
A.B. Spurr of Sturton - by- Stow was a Lincolnshire distributor, telling all farmers 'perhaps you have not got quite so much as '10 qrts. Per acre', but you might have had if you had used a Fisher Humphries Thresher'.
Ministry of fuel and power warned of Coal supply restrictions, they were intended to keep off the market for the time being, those who have stocks with which to carry on.

One birth was announced, *(my birth never warranted an announcement)* a daughter Susan, on 11th March at the Maternity Home to Mrs. Tarttelin wife of Sgt. Tartelin; Two engagements Bishell - Park, Johnson - Mawdsley; the marriage of Sgt. Moore, Royal Engineers to Alice Gray; deaths of Cowan, Glover, Harrison, Leeman, Reaveley, Tate, Taylor, Young, funeral arrangements no doubt ably taken care of by Marsh's, Wildbores or Walter Hammond. There are numerous acknowledgments, memorials and greetings.

The Grand Theatre and State Super Cinema were showing continuously each evening from 5.45 p.m. with matinees Wed. and Saturday at 2p.m. The Grand put a smile in your eye and a song in your heart with 'Irish eyes are smiling' in Technicolor, with Stewart Granger in 'Madonna of the Seven Moons' the next week. State screening 'The Thief of Bagdad', then the riotous comedy 'Up in Arms' with Danny Kaye and sweet missie, Dinah shore to look forward to.
Meanwhile the Kings Theatre presenting 'The Rotters' promised 'a promise is a promise' good entertainment in the ensuing weeks, with a footnote: -
'you ….the public of Gainsborough …
                    do not take the advantage of this theatre that you should. *(some things never change)*
Such a small town is fortunate to possess one.
If you do not want it to close it's doors.
    THEN IT MUST BE SUPPORTED BY YOU, THE PUBLIC.

Holiday's available, comfortable accommodation with full board 12s per day, near Keswick, Lake District.

Choice of dance's to attend: Tonight dance to the band of the Lincolnshire Regiment at the Drill Hall; Thursday 22nd Melody Makers band at Assembly rooms; Sat 24th R. A. F. band, students union at Technical College; with No. 7 Infantry Battalion Orchestra holding one on 27th at the Assembly Rooms.

At next Tuesdays practise of the Gainsborough Amateur Operatic Society 'Tom Jones' forthcoming production, parts will be allocated.

Sir Sydney Nicholson, M.V.O. Music Dor., Principal of the School of English Church Music, visited the choir of All Saints' Church on Sunday afternoon. In a few complementary remarks he expressed the opinion that Gainsborough was very fortunate in having such a good choir that sang extremely well. Sir Sydney also stressed the importance of church choirs making sure that the words of choral pieces when sang were audible to the congregation.

But while descending the stairs leading from the gallery that afternoon a member of the congregation, Miss F. Maltby fell and received a severe injury to the ankle.

Situations vacant ranged from numerous farmhands wanted; to Head Cook at Ropery road central kitchen; assistant nurse at Foxby Hill Isolation Hospital, salary £55 per annum. Domestic and Companion helps; in good class country hotel, general help wanted, waitress for Cleveland House Hotel *(later doctors surgery);* housekeeper, Queens Hotel Retford; junior clerk for solicitors office; milk delivery roundsman; shop work required a smart clean girl for bakery work; smart boy for fish sales; High School was looking for two instructors to organise swimming instruction to youth clubs.

Teachers, welcomed new salary scales: both heads and assistants felt that there was great danger of lowering the standard of education in the grammar schools, as few would be induced to go to labour of a university education unless the rewards for high qualifications make it worthwhile.

Hospitals were now better staffed as a result of improved conditions in the nursing profession, thanks to the training schemes inaugurated by the Ministry of Labour. With better conditions for nurses, staff problems at hospitals have now largely disappeared. In the early days of the war there was a shortage of trained nurses. The hospitals in the Gainsborough district generally are favoured with matrons who are both capable in their work and also understand staff.

An observer wrote of seeing many windows for over a mile with glaring lights, a splendid target for enemy planes, "do these people imagine the war is over or is it downright indifference? Surely there is a margin between absolute black-out and a glaring light"
Dim-out and lighting -up times on Friday was 7.37p.m. -6.45 a.m., each day, thereafter two minutes later each evening and two minutes earlier each morning.

In Gossip, subjects like these were reported: Trinity like the Britannia cricket club, is a town institution, it has been going for 72 years. Now its fate is in the balance. The directors placing the facts before the public, have made it known that they cannot extend the overdraft, which now stands at the bank against them. As a former Gainsborough man writes 'Gainsborough without Trinity would be unthinkable' wherever football is discussed you will hear of the prowess of Gainsborough Trinity. The lads at the front, who have quickly let their wishes be known, can do little where they are, so it is up to those left behind to do their utmost to keep the flag flying.

A Gainsborough councillor following a visit to an exhibition of Tarran bungalows at Leeds, says, "there is much nonsense talked about pre-fabrication, the public seem to have the idea that a pre-fabricated building will not stand up five minutes". He was greatly impressed not only with the lay-out and modern amenities provided but also with the outside appearance and durability of the whole structure. 'Gainsborough may have to take a supply, if a suitable setting can be found for them, why not?' *(Why not indeed - they served Gainsborough well for 55years)*

Well done Lincolns; marvellous work is being performed by the Lincolns on the western front. One particular battalion occupying a difficult an unusual sector in Holland is earning high praise for its offensive spirit, which is achieving complete domination of the opposing Germany. It has not been easy patrolling through deep and extensive flood waters, waist deep in icy waters, often drowning in deep holes or being blown up by mines and booby-traps beneath the water.

4. EARLY YEARS

It really comes as quite a shock
And dims my rosy glow,
Whene'er I write my date of birth -
It seems so long ago!

It can't be right. It isn't me.
There's something badly wrong.
The years are simply whizzing by
Where once they lingered long.

And deep inside my head and heart
Where no one else can see,
Appearances don't matter much,
For there, I'm simply me.

And if that 'me' has used the years
To love and give and grow,
Then I'll not fuss, for in the end
That's all that counts, you know.
                                Tricia Sturgeon

A further 6 pounds 19 shillings was paid to matron M. Brady when we left twelve days later. The National Health Act did not come into force until 1946, this established a free National Health Service open to all, with voluntary hospitals taken over by the state.
I was born under the star sign Pisces, symbolised by two fishes forever destined to swim in opposite directions, *(that sums me up)*, it should also have made me sensitive, artistic and creative, *(only the sensitive bit was right)*. fond of the countryside, happiest by the sea, escapes into own little world *(all true)* It was the Chinese year of the Cock, giving a quest for knowledge; *(true)* no one gave me a Bloodstone, which would have given me Courage; the planet Neptune gave me my flexibility, intuition, and imagination *(by the ton)*, My virtues were said to be generous, good natured, peaceful, perception, conscientious and trustworthy *(I'll let you be the judge of that)*. As a typical Piscean love is the only thing worth living for, emotional, feminine, loving and loveable, with loads of charm, kindness and sympathy, eager to give and receive affection.
I was baptized Christine (French, follower of /belonging to Christ) Caroline on 13th May 1945 at Blyton Parish Church by Rev. Davies

who had also joined mum and dad in Holy Matrimony.

Just before my first birthday we were on the move, dad took a new job with Jackson's and we settled in a tied cottage at Laughton - living in tied houses, meant the farmer provided a house with the job, the value of, a consideration reflected in the low wages paid, the loss of job meant vacating the house voluntary or you were evicted.

By 1947 - called austerity year - any happiness was not to last. The fighting spirit that had kept the country struggling on from 1939 gave way to a country that became plagued by the despondency of winning a war valiantly, then having to settle for a peacetime that was dreary, impoverished, anything but great. A country at peace but nevertheless under siege.

Living conditions in Britain was growing steadily worse . There was a world food shortage, acutely felt rationing at it's most severe remained a domestic problem. - clothes were rationed until March 1949; the rationing of butter, fats, bacon and meat remained until 1954. Potatoes were on the restricted list for the first time, although I expect dad being a farm worker could obtain them. It was said we were the "worst-fed" country in Western Europe. With two million unemployed, at least dad had a job. Millions were put on short-time working hours, dad suffered too as the ground was frozen for three weeks, which would have made farming difficult, if no alternative jobs could be found around the farm you were sent home, no work, meant no pay.

In that Siberian winter of 1947 The whole country was in the grip of the worst winter for years, the prolonged wintry conditions accompanied by fuel shortages increased the discomfort of the population.

Lincolnshire bore the brunt of some of the coldest weather ever seen in this country, with an easterly wind blowing, everywhere stood cheerless, grey and drab, snow was above the gates and hedges, depressingly the roads with enormous drifts - 20feet high were not unknown- were impassable for weeks. Villages and towns cut off , it seemed like it would never end. Snow hung menacingly from the eaves, icicles some six-foot long hung from the gutters. In March, following a rapid thaw, the floods that followed were the worst recorded in England, serious and devastating, the River Trent burst its right bank between Morton and Walkerith a torrent sweeping along thousands of ton's of earth and millions of gallons of water, flooding an area nearly to Scunthorpe.

Was that what contributed to mother walking out, leaving Dad and I, or was it solely a selfish love for John, her husband's brother. Divorce was out of the question, to avoid the stigma of a broken marriage they set up home in Bristol, and she wasn't able to marry John until 26 years later when there was a change in the law. Mother was 48yrs old when she married John on 3rd October 1973.

Did she ever love me? I have my doubts, how could she give up her child for another man. Did she have any regrets?

Dad never married again, I don't think he ever stopped loving her till the day he died, although they could never have lived together again, to my mind they were totally unsuited.

He was now a single parent. His sister, my aunt Edna came to live with us to look after me and keep house. I retained that bond with my aunt Edna for the rest of my life.

Life was a struggle for dad, farm labouring was physically demanding and badly paid. Long hours, 7am start in summer with an extra half hour in bed in winter. 5pm finish but not always home, harvesting and other busy periods meant many hours of overtime. Ever searching for better conditions - work, housing or both. In April 1948 we moved again, to 17 High St Corringham, a house next door to the local police. Dad didn't hit it off with his new boss, Mr. Johnson of Somerby, he only stayed at this job for 2 weeks, so being a tied house we were on the move again.

My fourth home in three years was now Sturgate dad got a job milking for Les Harris.

Dad told of a very loyal dog he once owned. Working in the hot fields he had removed his jacket, laid it under the hedge and the dog laid there, as it was want to do. Come evening dad returned home, completely forgetting the jacket, the dog was known to go off rabbiting, so he thought no more about it. Next morning the faithful pet was still guarding the jacket.

Life in those days centred around the large black-leaded grate, hot water from back boilers, cooking on the open fire and the only warm room in the house. In order to clean the grate every morning the fender had to be placed to one side to take out the ashes. It was here one morning whilst this was taking place; I tripped over the fender breaking my leg. Whilst living here, with my fertile imagination, probably for the first time, but certainly not the last or only time, I constantly inhabited a make-believe world of my own creation. I understand we lived a long way from any neighbours. Always more at ease in a make-believe world than in the real one, I was quite content to have no companions, except my imaginary friend, she, along with a shopping bag full of bits and pieces I carried, went everywhere with me. I once read somewhere that children's imaginary companions are intriguing, outlandish as they seem are a normal healthy part of childhood and it is said often indicate a child of above average intelligence. *What went wrong.* I might have become a great cook, I had plenty of practise making revolting mud pies. Once I gave aunt Edna a fright when I went missing, after a thorough search I was found asleep in the coal shed.

In 1949 there were still many shortages, but there was a lot to look forward to now that the world was at peace again, conditions could only improve. In May that year it was snowing the day we moved to HBB Cottages, Thonock Lane, bordering the northeast of Gainsborough, 4 miles from the town. Dad must have found the best available at the time because he was to work for Mr. Anyan of Corringham for 9 Years

At first there was still only dad, aunt Edna and I in our house. But I regret I remember nothing of this time, not even being a bridesmaid along with aunt Edna at her best friend Doreen's marriage on November 5th 1949. She married a Ukrainian John Sywulsky, at the Roman Catholic Church in Gains borough. I only have a photograph of this happy occasion, to be aware I existed in that place, at that time, aged 4yrs 7mths, I look cute, one foot peeping out, enclosed in little T bar shoes with button fastening from under my long dress with ribbon waistband. I have a large bow of matching ribbon cascading down my short hair; I stare bewildered at the camera, with fingers nervously clenched in mouth.

By 1951 Aunt Edna was courting and about to get married. They got lodgings in Gainsborough and started their new life. Gran's life with James Forrest at Wharton was ending, so she took over the household. Grans three remaining unmarried children Jeff, Bob and Annie came with her. Aunt Annie also had a son, my cousin Alan who was until his death in 2009 the nearest thing to a little brother I adored him, I'd do anything for him.

Although sketchy my earliest memories begin here. From the road it was the left-hand side of a pair of semi-detached cottages, part of the extensive hamlet of Thonock, were the ruined Hall, once the seat of

Sir Edmund Castell Bacon, the Premier Baronet of England stood in the extensive parkland estate.

A typical estate house with small square windowpanes, externally never altered. Two up and two down, I recall a large kitchen with a large deep white sink, a best front room, two bedrooms and a very large landing upon which stood a double bed.

We had a small front garden, with a lovely old walnut tree overhanging the adjoining large stackyard. An even smaller back yard, we shared with our neighbours. Mr. and Mrs. Bingham, a lovely couple, they had two children, a girl Valerie who was quite a bit older than me with a younger boy Tony. Only just across from the back door was an outside toilet and washhouse.

Uncle Bob, and uncle Jeff would bet on anything, they would even gamble on which of two flies crawling up the wall, would reach the ceiling first. Uncle Jeff was always great fun, he would pull me along on my home made trolley, round and round the garden and the stackyard, until one day he accidentally tipped me into a bed of nettles, I didn't trust him after that.

I had my share of childhood illnesses; the one I remember around this time was measles. My uncles teased me unmercifully, telling me it was really chicken pox, and I should be out in the chicken shed. The more I stamped my feet and protested it was only measles, the more they continued to tease.

Every year when the road menders arrived to repair and renew the A159, they set up base in the stackyard. The mighty steamroller, fired up, steam issuing from every orifice, pulled the heavy old, wooden box caravan living accommodation. Swarthy men reeking of tar from the searing boiler, shovelled the mountains of chippings.

Also in the stackyard stood the smallest bungalow, empty at first, but a family called King, mum, dad and children, Michael, Ken, Gerald, Raymond (Tubby), twin girls Lulu and Layla, occupied it during one summer holiday, until Mr Anyan, dads boss whom Mr. King had come to work for had a better house become available in Aisby, nr. Corringham. How they managed I don't know, they made the best of a bad job, it was great fun while they lived there, and being so many of us we had some great times. Our paths crossed occasionally until a few years ago.

On 6th February 1952, I recall vividly the impact of King

GeorgeV1's death. I was sitting on my dad's knee listening to the radio when the programme was interrupted to say the king had died. Our family were very loyal to the royal family, a picture of the king hung on the wall of the best front room. Dad had tears in his eyes, "it was the end of an era," he said. I did not understand then he had won the confidence and affection of the nation by his courageous example during the war. In 1952 television was available but not to us, we hadn't even got electricity. We gathered around the Bakelite radio the only way we were to receive coverage of the death and the subsequent coronation of Elizabeth 11. It is difficult to appreciate nowadays the impact it was possible to make without pictures, we listened as the service was relayed to the thousands gathered on the streets of London. I was eight years old in June 1953 when the Coronation took place. The queen was crowned amid great splendour, the grandest occasion in the whole decade. Gran took Alan and I to a celebratory Coronation party in a field at Morton, that was a blaze of colour, with Red, White and Blue bunting strung between trees fluttering in the breeze. Individuals waved tiny Union Jacks. There were long trestle tables groaning with food, various mixture of chairs and benches, most likely on loan from the chapel. Feasting commenced amid children's excited chatter, followed by sounds of laughter echoing through the air as children's boisterous play reached a crescendo. Fancy dress and games for every child to participate in closing with the community singing, before finally being presented with a commemorative mug.

If I close my eyes I can still see family gatherings, and hear our laughter ringing from party fun and games. Here my aunts and cousins came home to mum, many's the time we children slept, if that's the right word, top to tale in a double bed, we constantly fought over whose side of the bed we were on and who had the most of the blankets. Along with any visiting aunts and cousins we'd go for long walks down the fields. Along the railway embankment behind the house we'd gather the biggest dog daisies you ever saw, I'd swear they don't grow as large these day's.

Happy memories. Gone forever are those days when people did not burn the candle at both ends, but took time to live, to go for walks and to enjoy the life around them.

5. WHAT DO I KNOW
PRIMARY SCHOOL 1950 - 1956

When I was just a little child upon my Grandma's knee
The world was full of 'What's?' and 'Whys?' -
Or so it seemed to me
Well now I am a Grandma do I know it all at last
No, not a bit - those question marks keep coming thick and fast.

The world's still full of mysteries, and I could go on talking
Of Life - the Universe - Religion - works of Stephen Hawkin.
But more urgent than the scientific studies of Mankind
Are those everyday conundrums that keep puzzling my mind.

Can't people say, 'One penny' and not 'One pea' or 'Pence'?
And to put two Rs in 'Drawring' - does it honestly make sense?
Now why do people feel compelled, at every opportunity
To add apostrophes to signs and think they have impunity?

But the answer to one question there is just no way of knowing
How come I can't remember   Yesterday when I clearly remember Yesteryear.

Mrs M. Davey

About 8.15a.m each morning, I first had to cross the road outside our house, to await the bus, which ran punctual then. It was important to be outside before time or you were left behind. This was a public transport service bus, run to time-tables, bringing into Gainsborough children over eleven years old from the villages to various schools some private and some state, plus workers, shoppers and anyone else who had business in the town. I was the only under eleven on that stretch of road. The alternative school, in the village of Blyton, the opposite way, had no bus to get me there in time. Problems at the bus depot or the weather were the only time I would be late, seldom missing school.

The Lincolnshire Road Car bus was a double - decker. High at the front of the bus, a screen indicated a number with the destination, in our case Gainsborough, at the terminus the driver wound the handle to expose to view each change of destination, Scunthorpe for our return journeys, with accompanying route service number, in our case 101. Entry via a platform at the rear with stairs twisting to the upper deck, with no doors to shut out the cold. Schoolchildren travelled free of charge. A conductor or conductress, in smart uniforms, although known to sit between long stops, always stood up willingly to help young and old alike, the less abled and mums with push-chairs. They had the ability to take your fare standing in the gangway of a jolting bus, while punching you a ticket from a box mechanism slung around their neck, handing you your change, all with a smile. If you was lucky enough to be on board when the ticket rolls started showing the central pink line, indicating the end of the roll, as the conductor put in the new one, you would be offered the remaining several feet, (a useful aid to role play when a child). Buses had seats of cut moquette upholstery, when crowded, standing passengers, gripped leather straps, placed at intervals along a rail suspended from the roof. Notices reminded you not to alight until stationary, with how many standing and sitting passengers were allowed. Now and then a superintendent checking for honesty, would board, anytime, anywhere along the route, calling "tickets please". When wishing to alight, the conductor/conductress rang the bell notifying the driver to stop, placing used tickets in a tiny box near exit.

After the first day when my auntie Edna had taken me to show the way, I was on my own. After getting off the bus where Front street joins Morton Terrace - known as Four Lane Ends - I then had to cross the road to walk to school about half a mile. *Today's children are delivered by car, hardly knowing what legs are for. The car is taken to the post box or shops a couple of yards away.* Passing Morton House, the sizeable home of the Pumfrey family, which stood back in extensive grounds, with a long stretch of stone wall alongside the path. Next came the Lodge; a couple of cottages; the Vicarage; then Beech house; St. Oggs; Brooklyn; Crane house at the entrance to Belvoir Terrace - long gone; then on reaching School house (home of Mr. Plowright the headmaster), finally behind iron railings stood school. We left school at 3.30pm and the bus left Gainsborough at 4pm. I didn't have a watch so I couldn't dally, I returned to the cross roads, waiting on the triangle of green, where stood a wooden signpost, with the front facing the A159, the road to Morton took one side, the road out of Morton took the other. No school friends going my way so I had to do this alone. *Of course there was not as much traffic in those days and we children lived in*

a safer world. I often stared with awe and fascination at Morton house, due to my active imagination I once thought I saw a child stood in the window screaming, imprisoned trying to claw her way out. The mansion became the basis for many of my stories, I used it dynasty style with period balls and hunting parties or Cinderella style with wicked step-mother, deserted except for witches, even derelict with ghosts.
Making his way along between school and the bus stop, on winter evenings I saw the lamp lighter, with his long stick, reaching the individual gas lamps, pressing a lever down, the lights flickered into a dim light.
As the bus pulled away it was darkness, no street lights in the country. With only the buses headlights, it could be a difficult job for the conductress to ring the bell to communicate to the driver where to stop. Most of the bus drivers and clippies (conductors and conductresses) were regulars, worked on the buses for years, who knew their customers, knew were to stop, in really dark nights or thick fog the clippies would, to get a better view go to the front and speak through a little sliding window, to the driver shut in his own cab. But once on the way home, during extremely bad visibility the bus didn't stop till the bottom of Wharton hill, which was much to far. With tears streaming down my face, I had no option but to put one foot in front of the other to make for home, luckily Uncle Jeff happened to be passing, needless to say I was very pleased to see him, I know my dad, his brothers and sisters had to walk much longer distances, but that's just it they had each other, it was very dark, very cold and I was alone.

It can be a lonely life living in the country, no after school friends, no one lived near us - except the few months of the Kings - with the only other children for miles considerably older or younger than you. My school life was very happy though; there I had company of my own age. As I grew older I made friends who met me at the school gates in the mornings, with time, if anyone had any pennies, to spend at the small Co-op shop conveniently next door or the little post-office shop around the corner in Dog and Duck lane. We would buy, a bag of mixed penny selections; lemon crystals; or tub of sherbet with a Liquorish stick to dip; Aniseed balls; Gob-stoppers, which changed colour as they were sucked, so were as often in the hand for inspection as in the mouth for tasting; believe it or not confectionary cigarettes, made to look like the real thing, same size, white with a red tip, complete with the packet, we all puffed away, copying adults; love hearts, sickly sweet pastel coloured heart-shaped tablets, overprinted in red words, coyly offered to the boys with 'be my love', 'I love you', 'kiss me', 'sweetheart'; fruit salads; or best of all my favourites the biggest and best Wagon Wheels, the size of a saucer - *not to be tasted again for 45yrs, till I went to Turkey.*

After a while I had a special friend, I would call for her on the way to school, she lived on the right-hand side at the end of Belvoir Terrace. Often when I arrived she was still in bed, she didn't like getting up and her mum had to call her more than once. When she came down, she grabbed a round of toast and we then had to run, but I don't recall ever being late.

Morton Primary School, then on Front Street, consisted of four rooms stretching in a long oblong, one after the other from the road down to the playground. To get from one classroom to another you went outside along a wooden veranda, which ran the entire length of the entrance side. To the west side of school was a narrow strip of land left for the purpose of allowing extra light into the windows, then considered necessarily high so pupils were not distracted. These were opened and closed by a long wooden pole with a hook on the end. In the middle of the run of classrooms were the cloakroom, coat pegs and washbasins only. To the side of these were a set of open fronted concrete steps, which rose to the headmasters study, the only part of an otherwise single storey building.

Separate blocks of toilets, for boys and girls were outside, across the playground. These water closets connected to mains drainage, consisted of separate cubicles containing a low white bowl with varnished wooden seat, an overhead cistern, full of water worked by a ball and chain to flush, the latter striking you a sharp blow on the back of the head if you left it swinging as you went out. Austere, shiny, stiff toilet paper, hung on a roll at the side. If you wanted to go during lessons you had to put your hand up "Please Miss may I go to the toilet". *This brings to mind a childish joke, teacher says to pupil "Johnnie stand up and say your alphabet" Johnnie starts "A B C" and continues to "Z" omitting P, "where is your P Johnnie" asks teacher, "running down my leg miss".*

Electricity had arrived in the form of one single light at the end of long flex dangling from each ceiling; heating was a pot-bellied stove in each classroom that burned coke.

The day was spent sat at your own desk in the one classroom

organized according to age. Each desk designed to seat a pair of children, were made of wood in metal frames with lift up lids used for storing your books, pencil and crayons, at the front groves for pen or pencil with a holes for removable inkwells, accompanied by a small hard wooden chair for each pupil, also in metal frames. No streaming, no tests until 11+, ranging in size as you progressing through the years, all were in neat rows facing the front where teacher sat in a similar desk but single and high above us.

For best I often wore thick kilts with crisp white blouse, accompanied by a hand knitted cardigan. For school it was navy-blue gymslips - bare legs even in winter, no trousers for girls in those days not even at secondary school - *don't forget the cotton handkerchief to tuck in the pocket - tissues did not exist in my world until about the 1970's,* twin-sets - short sleeve jumper plus matching cardigan - almost always in drab brown or dark green; cream woollen vest; white cotton petticoat with beautiful embroidered edge; always navy blue cotton knickers with elastic banding, that left red circles around the legs. White, turned down ankle socks; together with strong - not much cut away - sandals or shoes with one strap and a button in summer; stout leather lace-up shoes in winter, studded with Blakeys, little metal tips on toes and heels to make them last longer. It was fascinating to watch dad do this, with the cobblers last - a metal three-legged upturned iron foot for different shoe sizes - between his legs, take a handful of sprigs, pop them in his mouth - yet never seemed to swallow them taking them - one by one to hammer into pre-arranged holes. Footwear with worn soles were repaired with a piece of leather cut, shaped, stuck in place. Anything put on inside out, had to be kept that way all day because it was terribly unlucky to change it, a habit difficult to defy. In summer cotton print dresses with peter pan collars were the order of the day. Black plimsolls for P.T. worn indoors on rainy days hung on your coat peg, in a nice little drawstring bag made by yourself, embroidered with your initials.

When very young I had two long plaits with middle parting, tied with lengths of tartan ribbon. Later I had ringlets, which entailed winding sections of hair in strips of rags till my head resembled a cauliflower, sleeping in these all night, brushed out in the morning this achieved the floppy heavy curls to normally straight hair. One unpleasant memory I have, is of the dreaded nits, the female insects lay eggs, which attach to hair near the scalp, hatching eight days later. It did not matter how clean your hair was kept, as most girls like myself had long hair, close contact passed on the horrid creatures. The search began when seen itching my head, it was time to get out the special shampoo, the combing with the very small fine-toothed 'nit comb', with head bent over, cracking them under the thumb as they scurried across an opened newspaper placed on the table, absolute murder when you had long thick hair.

The bottom two classrooms were divided by a partition of glass and wood, this allowed when folded back for a large area used for gatherings necessary for larger numbers when more space was needed, for example when the whole school partook of an activity. Promptly at 9a.m.every child filed into this room, the teachers sat on wooden chairs, children sat cross-legged on the floor to sing hymns, say prayers in compulsory morning assembly, this united pupils and teachers and gave us a distinctive religious culture. Traditional hymn singing had the power to improve children's attitude to school, was at the heart of every child's musical experience. My favourite's being, "Morning Has Broken", "Now Thank We All Our God", "The Lords My Shepherd" and "We Plough The Fields And Scatter". I learned hymns and carols easily and loved singing, always heartily and with sincerity. Music played a large part in our school I loved the simple percussion instruments. Starting with the metal triangle struck with a metal bar; cymbals; then progression to a recorder. I can still manage to play "ding dong bell, pussy's in the well ".

No inter schools activities in those days. The only time we saw pupils from other schools was when we took part in the annual West Lindsey and District Music Festival at the Gainsborough Town Hall, were our voices sang happily to the school pianist, to defend our schools honour.

After assembly the attendance register was taken daily in your classroom, called in alphabetical order of surnames, (sit up straight, arms folded) not a sound except your turn for "yes miss". Mondays we quietly took out our "busy book" a notebook of our own making used for writing stories of anything which interested us, or copied down the weekly poem, multiplication or spelling list chalked on the blackboard, whilst each child came out in turn to pay the weakly dinner money.

Quaint little milk bottles containing one third of a pint of fresh milk, free for each child was delivered to the school each day the glass bottles clattering in the metal crates. The contents of which were taken mid-morning at the first playtime, consumed by the supplied straws the end of which quickly became blocked. Refreshingly cold in winter but with no refrigerators horribly nauseating warm in summer.

At playtimes we children scampered eagerly outside to the playground our games followed through the year by unwritten laws of succession, when spring arrived out came the 'whips and tops', with everyone vying to have the best decorated, drawn yourself with chalks which swirled in colourful patterns as they spun.

Multi-coloured 'marbles' would appear with bags of potters and shooters each player first putting a chosen marble in the chalked ring in the playground then vying to be the champion by knocking all the opponents entries out the circle, the game ending when the circle was empty, the champion gaining a bulging bag of gaudy treasures. When only two players were available, an alternative version was played. The large marble 'chuck' was rolled as far as possible, the opponent made an effort to hit the chuck, when a hit was scored, a smaller marble was your winnings from the chuck's owner.

'Handstands' against the wall, cartwheels, or if really clever, a complete flip over to stand tall again. All without perverts watching as skirts fell over heads and knickers flashed.

'Hopscotch' was played by chalking out a series of squares, starting with your first square no1, squares 2&3 side by side, were placed above, meeting in the middle top of square 1, square 4, again placed above, ½ overlapped squares 2&3, continuing in this pattern 5&6, 7, 8&9, finishing with square 10. A flat stone is thrown into each square in turn, to be retrieved while hopping the whole course there and back, without touching any lines or putting your other foot on the ground. Handicaps could be imposed such as hand on hip or behind your back, then the more difficult, twirl on one or all squares.

'Leapfrog', which I was good at, played in pairs. One child bends to touch their toes, making the arched back higher as the hands are brought higher up the legs, tucking their head well in, while the other child runs to leap over placing two hands on the arched back. Alternate turns were taken or if more than two taking part, (there was no restrictions on how long the row could be), the first leaper taking his place in the line when the last "frog" is cleared, then the first "frog" is next to be the leaper.

'Skipping' individually with your own rope usually a length of clothes-line was popular, performing forwards, backwards, with a partner, how fast or performing certain tasks without breaking rhythm.

Communal skipping was often a long rope owned by school, borrowed, with teachers persuaded to be "turners" each end of the heavy rope, how many children one at a time could join and leave, before stopping the rope. proceedings.

Another we attempted record breaking entries and exits as we **Chanted**

"All in together
Fine and frosty weather
When the wind blows
We all fall out."

'Ball games' were always popular, thrown against the wall to jump over, under one leg, or if really clever round one's back, all whilst continuing to bounce and catch. Rows of girls individually juggled two balls against the wall, three if you were really clever reciting ditties and completing actions.

Chant   **actions, keeping the two balls going**

"One-two, buckle my shoe   reach hand down, whilst rising foot, make out fastening shoe
three-four, knock at the do   simply clench fist and knock imaginary door
five-six, chop the sticks,   replicating striking axe
seven-eight, lay them straight   hand movements to arrange them neat
nine-ten, a big fat hen"   make exaggerated sweep of tummy

"I'm a little girl guide dressed in blue these are the actions I must do, stand at ease, bend the knees, salute to the queen, bow to teacher, turn your back on (here you named whoever you disliked)".

Another rhyming game was 'French Elastic' - two children stand inside a loop of elastic and stretch it into a rectangle round their ankles. A child then jumps in and out of the elastic while chanting.
"Lady, Lady touch the ground

Lady, Lady turn around
Lady, Lady point your toe
Lady, Lady out you go"
Children do not seem to commit to memory these days the traditional chanting rhymes involved in games.
Teachers kept a watch for bullying (the worst I recall was "what's matter cat got your tongue" or the occasional reply to name calling "sticks and stones may break my bones, but words will never hurt me"), or soothed the tears from grazed knees, before the growth of the compensation culture the rough and tumble of cuts, bruises and scrapes were part of growing up. Loners or an occasional idle dreamer were encouraged to join other popular singing action games, Any amount of children performed in groups or teams. 'Nuts in May'; 'Bingo was his name'; 'I sent a letter to my love and on the way I dropped it', a hankie dropped behind some one; 'This is the way I wash my face'; 'Farmers in his den'; 'What's the time, Mr. Wolf'; all played in a circle. Pairs skipped in line to 'oranges and lemons' - two players forming an arch with their arms as the others file through. On the last word of the song, the arch children drop their arms to catch the pair passing through..
Another team game, involved any number of children, all lined against the wall. A chosen child a few feet away starts with their back to the line, frequently looking over the shoulder .The object being to touch the solitary child without being seen advancing, if spotted, name called out, you had to return to base. Taking turns was done diplomatically pointing to each child with a "one, two, three O'Leary, out goes you", or the alternative "dip, dip, dip out goes you".
Then autumn came with it 'conkers', followed by 'sliding and snowballing' as winter arrived.
Other old favourites included 'tag' - a chaser runs after other children and 'tags' them, the person who is touched becomes the chaser. 'British Bulldog' - the first team lines up at the side of the playing area while the other team is dotted in the middle. The first team runs to the other side, trying to avoid those in the middle. Those caught join the catchers.
The beginning of the day, plus the end of playtime was signalled by the ringing of the bell, everybody had to freeze, not a murmur as lines were formed according to your class for marching back indoors.
On rainy days, playtime was taken indoors, with jigsaw puzzles,

beads, plastercine, picture books, crayons and paper, to keep everyone engrossed.

The clanking of big, heavy heat - retaining metal canisters could be heard announcing the arrival of dinner, delivered from a central kitchen in North Warren Road, were it was cooked fresh daily for all the town primary schools. Washing up was done in our own tiny 'wash up' built on the northern extremity of the school. Most children stayed for school dinner in those days. Hands were washed, then we took our places for good, nutritious food enjoyed by all, served up by the dinner ladies. Stews or shepherds pie, always with mashed potatoes and fresh vegetables, puddings and custards, seconds could be requested. My favourites were always puddings, particularly bread and butter and rice, and we had jam to stir in semolina.

I always had the ability to amuse myself, poems and rhymes, I learnt so effortlessly, reading gave me quite and relaxed time, so important when you are shy.
I started in the second room down, reading, writing, with the rules of addition, subtraction, multiplication and division, working with ten's and units, shillings and pennies were all taught.
Advantage was always taken of hot sunny days, chairs were picked up, the large wooden framed blackboard with a rolling canvas was wheeled outside, to enjoy lessons in the sun.
A feature in this class was the nature table, an important start to wildlife; I would scour the area around home for things to contribute. On my daily walk from the bus stop to school, I picked wild flowers that grew in abundance, from the hedgerow that surrounded the allotments (now housing) to take to teacher.
The last period of the morning in vest, knickers and prim soles would be physical training (P.T). Movement to music, transmitted on the school wireless or games with hoops or bean-bags, outside in the playground in all but the very worse weather. This left this classroom empty to prepare for dinners, two small desks placed back-to-back, therefore seating eight at a time. As we progressed through school rounders, (no netball) and vaulting the wooden horse, which is really an extension of leapfrog, over the horse (box) instead of fellow pupils, a bit higher with mats provided for a soft landing or to roll away. Even today, in my minds eye I still see and feel the pleasure I had Country dancing, in foursome's you joined

hands, circled one another, passing each other, weaving in and out, then circling back to back. What a pity today's children seldom if ever enjoy such simple pleasures derived from old England traditions.

I was very fond of my teachers and early schooldays, although formal. Classrooms were not brightly decorated, no cheerful posters or children's work adorned the walls, no day trips or holidays away with school in those days.

With little activity except in the playground the event of the year eagerly awaited, the only event attended by parents, was Sports days, which was always on a glorious hot sunny day. No playing field of our own, so chairs for parents, mats for children, were taken across the road, to an area of field, with lanes marked out. After dinner the fun began, as we walked across to the field in orderly procession. It was all about the team, each child proudly wore its team's coloured (red, yellow, blue and green) sash. 3 points for a win, 2 points for second place and 1 point for a third. Totalled by a teacher at the finish line. Cup for the winning team to be displayed in school till next time. Every child in individual age groups competing. Running; relay; sack race, for which you put your feet into old hessian potato sacks and waddled or jumped towards the winning line; in the potato races, you picked up a row of six, one by one, returning to base each time to place in a bucket; wooden spoons and pot eggs were used in the egg and spoon race; most difficult of all, the three legged race in pairs bound together at the ankles, as best you might, you fell and struggled collapsing in heaps. A day of endless bliss, to be enjoyed by all a day for children to remember and there must be many who still do.

We put our hearts into singing "We Plough The Fields And Scatter" at our harvest festival, still one of my favourite hymns. We marched in single file to the vicar who was stood amongst the corn sheaves, awaiting our wholesome offerings of fancy plaited loaves of bread; fruits and vegetables in small, fancy baskets; a jar of homemade jam or pickle with pretty gingham covers around the neck of the jar; often a child staggering to the front carrying a large marrow stretched across two arms; all home grown produce. Later distributed to the needy people of the village.

Christmas brought carol singing, a time for making paper chains, strips of brightly coloured paper, interlinked and pasted together, cascading in rustling heaps on the floor, along with smudgy calendars and cards as individual as the children.

Next class was the first room nearest to the road, were the basics were improved upon, multiplication tables were chanted, music scales practiced. As a child needlework began with simple sewing lessons progressing from woven raffia mats to kettle/iron holders, these were simply two knitted squares, joined together with loads of padding enclosed to protest fingers from hot handles; next would come the making of your own lovely needle case, two small rectangles of felt were cut, one in white slightly smaller than a coloured one. Folding the two in half, the inner white one held your differing sizes of sewing needles when complete. The two pieces were joined together on the fold, the outer one was embroidered on the front with your initials. Making your own P.E. bag was a work of art, from a few basic stitches it could be as plain or as elaborate as your capabilities. Each child working according to their own ability, how proud we were to take home our efforts, despite uneven stitches or knitted items even with the odd dropped stitch. This teacher although her name alludes me, I always remember had the time and patience to listen to all children eager to tell of weekend activities; family visit's; adventures; all important happening's to a young child, then wrote down in storybooks.

Then progression to the bottom of two rooms that were divided by the partition. Religious studies, the Commonwealth, Saint's days all now added. Up till now writing had been done with pencil, the heavy metal pencil sharpener, a contraption about the size of a can of beans was fixed to the edge of teacher's desk for use by all. Around this point the use of wooden shafted pens were introduced, (no biros) - a length of wood approximately the length of pencils, with a steel nib you dipped into a bottle of blue-black ink - messy blotchy, splattered clothes, with permanent inky fingers - joined up writing was practised and practised until copper plate quality writing was achieved, then as you wrote you used blotting paper which retained the mirror image of your incomprehensible, squidgy work.

I therefore ended my primary school days in the remaining half of the divided classroom, arithmetical problems, understanding written questions, how to set out answers and express ourselves generally, in clear and straightforward language were the order of the day. (No calculators, no computers)

Domestic science was taught in the final year for which we had to walk in crocodile lines around the corner to the Primitive Methodist Chapel where a large room was fitted out, with more than one cooker and large tables. I recall windows were high, in elevated walls, It was more home craft than cooking I cannot recall one lesson. I am not particularly interested in cooking now, is it because that teacher didn't inspire me?

It was also in my final year I became school monitor which entailed distributing the registers to each classroom in the morning, collecting them after marking and returning them to the headmaster for checking. When you started school you were placed in a team, points were allocated for good behaviour, work, attendance etc., the list of points awarded in each classroom was collected Friday afternoon break, and also taken to the headmaster to be entered and totalled on the master chart for the end of term winners cup. This had always been done by the headmaster, once when he was late I thought I'd have a go whilst waiting, I must have impressed him, thereafter I was allowed to do this, but I dare say it was checked again. But I considered it a great honour to be the first child to be allowed this privilege.

One bitterly cold morning, when *I* was 10 yrs old, it was impressed upon the whole class, the solemnity of the occasion, the need for complete silence as we sat our eleven plus exam. The exam was a big deal at that time, it determined whether you got to High School or were consigned to the Secondary Modern, the difference between success and failure in life. But I did not then know the consequences, but I wanted to do well and tried hard.

Many years later I was told I had indeed passed, but the decision was taken that the finances could not cope with the expenses of uniform, extra books, hockey stick and other essentials that being at High School demanded. Higher education had not been readily available so not rated highly in our family, my great grandfather never learnt to read, he could not even sign his name, but marked with a cross. Gran had six years of schooling at most, Dad who left school at fourteen, faired a bit better with nine years although a fair amount of time he would have been absent, (the farming year took precedence over schooling) expectations for me were not high. For girls like me, school was just something compulsory until you were legally old enough to go to work and earn a living. Nevertheless the end of my primary education, ended in what I believed was failure. I always blamed myself thinking the essay paper was my failure. The topic was a train derailment, I knew I wasn't doing a very good job of describing something I'd never seen, or read, or heard of. Today that lack of information still haunts me, which is why I thirst for knowledge and set myself the quest of cultivation and reading with such voracity.

My first school has gone now, demolished by the bulldozers, all that remains is a stone in the wall of the new Co-op supermarket that stands on the site. It stood empty for a long time, when I passed I used to stand and gaze, memories would come flooding back. I'd wish I could buy it and convert it into a bungalow, to live in forever.

Today's pupils have a brand new building on a new site, with it's own playing field attached, central heating and all Mod. Cons. I wonder sixty years from now will someone stand and stare with affectionate memories.

One memory does still haunt me from my primary school years, a vague recollection of a girl losing an eye in an accident involving a pair of scissors. Thankfully today children's scissors are plastic and blunt ended.

SECONDARY MODERN 1956 - 1960

Now four feet five inches tall, with darkish short hair, my eleven plus education as it was then called, began in January 1956, at North County, Secondary Modern, Ropery Rd. Gainsborough. Two large adjacent, Victorian buildings Our block was set back from Ropery Road, with the boy's playground in the front, the smaller block at the rear accommodatating primary children, separated by the well-remembered girls bleak playground. How I hated being compelled to spend a certain amount of time each day in this location, now virtually outgrown our childish games, 'playtime' became a ceaseless hanging around with difficulty finding a corner to shelter from wind or cold. One funny anecdote I recall often lightened the boring outdoor break. Toilets were still an outside building. Boys being boys they would have competitions to see who could pee the highest, great hilarity followed when one managed to sprinkle over the high wall.

Apart from the headmasters study being up a flight of stairs, the building was single storey, shaped like a roman numeral two. Four classrooms, at the outer edges, plus cloakrooms, and entrance/exits, a further three classrooms, one with large N. S. E. W. painted on the floor, were either side of the central hall which consisted of a folding dividing wall, this provided a central space for larger activities. I recall these six classrooms being very light as one side had large windows to the road, the ones on the opposite side of the hall had windows to the rear playground, with both having top-half glass partition windows to the hall.

Taking my brand new satchel, holding my pencil box, a wooden contraption, you slid the lid out, for the first layer containing pencil, pen - now a fountain pen which required you to load occasionally with ink by a process of suction triggered by raising a small lever - rubber and sharpener. Swinging it sideways revealed another layer containing your crayons. (No felt tips then) Exercise and textbooks were handed out and collected, unless being taken for small amounts of homework - hence the satchel.

Throughout life dancing has played a very important part in festivals and celebrations, many of which go back to ancient times of darkness, fear and superstition. Many of the dances were concerned with the death of winter and birth of spring. Here I was introduced to Country dancing, we learned to express feelings through dancing, this I loved, one of the highlights of my time at this school. Usually danced in sets of four, first all holding right hands above the centre, skip clockwise, then change to left hands steps anti-clockwise. You and your opposite number then joined crossed hands swinging round, circled one another back to back, returning to the arch of four, continuing likewise until you had partnered each of the group.

Before this school acquired its own playing fields, we had to walk crocodile fashion a mile each way, up North Marsh road, crossing Morton terrace, continue until turning right at Morton cemetery, on the left hand side just before the railway embankment was a playing field were we changed in a wooden hut for games.

One occurrence that stays in mind, I learnt by heart a poem of many verses, unfortunately before I had my chance to recite it to the whole class, the teacher, whose name escapes me, had to go into hospital to donate one of her kidneys to her twin sister. Three teachers names from that school that I do remember. Mrs. Larratt, nicknamed Moggy Larratt she was a very strict and greatly feared, she brooked no nonsense, ruled with a rod of iron, even toughies trembled at the knees in her presence. She probably retired, when that school ceased to be a secondary school. Mr. Gray and Mr. Little, they transferred to our new school and would remain my teachers throughout my school years.

Two years later, due to the rising population this building became the primary school. Along with children from Scotter, Laughton, Blyton, Corringham and parts of Gainsborough, I was transferred.

At 9a.m. prompt on 7th January 1958 the doors opened to Castle Hills Secondary Modern, - quickly nicknamed "Cassies" - for the first intake of 480 pupils.

This was a whole new kettle of fish, new friends, new subjects, new words and ways; playtime became break, toilets now became cloakrooms. Not to mention the long journey to and from school.

On our first morning I arrived by bus at the school gates on the avenue. Following a walk down the drive, this enormous building loomed before me. Built to accommodate 480 pupils, brand new, modern, steel framed, large open plan staircases rose to light, airy classrooms. A lofty all glass three-story building built on the site of an ancient battleground where King Swegn is said to have been killed, and where his son Cnut was proclaimed King of Denmark.

Wearing our brand new uniform. Grey skirt, four inches below the knee - which all girls soon learnt to roll over at the waist to make them shorter, gold and white striped blouse; royal blue tie with gold stripe; royal blue cardigan; royal blue blazer with school badge; white three quarter length socks; uniform even meant the same black shoes - no heels for every pupil. Summer we wore gold or blue check gingham dresses. Boys wore grey trousers, girls never wore trousers. I for one enjoyed wearing my uniform from the first day till the last. Everyone wore the regulation attire, purchased from the same suppliers there was no difference in quality, so everyone was equal. Kitting out represented a major investment, grants were available to help with the cost, but no one knew who had received these. Everyone was smart, pride in wearing the uniform was instilled throughout the school. Blazers and hats were compulsory at all times between home and school, breaches of policy were taken seriously and punishment meted out.

Gathering, for the first and only time we would use the impressive main entrance, we all felt lost, no one knew where to go, what to do or expect. Collectively we assembled in the hall, with cathedral size windows for a welcome speech by the headmaster, Mr. Underhill. A tour was then conducted in groups, of this, shiny, light, airy, school of ours. The first in the county, that was newly built, specially designed with every modern facility, things I'd never seen, things I'd never used, the only child in school, living with no electricity and only an outside toilet.

On the ground floor at the end of the large hall, were we stood for assembly every day, there was a raised stage, with large lights projecting onto it, and luxurious curtains with dressing rooms and backstage area.

The school had its own kitchen to cook on the premises that morning, divided by a counter from the dining area. You collected a tray, formed an orderly queue to be served by the dinner ladies, (another coincidence, my aunt Joan was one of them) mother hens who knew all the pupils and clucked over their chicks, to serve you your own choice from a selection of fresh, hot food. You paid your money and chose a table, which placed together formed a three penny bit shape, seating eight, set with drinking glass and cutlery, a jug of water placed in the centre of each. If you were lucky, your friends joined you and your table was full, if you weren't quick enough a teacher joined you as they sat and ate with pupils.

A Gymnasium with attached showers, a gigantic cubic vault of polished wood, with every conceivable apparatus. A massive

structure of beams filled the wall of window, swinging out into the room for climbing activities. Following P.E everyone had to take communal showers, invariably cold. I found this compromising and immodest exposure difficult. Thankfully at school you were excused P.E. when "on" as periods were called. It could be used as an excuse to avoid games, but care was needed as teacher kept a record.
Marked out playing fields for track events, football, netball, hockey pitches, hard and grass tennis courts.
Library stocked with rows upon rows of fiction together with books on every conceivable subject, providing a quite area for study.

Fully equipped Science laboratories complete with banks of sinks, including large work surfaces with gas taps. Art rooms contained every possible medium, Metalwork, and Woodwork rooms for the boys. Girls had beautiful laid out Domestic Science rooms, with large tables, new state of the art gas and electric cookers. Barrels of basic ingredients i.e. sugar, flour, dried fruit etc. that was weighed out by the pupils as needed in lessons, fresh ingredients purchased according to that days recipes, small payments made each lesson to cover costs. There was an attached sick room, were any pupil in school feeling off colour was sent to lie down a while, thereby providing small-time nursing skills.

Following our move to Scotter, school mornings I rose at 7.30am, first cycling to the village, prearranged I left my cycle in a ladies garden shed, then walked around to the small local private bus depot, (specifically hired for our school run.) Unlike the earlier days when I was the last pupil to board, with a straight run to school I was now one of the first to board facing a one-hour journey, many children from outlying villages were collected, our route taking us via Scotton, Northorpe, visiting the crossing for one child resident there, then turn around, along the B1205 for a stretch, then back roads to Corringham where we crossed the railway, awaiting the man who operated the always closed gates - no automatic barriers then - arriving at school for 9.45 a.m. The school day ended at 3.45pm so I was seldom home before 5.30pm.

Learning was a serious business, the amount of homework increased. A whole new language, a range of new and varied subjects, with properly trained specialist teachers, swiftly moving to different classrooms for each subject. With no talking on the stairs, in the corridors, reprimand for violation of regulations was followed by conduct marks, lines, detentions. Truancy, vandalism and graffiti were unknown. No longer was a desk allocated to you, free to choose your own, each and every lesson, no chattering in assembly, or lessons, only speaking if spoken too. The days were divided into periods, two taken before mid morning break, one more before dinner, again two before afternoon break, one further before hometime. Each period a different subject was taken, over the week, four lessons each of Geography; History; Maths; English; the Sciences, Biology and Physics; the exceptions being Needlework, with use of the sewing machine introduced, and Domestic Science, both given a whole morning each. R.K. (Religious Knowledge) only rated one period; Mrs. Jennings took us for Games and P.E. (physical education) twice a week. Gradually satchels became obsolete along with the wooden pencil case. Nylon rucksacks became the cool new way to carry everything from books to P.E. kit to cookery. Plastic tubular cases with a zip, now held your pens, along with persplex protractor and set square. Each pupil was allocated a locker, (no locks needed - nothing of value was brought into school, no I-pods, calculators, mobile phones, designer gear) used for anything and everything between lessons and not needed at home. Exercise books were neatly covered in scraps of wallpaper, to brighten, and allow easy identification quickly, as they were changed between lessons. Even the blackboards were different, no longer free standing, each one was fixed to the wall, often upon entering a classroom a view of the previous lesson could be glimpsed before erasure took place to begin again. Desks resembled tables no longer having lift up lids.

The class you had been allocated had been based on reports from your previous school. No more all one age group together, for the first time we became acutely aware of competition and selection, placed in one of three streams from the highest A, to C, giving pupils chance to progress at their own pace best suited to them. I was to go into A group. I wasn't the cleverest but I wasn't bottom of the class either, in exams my position in each subject remained consistent, hovering around eleventh to twenty eighth in classes of thirty pupils. Term mark ranged from C+ just above satisfactory to a creditable B, rated good. Points were awarded for subject work, sports results even good manners, these went towards your allocated House, counted for silver cups on Open Day. My House was Kenilworth; the other three were Conway, Edinburgh, and Warwick all chosen aptly because they were castles.

I didn't enjoy P.E. at all. Reports range from showing an early interest; deteriorating to "not enough effort made" finally "weak, makes very little effort" I hadn't had much chance to be a team player, so Netball left me cold. Hockey I hated, being bashed around the shins by a stick didn't hold any attraction for me. Tennis with white primsoles that needed whitening before each games lesson wasn't too bad, but I never managed to get the hang of scoring.

Never very physical - races, hop, skip and jump; long jump; high jump; javelin and discus throwing, none appealed to me - I never had aspirations to be the first over the line, highest or longest. As for long distance running, round "Big Belt" (turn left at school gates, turn right joining the Belt road, proceed to Corringham road turning right again, continue until on the right hand side you encounter The Avenue, bringing you back to school gates) how boring can you get? Why run when you can walk and take in the wildlife, also while lingering you could chat to like -minded dawdlers and miss something equally hated back at school. The one thing we didn't have was a swimming pool. Although I'd never had the chance early in life, when I did learn to swim years later I thoroughly enjoyed it, and maybe just maybe that was were in sports I might have excelled. We'll never know. At primary school I had found vaulting the wooden horse easy and enjoyable, but now in the Gym, everything was bigger and higher and not so easy or maybe I'd just become lazy. I never got the hang of climbing the rope, try as I might I just could not do it. I was quite good at floor gymnastics and balance on the beam. I must admit that I am by nature a timid person, cautious, and easily scared. Filled with admiration for those who are fearless, will have a go at anything, and pick-up things easily.

All the teachers loved their chosen subjects, they were strict but we respected them. Mr. Gray our old teacher from Ropery, was a fascinating teacher, he took us for Physics which enthralled me, all those experiments, bubbling liquids in test tubes. He took the time to explain things so you understood, pushing me into a very good position in class, but exam results were always disappointing, attentive as I may be in the classroom, enthusiasm was no substitute for ability to remember facts, memory failing me every time.

Magnification of soil samples taken from Scotter and school, in experiments in Biology, led to results determining profile types.

School soil being clay, Scotter soil revealed slightly clay but high percentage of sand. I struggled to keep up with osmosis, food storage organs, transpiration, photosynthesis of plants, strange words leaving me with my lowest marks in any subject, at best C+ worst D - with a scattering of "see me's ". I faired better with fruit and seed dispersal; amoeba; recognition of pond plants; non flowering plants such as seaweed, mosses, ferns, bracken, lichen, toadstools; along with birds, this was closer to nature as I knew it, this was all around me. All things creepy crawly, earthworms, millipede, centipedes, wood lice, slugs and snails, I had great fun seeking these out for examination. Next followed human biology, if I was bad at all that plant theory, this was worse. The organs of the human body were an easy start, but bone structure, the skull, joints, skeleton, too many long words, how many vertebrae? just not interested. However on hygiene I received a B*merit, with an A+ for my plans of a bungalow for one child and parents.

I particularly liked Art, in or out of school I spent many hours drawing or painting. Making the most progress, rising from C to C+ to B, comments ranged from "should do well" to "careful craft work" Numerous times we were allowed out for lessons, to sit - where the Leisure Centre now stands - and sketch. The view over the old railway gave many opportunities. If old sketches had been saved, how would today's view compare? In year four exams, from the list of subjects given I chose gypsies, towards the end of the period I became dissatisfied with my painting, dipped the paintbrush in the murky water and washed over the paper. Next lesson, the results were read out by the art teacher, Mrs. Brown, in reverse order. As was usual my name was not the first called, my first thought was "that makes a change" after the next few names continued to be read, with no mention of me, my next thoughts were "I'm in trouble at the end of class " expecting to be told off for not making an effort etc, etc. I sat terrified, head down, ashamed, drifting into a world of my own, only to be brought back to reality upon hearing "Christine Matthews receives first place for her remarkable gypsy painting, the smoke effect is so realistic". I could not take it in, sadly it was to be my first and last great artistic work of art, unfortunately I was never given the great masterpiece.

Domestic Science, I was a meticulous student, paid attention to detail, measured accurately, but was heavy handed and lacked the necessary flair, marks remained at B throughout. To this day I am a very basic cook, I can't abide the mess. Needless to say I enjoyed everything I made, if it was something sweet like cake or biscuits by the time I got home there was only a very small portion for dad and gran to taste. If it was savoury it arrived home for general eating I don't recall anything being refused or not eaten. A couple of early lessons were given over to nutrition, metabolism, calorific values, digestion that sort of thing. The very first lesson was spent impressing the importance of how to look after yourself from hair care to nails and cuticles. A visit was made to Mr. Therms Home Comfort Exhibition on 11th March 1959. Organised by the East Midlands Gas Board, demonstrations included, the use of a gas cooker, use of a gas washing machine, how to make a fruit flan, cook fish cakes, with tasting of fish cakes, Heinz soup, and a free bottle of Coca-Cola. A selection of gas appliances were displayed, cookers, from £23.18.6d - £68.16.0d; refrigerators, cheapest £29.19.6d - £63.3.8d; water heaters average £14; with washing machines ranging from £20.13.8d to the super servis at £70.0.0d, which could be yours for £7 deposit with 11 quarter payments of £6.17.2d.

Needlework I never got a mark above C+, but was consistent with my C's, despite my many hours of sewing at home, I failed to meet the standard required "must try to raise her standards", "inaccurate" the comments made. Were the other girls remarkably good, certainly a number exhibited garments made, at a fashion show on 18th March 1959. Two of my class mates paraded, Angela Wheeldon showed pyjamas in 'Dayellon', cost 5/11d per yard, with Margaret Winter in a bouffant dress in Ferguson's 'Derwent' at approx. 6/11d per yard

English one of my favourite subjects I worked hard at, making the most progress in. In my first term I was seventeenth out of thirty, finishing second out of thirty-seven in my last year. I had a vivid imagination, so produced good essays and was a good storyteller, as my cousins would testify, I always kept them enthralled. Years later the computer has made life easier for me, written work was for me the hardest, my brain always appeared to work faster than my hand. I had pages of scribbles with inserted words and arrows moving paragraphs, until the whole was something only I could read. I then had to rewrite the whole to make it presentable. A very good piece of work I did was an account of an author's life. I chose Charles

Dicken's, extra's included drawing a picture of him, listing his books, finishing with a synopsis of his first book, Oliver Twist.
Words fascinated me and still do, I attempt the daily paper crossword most days, if I miss, I save to do another day. I was good at spelling, average at grammar and I had a remarkable good memory for learning a poem, hymn or song I liked. My number one poems were "Hiawatha", "Old Meg She Was A Gypsy", and "I wish I lived In A Caravan" all of which I can still recite all the way through. I could read for England, everything I could lay my hands on, even the proverbial corn flakes packet on the breakfast table, over and over. *Just in case it was changed you understand.* Although there was a town library, at this age I did not know this, but living in the country in those days would not have given me much chance to visit. The library at school was just waiting to be discovered, opening up a whole new world for me, a world filled with revelations, giving me my first chance to borrow interesting books, until then I'd only had family to bring me a book that would make a valued present.

Geography was my preferred subject, each lesson eagerly awaited, my exercise books being littered with A's. The study of our lives in the world, our country, county, town or village along with the people and things in that world. Here we started with how to read maps, making a scale layout of school and grounds.
Moving on I did a project on Gainsborough, being very proud of Our Town. A place of endless interest and delight.

Just after the year 1,000, Swegn, King of Denmark, sailed up the River Trent, to land at Gainsborough. When Swegn was killed by King Ethelred, Canute was forced to flee. In 1086 the Doomsday book records that the Saxon landowner, Ledwin, was dispossessed with the lands of Gainsborough given to the Norman, Geoffrey De. Wirce. Gainsborough was the scene of several battles during the Civil War and changed hands several times.
The Trent the mainstay of Gainsborough's existence is the third largest river in Britain. It rises in North Staffordshire 1100 feet above sea level, of its 200 miles length, 52 miles are tidal. The latter has been its greatest asset carrying shipping and merchandise sixty miles into the Midlands. River craft of all kinds sailed the Trent, from the coracles of the Roman's, the Danes who came in their dragon ships, three masted sailing schooners, small one sail open

trading boats, steamships, barques, brigs, keels, barges, and sloops were seen in the river until the First World War. As a major river-trading centre through the 17th century it grew as a river port, the river frontage of quays and warehouses making Gainsborough, Britain's most inland port. Many industries flourished, including malting's; rope works, Ropery road a reminder of this industry; milling; a thriving hub of the engineering world, agricultural and packaging, Rose Bros. making wrapping machines for cigarette packets, sweets and razor blades, during the second world war, one of the major munitions factories in the country, continuing until the building of the railways in 1849, saw river traffic and cargoes decline. Now, can be seen passing boats of 800-950 tonnage, carrying oil.

A local phenomenon of considerable interest was the tidal bore, known as the Aegir. Twice daily it comes from the lower reaches of the Trent, achieving a height of several feet, but somewhat diminished since the serious floods of 1947.

Gainsborough greatest architectural building a late mediaeval Manor house is the Old Hall. Much of the house was built by St Thomas Burgh, in the late 15th century. He lived there from about 1433 to 1496. King Richard 111 was entertained there in 1483. Henry V111 stayed at the hall twice, meeting his last wife Katherine Parr there. In 1596, the 5th Lord Burgh sold the hall to William Hickman, a London merchant who resided until 1720, when they moved to a newly built house at Thonock. In 1970, the owner, Sir Edmund C. Bacon, generously gave the building to the nation.

In the 18th century John Wesley is known to have preached both inside and out. Gainsborough also had strong connections with the Pilgrim Fathers, the Puritans who left England for America.

Henry 111 in 1242, licensed the first recorded fair, then Edward 1 granted another license in 1292 for a fair around All Saints' Parish Church, but these were discontinued before a grant for two fairs or marts was given for Monday, Tuesday, and Wednesday in Easter Week. Followed by October 10th and 11th, granted by Queen Elizabeth 1 in February 1592. Each increased to nine days by Charles 1 in 1637. In 1818 the first annual cheese fair was held, at the October mart, five years later, in June, an annual wool fair was introduced. Gainsborough fat cattle market was first recorded in May 1799.

Catapulting my mind back in time to scenes long ago I see, standing outside Elm Cottage. the old horse trough, once a common feature as it was essential to provide frequent supplies of drinking water for horses. Behind the Elm Cottage stood the Gas works supplying the town with its own supply before the introduction of a national grid supply system, with the gasometer tanks that always delivered a strong smell of the stored town gas.

As expected we moved on to our beloved county of Lincolnshire, which I think is the loveliest county in England, with its variety of coastline and rich fertile countryside fields of corn, cabbages, potatoes, and beet stretching as far as the eye can see. Savagely the North Sea roars against the sandy shore, from hills on high to flat fens where keen winds blow, meandering rivers large and small, ponds reflecting wide open sky. Roads like lines of stitching link ancient markets towns and sleepy villages. Off the beaten track lies woodland full of delights. The wild geese fly on high, cows graze on rich pasture and foxes prowl on moonlight nights.

Then logically following on, the Great British Isles. Getting to know your country included the physical landscape, many kinds of rocks that make our scenery so varied, so much beauty in such a small space. The South Wales coalfields; textile factories in the Pennines; seaports, with for some now unknown reason even the shipping forecasts.

Going on to study the world at large, populations, capitals, area, climate, vegetation and crops; from New Zealand wool and lamb; South American cotton; Canadian wheat; to sugar canes in Australia; to India's tea plantations. Followed by Africa, Sweden, Ghana, Spain, Poland, Ireland, Burma among others. Lots of free literature could be sent for from each country Embassy. We were encouraged to draw pictures, adding postage stamps, tea cards, or: eating an orange, the little stickers from each, stating country of origin we saved to illustrate our work as were labels collected from tins of fruit etc. No wonder my exam results rose from twenty-seventh to tenth. This gave me a desire to one-day travel, to all those strange faraway countries.

A subject taken occasionally, Current Affairs was a different matter. I loathed it. I knew the country was governed by the Queens 'ministers', who were chosen from among M.P.s whom everyone over the age of 21years was allowed via voting to elect to parliament. The sovereign, head of the 'family' of nations that made up the British Commonwealth never acted against their advice. Ever since Alfred's time our country was united, Wales, Scotland and

Ireland were joined to form the 'United Kingdom'. The teacher asked a question and chose a pupil to answer, I lived in constant fear of being chosen. I did not know who was current Chancellor of the Exchequer, my world revolved around who was head of our family. We had no daily newspaper and the radio was used sparingly it wasn't considered something to waste the battery of. This probably accounts for why I now read the paper so avidly and like to hear the news at least once a day.

Ballroom Dancing - replaced my country dancing and how I missed it - was limited to a few lessons for the first few terms and I never got the hang of it, I was the child that needed lots of practice, and repetition, to remember new things. I appeared to have two left feet, and was always self-conscious, and painfully shy.

Drama produced the same feelings; I could not show my true potential, which was definitely there. In private at home, left to my own musings in scenes where I was the chief actress, I gave some remarkable performances. I had difficulty expressing myself in front of strangers, I was afraid of being laughed at, a sense of failure always lurked.

But when I was sure of myself I could command remarkable feats, like morning assemblies, I was confident enough to stand on the stage in front of the whole school and do the mornings reading from the bible. I loved assembly and hymns, the beautiful language of religious devotion with music that could truly touch the soul. I sang heartily, some of my favourites being "There is a Green Hill Far Away", "The Lord's My Shepherd" and "All Things Bright And Beautiful".

R.K. Religious Knowledge was taken weekly, probably the last generation for whom Christian traditions formed a central part of our education. We had bible readings, which entered our brains even if we thought we weren't listening, their message remains. Thereby enriching our lives, helping us understand our past, teaching us who we are and who we have been.

Mr. Skepper who taught history said, "I was a good worker", twenty-sixth position that year; "A trier, with disappointing exam results", twenty-eighth position; rising to twenty-second position, "worked well, showing considerable improvement" in third year. A

difficult subject for me when at school, it was all jumbled up, disjointed, out of order, with no connection between one time and another, it did not fit a pattern. I really hated all those dates, so boring - the Saxons; Danes; Normans; medieval; 1066 and all that, meant nothing to me. At point in life, yesterday meant nothing.
In 1985 I became interested in my family history and the further back I got, the more interested I became in history. If lessons had started with me and worked backwards I think it would have been more beneficial. Now I know were it all fits into the scheme of things.

Mathematics to give it it's full title, "shows an interest in", "worked well (in class) deserves a better result (exam)", achieving my highest term mark of my school life, a B+ in maths in my final year. I was good at Maths, except mental arithmetic, to this day, remembrance of numbers elude me, telephone-even my own bank a/c nos., all has to be looked up when needed. Calendar has to be checked daily for birthdays, and important appointments. Give me a pen and paper though and my books testify I could work out with accuracy the most complicated arithmetic, going on, in later years to pass my accountancy exams with credit.

In music I showed an early interest "could do quite well", progressing to "I think she could do even better". I desperately wanted to play the piano, but on trial I was obviously no good, as I never received lessons. Although I never learnt to read music, learning by rote, I did play, the violin in the orchestra for a time having recollections of playing at a school concert. But what went wrong? Year three "not always at her best".

Clubs and societies were started. Not more than four could be joined, 6d. per club, per term. On offer, discoveries, drama, puppetry, sketching, photography, dancing, stamps, chess, also sports from Athletics to Table tennis. One activity, which met during lunch breaks, I did join and completely enjoyed. Unfortunately after two editions, summer and autumn, the decision was made to move the magazine group like the rest, to after school hours, it became out of range for country folk like me to benefit (no buses out of school hours from school to home, no parents to deliver and collect from out of school activities). Reports of educational visits; club activities; quiz's; puzzle; jokes, one of my contributions, Q. Why is

74

a policeman the strongest man in the world? A. Because he can hold up a line of traffic. *Corny or what?* Riddles; stories; and poetry were all included, for a cost of sixpence an issue. My responsibility in the second issue was the diary.

Another novelty was the tuck-shop opened 10minutes each break, selling pop, crisps and chocolate, tucked under the stairs, run by the pupils for the pupils.
Breaks had to be taken outside - with prefects patrolling corridors to make sure - hanging around the playground, or use could be made of the playing field in good weather. We lay on the grass in groups discussing television programmes, like 'Oh Boy', or out of school activities. New music for teens with teen magazines, started to play a part in our lives; dialogue centred on who was the most gorgeous, both in real life, stage or screen. My scrap-book was littered with cut out pictures from Musical Express, which was now bought weekly for me. Cliff Richard, Tommy Steele who had his first hit in 1956, Paul Anka who had a big hit with Diana, when he was only fifteen, along with Brenda Lee who first came to fame at twelve. Favourite film stars included James Dean, Marlon Brando, my favourite at the time being Rock Hudson. At an age when hormones were raging, most knew very little about sex, intensely fascinated with boys, some did brag about a 'snog' with hands slipped under jumpers, or roving under skirts to the 'laughing gap' (so called by boys who boasted if they got to the bare flesh beyond the stocking top they were laughing), discussions included who was supposed to be doing it, who wanted to be doing it, but I doubt if anyone really knew what 'it' was. Some girls with boyfriends (at same school) took advantage of being together at breaks to lie kissing and cuddling. I had a crush on Peter Drewery who I named as my bridegroom in an imaginary newspaper report we had to write for an English lesson. We were married by the Bishop of Lincoln; the hymn sung was "Love Divine All Love Excelling", the bishop reading Matthew chapter fourteen, verses eleven to fourteen. *I wonder where he is now and what he would make of this confession?* The group I hung around with consisted of Jacky Cooke, Joyce Parish, Christine Hancock, Christine whose father was in the forces, went to live in Aden, leaving me a spare. This made things difficult as anything with partners produced long-term friends Jackie and Joyce. In team games, always the dregs I was the last person left for the unlucky squad. I was always the outsider, I longed with all my

heart to be accepted to be part of the whole group, leaving me with feelings of being tolerated rather than accepted, a terrible fear of rejection, inadequacy which lasted till old age, I now realise I was a victim of my own fears, the workings of the young mind, often unreasonable and illogical to the mind of an adult. The hopes and disappointments, the very real fears and joys, a bewildering time. Throughout my life I could relate to very small numbers of people, but large groups intimidate me, always happier in the company of boys/men than girls/women.

When Christine went to live in Aden we corresponded regularly, envelopes would be carefully addressed to Steamer Point, Aden, B.T.P.O. 69. Then the flap would be adorned with little ditty's like,
Postman, Postman
Don't be slow,
Don't be late
Be like Cliff, (Richard)
Eat your cornflakes
And go man go.

D...... Liver D...... Letter D......Sooner D......Better

In 1959, my fourteenth year, never consulted about our future, our routes were decides for us, divided into the chosen few, who went on to have the last year with more specialist tuition to pass external examinations, the criteria of success for well paid jobs, secretarial training or further education. Although consistently in the top stream, there was an unspoken assumption that the working class child would never amount to much. As far as I was concerned I'd been written off academically. I now found myself consigned to a practical class, with the B and C streams. Admitted I was a down to earth country child, with a practical attitude, made strange by my shyness, but I did not deserve this. My grades appeared to improve, showing some of my best work, rising that term to seventh in a class of thirty-seven. In internal exam's I'd received a first in art, second in English, tenth in geography, eleventh in maths. But being downgraded I'd stopped trying, I'd lost all interest. I know I was capable of even more and improved results.

Those that have real intelligence have the capacity to retain facts, then there are those like me who malfunction a brain like a door, which swings backwards, and forwards in the wind, a lot of things blow in, but seldom stay. I scored high in daily work and projects, doing badly in exams. I was always in a nervous state when taking examinations never feeling confident, trying to find at short notice, the right words to express myself. But exams only prove one thing, who can remember what on any given day. The first terms work was good, trying really hard, but examination results were disappointing, so said my form teacher. Next reports said Christine works well and shows interest, continues to improve her work. My last form teacher wrote, "Christine is to be congratulated on the great improvement in her class position. She has shown interest and worked hard to achieve this". So what went wrong? I now believe I went to school at a time when it was a biased world, children from poorer families were wrote off, didn't fit, didn't need higher education, some-one had to do the cleaning, the factory work, the menial tasks, the labouring jobs that were of much lower socio-economic status.

In January 1958 I'd entered Castle Hills School as a quite and willing girl, always ready to assist in any way. (form teachers words) My attendance was noted as regular, conduct excellent, progress satisfactory. With the benefit of hindsight, I can see some teachers were very good, inspirational, made lessons motivating and enjoyable, all teachers did their best, doing an enormous amount to inspire pupils, but they failed me, pushing development in the wrong direction.

One joyful memorable event of my last year, the weekend of 14th March 1959 was a school trip to London, for the princely sum of £3.10.9p. We travelled by train alighting at Kings cross; we went directly to Wembley to watch the women's International hockey match, England v South Africa. Entry to the west standing terraces cost 2/-, the programme 6d. Opening with the Central Band Of The Royal Air Force, then the Central Band of the Women's Royal Air Force. A free song sheet had been given to take part in the rousing community singing, which followed, patriotic songs like Land of Hope and Glory, with favourites of the time like 'when the saints go marching in' to my favourite 'the happy wanderer', which went like this
I love to go a-wandering,
Along a mountain track,
And as I go, I love to sing,
My knapsack on my back
Val-deri, val-dera,
Val-deri,

Val-dera-ha-ha-ha-ha-ha
Val-deri, val-dera.
My knapsack on my back.
After the final score of England 4, South Africa 1, we made our way by bus to the Hotel Caremel. After tea we went to the theatre by underground (*along with the hotel, the lifts and escalators my first encounters with*) to see 'Around the World in 80 days'
I being an odd number was allocated a room alone on a higher floor, but on going down to my friend's room for a midnight feast, Jacky and Joyce pushed their single beds together, so I could join them. After breakfast Sunday we visited Trafalgar Square, feeding the pigeons, before visiting Buckingham Palace to watch the Changing of the Guards. A touch of pageantry and colour to the London scene, each morning the new guard marches to the Palace from the Barrack's and the band plays in the forecourt as the new guards march in, those who have been on duty stride away. We had dinner in the dining carriage of the homeward bound train, arriving at Gainsborough Central station at 4pm. Tired and slightly tipsy from drinking ginger beer, which left me quite ill. (*So I've never touched any kind of beer since*). One incident marred my trip. We had a list of things we had to take with us, one being a raincoat which I did not possess, so one was borrowed from a teacher Mr. Cavill, unfortunately I mislaid it somewhere, I felt very guilty, one benefit was it taught me to be more careful and to this day whenever I leave anywhere I always glance behind to check if anything's been left.

The importance of the teacher cannot be over-estimated. I was profoundly interested in the world around me, setting one teacher on a pedestal. The innocence of these years' colours all your actions, the world has not yet disillusioned or disappointed. With the love, awe and admiration, of an adolescent, like many impressionable young girls, I had a crush. He became the centre of my affection and adoration. There was nothing abnormal about this relationship, later interests centred on boys of the same age and my emotional life developed properly.

Little miss average along with other miss averages, it was a day like any other when I walked out of school for the last time. Friends wished each other luck, with (broken) promises to keep in touch.
But I picked myself up, dusted myself down, my education in life was just starting, the real learning was to come later.

6. COUNTRY WOMEN AT HOME
1953 - 1958

What happens to the time we save
By cooking in a microwave?
More time to watch TV?
All this 'time saving' baffles me.

Granular tea for an instant brew,
More time saved - now what do you do?
'Just add milk' for instant whip,
That's two more minutes - have a kip!

Frozen puddings, veg and cakes, how little time it takes
To get a meal prepared and eaten -
Is there some record to be beaten?
Fast food outlets, takeaways, all saving minutes, even days!
Instant mixes, packet sauce,
More precious seconds saved of course.

Foil TV dinners, soon oven-heated,
In no time at all you're seated,
Before that square, cathode chat stopper
Rather than the dining room proper.

'Instant' custard, boil-in-bag-bag,
All designed to relieve the drag,
Now there are no spoons to lick,
Food is bought because it's quick.

Soup-in-a-cup, chocolate drinks,
Produced, it seems, in just two winks,
Poor Mrs. Beetons' fading fast,
Are recipe books a thing of the past?

Eventually, at this present rate,
Soon all there'll be there on the plate:
Three coloured tablets; green, blue, and red,
Main course, dessert and off to bed.

John Hyde.

During 1953 Dad was offered a larger house known simply as

Thonock Lane, Gainsborough. *Can you imagine getting your post there nowadays, with such a simple address?* It was about half a mile further down the road towards Blyton.

We arrived at our new home, sat atop our worldly goods carried on tractor and trailer. Viewed from the road as we approached, it had once been, one large brick - built square house. Nowadays reverted back to one house, known as Westfield cottage. With a front door facing the road, currently used by our neighbours. The back door our entrance then, in those two back-to-back homes. Turning off the road onto a hardened compacted soil drive, the front one (lived in by Derek's - chapter 12 - Grandma, but of course I didn't know this then) ran parallel with the road. Ours at the rear was in my opinion in the nicer position. Fields beyond, with trees interspersed amid the hedges , in the distance the woods. A spinney of lilac trees, quite the loveliest things ever seen when in full flower, edged the drive on the right hand side with two laburnums raining fountains of droplets to the left; the drive continued the length of our large garden with access (these days redundant) to the fields beyond. Snowbells, aconites, bluebells that grew in abundance made their carpets in the spring beneath the trees. Violets, Gran's favourite flowers (being her name) grew under the roadside hedge.

We had a small orchard, two apple, a pear, a plum. A number of gooseberry, raspberry, blackcurrant bushes, when fruiting all netted with muslin to deny the birds a feast; with a large clump of rhubarb that was covered with old buckets, to force, in winter. Outside, Dad's domain, was always a busy place, always a task awaiting, every evening after work would find him there.

Just outside the door was a square of lawn, but by far the largest part of the garden, was neat rows of vegetables and fruit bushes. A portion was available for the wooden chicken shed and run, moved periodically for the next vegetable plot, dug and turned over it was satisfactorily fertilized.

Away from the house a brick building divided into three stood at the end of gravel paths, which were made for perfect grip in winter ice, and repaired when the fire grate was cleaned daily, ash and cinders were put through a sieve, the largest lumps placed on the fire back to be raked down for re-use. In the shed where hung assorted tools neat and ready for use, the hoe, rake, spade, fork for the gardening, push along mower used for narrow strips of grass criss crossing the different areas. Grim reaper-style scythes to cut long grass. Cross - cut saw, with hefty axe used to split the larger logs, smaller one to chop the sticks. Next the pigsty, inner sanctum with outer pen surrounded by wall over which we tipped the swill (all waste food). Last but not least, perhaps our greatest hardship, the outside privy, (lavatory) an earth closet, you sat on the wooden bench over a pan, the men's (usually fell to dad) worst job each week was digging the hole and burying the contents. A creepy place, the largest spiders you were ever likely to see; at night a foreboding, sinister, treacherous journey in the dark; a most unpleasant experience, best avoided, too far from the safety of the back door, a long journey if in a hurry. In summer you had to hold your nose as no amount of disinfectant powder could counteract the smell and keep the flies at bay. In winter, day or night, dressed for the artic donning top-coat, hat, scarf, gloves, boots down the frozen cinder path you trudged. Toilet rolls were unknown, the local newspaper which was stiff, coarse and irksome, was carefully torn into squares and fixed to a nail on the back of the of the door, upon use it was necessary to scrunch each piece into a ball to break down the fibres. Reading was out of the question because there was no lighting, or heating which deterred people from lingering any longer than was absolutely necessary especially when rain dripped through the roof. Doors, peculiar to privy's always had a gap at the top, often to fearsome effect used by an escaped chicken to perch upon, also at the bottom bringing snow blowing under, ours had a diamond shape cut out of the wood about adult shoulder height. Beside the house door stood a wooden barrel below the downspout from the roof, collecting rainwater believed to be the best to use for washing our hair, making it soft and shiny, in winter capped by a thick frozen crust of ice. Adjoining was the lean-to brick washhouse, complete with built in wash boiler, a large round bowl 'the copper' as it was known, a fire grate inserted beneath it at floor level. Fire-wood was neatly heaped under a makeshift roof to protect it from the worst of the elements, with a manure heap of the pigs litter, rotting down at the furtherest extremities, awaiting distribution to the garden this completed our outside space. The whole was enclosed, fences of assorted timber, corrugated sheets or anything considered suitable for running repairs to the original hedges.

'Welcome' the cosy rooms seemed to say. Generations had sheltered here, what stories it could tell; these old walls had absorbed the sounds of many joys and sorrows, and were sturdy enough to absorb them for many years to come. This old cottage had character, the hands of its humble builders, workers that were proud to make a home with simple tools and supplies available, showed in its irregular corners, bulges and crevices.

The first room you entered was the hub of the home. When you came in from the garden, through the one and only old solid wood back door, which normally stood partially open except in the very coldest weather, it would not go all the way back because of the working coats hung behind on a nail, There was no entrance hall upon entering; you stepped into a small square. The under stairs cupboard was in front of you, immediately to your left the door to the "Best" room. Open to the right, a mixture of kitchen and living room, sitting room, dining room all rolled into one. Look down you see the red quarry tiled floor liberally spread with home-made pegged rugs, look up you see the oak beamed ceiling which throughout the downstairs are actually the floorboards of the bedrooms.

Doing service as the bathroom on Sunday nights. Filling and emptying the bath were laborious chores. The large copper in the attached lean to was filled with water, and while it heated the large galvanized zinc bath that hung on a nail by the back door was fetched in front of the roaring fire, then the hot water was tipped in bucket by bucket, having to be bucketed out again at the end of the night. Children first, the temperature tested by grandmas bare elbow, then rubbed dry with large fluffy towels kept warm on the fire guard, bundled to bed in deliciously fragrant pyjamas, chanting "up the wooden hill to Bedfordshire, into blanket street" "night, night don't let the bed bugs bite" whilst the adults had theirs.

Stood in the centre of the room was the large pine table the most used item in our home, it served for all purposes. Covered in newspaper, vegetables were prepared, fruit bottled, pickling, baking, fire irons, brass and silver polished to gleaming perfection , ironing (no ironing board), all took place. I turned the handle of the large mincing machine screwed to the table when sausages were made. Children made things, games were played, how many were entertained and practiced their artistic talents throughout the years? The laughter, the tears, the quarrels, and the tales this piece of history could tell. Covered with a tablecloth at mealtimes with cutlery and condiments laid, standards were always maintained, respectability was a virtue, which was preserved at all costs. Some wood chairs were tucked under the table and others filled available spaces around the room.

Eyes right, as we look around the room, placed under the twelve very small paned, sliding wooden window we had the old, brown salt-glazed sink, with wooden draining board, mounted on two brick piers, plus the one and only cold water tap.

Next came the substantial fireplace with a high mantle-piece, enclosing the black- led grate, with no electricity, our sole source of heat and cooking, it dominated our lives. A raised open fire, with trivet ring upon which lived the old black cast-iron kettle kept simmering with its gentle hiss, to be swung over the fire to make the ever-ready pot of tea. When anyone visited, or minor accidents took place, the first thing said was "Put kettle on lass", (meaning bring to boil and make pot of tea) a cure for everything. A small boiler, upon which I recall dad always putting his mittens to dry. A square container to one side of the fire kept full of water, provided a rusty brew of hot water ladled out for personal use. The oven on the other side of the fire held three heavy iron shelves, many a time one of these (first wrapped in an old towel), warmed our bed when we'd forgotten to put the normally used brick, in the oven early enough.

Slack (the very smallest coal, dust and recycled cinders) was banked to the sloping rear and raked down as necessary, to prevent it burning so fiercely, economically conserving heat when a blazing fire was not needed. In the hearth lay kindling (sticks) a pile placed there each night, so that in the morning it was dry to burst the fire back into life. If for any reason the fire was in need of a boost, with no kindling to hand, firelighters were made from newspapers, folded and screwed very tightly, then the shovel was fixed in the bars to hold a large sheet of newspaper, sealing the fire to cause a suction. Great care had to be taken, when flames were seen the shovel with its wooden handle had to be whipped away pretty smartish.

Upon the mantle-piece centre stage stood the big heavy old black marble clock, wound religiously each night before dad went to bed, rhythmetically ticking, regulating our lives. Either end stood two heavy spelter decorative ornaments, heavy enough to wedge behind them few letters or bills received, as I recall they looked something like the statue of liberty. The pot of spills was placed here too, long tapers rolled very tightly from newspaper and then twisted at the end, used instead of matches, to take a light from the fire for lighting the lamps in the evening or light gran's and dads cigarettes. (both smoked in those days). For a short period of time the small carton of goldfish food was on the corner, but the poor fish jumped out of its dish overnight and was dead on the floor next morning - no more fish for me. Under the shelf was stretched a line, which always had some item of clothing, mostly underwear airing. From a hook hung the padded kettle holder.

Here I first attempted cooking. Toasting, an enjoyable task in winter, *now there's an art*, fixing a slice of fresh bread, *the difficult bit*, onto the long handled, two pronged fork, holding the bread close to the hot embers, not flames, *not too close*, checking until golden brown, except for the visible white marks from the fire bars, then turn over, *now easier to keep on the fork*, and repeat. Spread with butter whilst hot and enjoy, toast never tasted so good. Burnt toast was said to make the hair curl. Later my speciality meal for myself, fried egg on fried bread done in the big heavy frypan over the hot embers.

Two Windsor chairs (one being Grans - woe betide anyone else sitting in it) with comfy cushions, either side of the fireplace, swung around for mealtimes.

Next came the pantry cooled by the breezes which came in through the pierced metal of the fly proof small window, one of the nicest places, always the aroma of fresh baking to tantalize the taste buds, things did not last long in our household. A small square room; it had a red tiled floor and whitewashed walls, with thick, chunky, strong wooden shelves all the way around, lined with assorted surplus wallpaper . Each spring this job was turned into a much prized contest to see who could make the prettiest fancy cut edging. About a foot from the floor running the length of one wall, was the cold slab. The whole designed to keep as cool as possible, important in the days before fridges and freezers. All the surplus things grown from our own garden, gathered, bottled, preserved, salted, stored. It had to be well stocked for emergencies, last the year, and provide the odd jar to take to other family members. Staple goods like dried fruit were kept to be weighed out for home-made cakes, puddings, and plum bread.

From the ceiling hung ropes of home-grown onions, dried sage and mint tied in bunches, aromatic when pinched between finger and thumb. Home-made jars of tomato sauce, piccalilli, chutney, pickled onions, red cabbage in spicy vinegar. Bottled fruit in Kilner jars, plums, blackberries, pears, gooseberries, row upon row of jars of lemon curd, jam and jelly, all labelled, dated stood in ranks. Large crocks containing surplus runner beans salted, stood on the floor. Marrows; apples carefully picked, so not to bruise were placed not touching in wooden trays, to last until the following season. Windfalls used first for pies and puddings.

Continuing we had a big old fancy dresser upon which was positioned the wireless, it had a mirror back, around which was small decorative shelves, in the cupboard was hidden the home-made plum bread, brought out for special treats, a slice thickly buttered, served with a chunk of cheese. At Christmas twelve loaves were made, each to signify a happy month. The radio was a necessity, the only contact for news of the outside world, but used sparingly to conserve the battery. Gran loved boxing and would set her alarm to rise at outrageous hours to listen to matches live. Through these years the wireless was my passion too, sometimes when the battery was low it would be placed in the warm oven to heat it a little to squeeze another hour until a new battery could be fetched. Saturday we listened in to 'Jimmy Clitheroe Kid'. Sunday lunchtime Jean Metcalf's voice preceded the signature tune, 'With a Song in my Heart', "In Britain it is twelve noon, and in Germany it is one pm but at home and away it is time for 'Two way family favourites'". An exchange of friendly conversation, the tunes were requested, week after week, an important link between families at home and the forces abroad. Broadcast between the BBC in London and British Forces Network in Germany.

Each night Alan and I went to bed at the same time, I would then read Alan bedtime stories or make up my own far-fetched tales to thrall him with. If I was lucky and he went to sleep quickly I was allowed down for another hour to listen to radio, the likes of Wilfred Pickles with wife Mabel with Violet Carson - who later played Ena Sharples in Coronation Street - at the piano toured the country, calling at cities, towns, villages and hamlets, to get the greatest variety of accents and experiences. Requesting ordinary homely everyday steadfast people with humour, courage, and ideals to volunteer to 'Have a go' general chat was followed by a few questions with Mabel at the table to "give 'im the money, Mabel ". The funny answers and the serious ones poured from the people. Pity there isn't something like it nowadays. This island is full of individual people with different dialects, and accents, and a wicked sense of humour. Individuals with stories of exploits, and great daring. How terrible to think that it is not being recognised and preserved.

The enclosed staircase, rose between each room, with a narrow strip of jute carpet top to bottom, fixed firmly in place on each tread with brass rods held by fancy claw clips. Ascending from the left at the back of the kitchen/living room, two bedrooms were placed, one each side of the small landing (top step), both large, one over the kitchen looked out over the garden, were the men slept, and the other in which women and children slept, over the best room were the window looked out over the side of the house down the road.

In our early days in this house in one bedroom there was my dad, uncles Bob, and Jeff who all had single beds with wooden bedsteads, the only furniture in the men's bedroom was a built in wardrobe over the stairs and a set of drawers.

In the front bedroom was Aunt Annie and her son Alan, in one bed, Gran and I another, but Alan spent more time with us. Ours were double beds placed feet to feet, slightly offset to fit the room, with brass knobs at each corner of the big black bedsteads. Still room was found for a large double wardrobe, a set of large mahogany bow fronted drawers plus a marble topped washstand upon which stood matching ceramic basin, soap-dish, tall jug, all decorated with sepia country scenes.

The mattress's covering large cumbersome wire mesh/springs foundations on iron frames were thin; with another cotton ticking flock mattress overlay that was shook and turned each day. Bedding always consisted of pure white cotton sheets and pillow cases - no variety of colours, no easy care fabrics - grey wool blankets; or those homemade, of knitted squares sewn together; then a candlewick bedspread topped with a fluffy feather square eiderdown encased in glazed cotton cover with its very light filling, ventilated at intervals by small stitched holes. At the head of the bed was a bolster, a cylindrical feather pillow, one complete length of the width of the bed, over this came one or more softer, rectangular feather pillows, encased in white pillowcases with intricate, colourful hand embroidery.

Embroidery transfers could be bought at the haberdashery shop for a few pennies a sheet. These patterns were of delicate flowers, birds, strips of bordering, ladies in wonderfully old fashioned dresses or exquisite letters of the alphabet for use as initials, printed on tissue paper, which when pressed with a hot iron left the black outlines on your chosen fabric. Many colours of thread could be purchased adding them to your collection, held in a pretty tin that you once received full of sweets or chocolates. From simple running stitch, to blanket stitch, herringbone, chain stitch, featherstitch, satin stitch along with French knots the picture became works of art. Cross stitch mats; initials embroidered on handkerchief corners;

progressing with age to ever more elaborate designs on pillowcases; pinafores; then tablecloths. One of many skills no longer practised in this mass-produced society.

Downstairs again we had a horsehair sofa placed with its back to the stairs wall. Round the corner, the door to under stairs, the door to the front room and completing the circuit back to the door.

The front room was always known as the 'best' room. No one in working clothes dare go in, this was an age when workers did not change out of their working clothes for the evening, unless going courting, which incidentally they did not do in the front room. It was reserved for high days, holidays, and funerals, Thankfully it only has happy memories for me, only used for Christmas. With it's brass coal scuttle, fender and fire irons, all kept immaculately polished till your face shone in them, taking on the flickering reflections which added so much to the cosy appearance of the room when the open fire which with the addition of a match, was always laid ready to instantly burst into life. On the right hand side of the fireplace was a large built in cupboard that contained all the best pottery and precious china, collectables from visits to the seaside, that sort of thing. Hidden at the back a bottle of port and bottle of sherry, kept for funerals, weddings or Christmas. Gran's large mahogany table, that extended to accommodate visiting relatives, opened-up by turning a handle to enable two further leaves to be inserted, always protected from scratches by its soft green, chenille, tasselled cloth. *To my utter regret I had to part with it a number of years ago when I no longer had room, were I was then living.* An old, well worn, comfortable settee and 2 arm chairs; the piano which I never touched, it was auntie Annie's, and though she didn't play it very often, we did have some good sing-alongs at Christmas; and a bookcase containing a few books, completed this room. One book to survive, I still have is The Mystery Of The Squires Pew and other stories, presented by The Salvation Army to my dad 'For Good Conduct, Diligence and Regular Attendance 100 marks out of 100, April 1931 (7yrs old). On the wall hung the only photo I ever recall seeing displayed, years later I was to find underneath it my mum and dad's wedding photo. Aunt Edna explained she covered it up to save further distress when mum first left me because I was constantly pointing to it repeating "my mummy". There was a door which led to a further downstairs room off this best room, but it was very small and narrow, rendering it useless except for storage, until I was older when I was given a table and chair spending many a wet day writing and drawing there. Next door got the better deal here having this very small room upstairs above ours. Perhaps if things had been the other way round I may have had my own bedroom.

All the doors were planks of wood, battened together on the back with a Z; hung from the frame with large black hinges, opened and closed by holding the handle, pressing down with the thumb which lifted the 'sneck', (a latch and hook). All my childhood we never had a cat, but always had a dog for a pet. One dog-called Scottie caused us to trip up many a time; he was indisquinshable from the pegged rugs.

In winter the kitchen was a wonderful steamy warmth when cooking. Evenings too it was soon warm and "snug as a bug in a rug" as Gran used to say. A lovely roaring fire, the curtains drawn, a thick curtain on a pole pulled across the door to stop some of the draughts that came from apertures you never knew existed, until someone entered or went out then a icy blast entered with them "Shut that door" still rings in my ears. The chilly mornings were not so good, bitter cold pervaded, fires banked down at night with a generous sprinkling of slack dampened with tea leaves, were raked into life, or relit with the ready supply of sticks called 'kindling'. When the fire refused to spring into life, the shovel was carefully wedged in the bars and a sheet, or two of newspaper was held in front forming a suction, eventually the silhouettes of a few flames danced into sight. Whilst waiting for warmth, huggled close the legs burnt and the back was frozen cold.

The same could not be said for the rest of the house. Bedrooms, linoleum covered floors with home-made bedside rugs, very cold to bare feet, were unheated and bitterly icy cold in winter. Inside and out the feather and fernlike etchings of frost lay thick upon the tiny wooden window panes, net curtains froze lace-like cobwebs which glistened like diamonds in the moonlight. Shivering as the chill seeped into my being , often resulting in having to wear an old woolly with your nightdress, I perfected the art of dressing/ undressing beneath the bed clothes. On windy nights the 'bogey man' came knocking as the ill fitting windows rattled. (a frivolous jest "the bogy man will get you". At night, bed was entered quickly snuggling deep into the blankets, the feather beds were cosy. Stone hot water bottles with screw stoppers warmed our toes the brass knobs on the bedstead shone in the dim light of the eerily flickering candle. Morning came with the daily crowing and strutting of the cockerels while the hens scratched for buried worms and handful of corn scattered to them.

One of Grandmas prized possessions was an oil lamp a beautiful thing which when lit it provided a subtle glow. These consisted of a fuel chamber on a Brass stem and base. A wick, adjusted for efficiency, soaked up the fuel and rose through to the burner, a clear glass funnel was added for safety it protected the flame and controlled the flow of air. A white or sometimes a coloured shade was added, perhaps for decorative purposes or more probably to spread the light. These I understand were the most efficient option, but oil was expensive and fear of breakages was great so usage was restricted to occasional use in the best room. Our nights were lit by Tilley lamps, they were more practical and brighter. Both lamps, over the course of an evening lost up to 40% of its illuminating power as the glass accumulated soot. They had to be filled each morning, glass cleaned, with the wicks trimmed evenly, removing any tiny charred cinder If maintenance was not carried out correctly the light did not burn brightly that night. If the wick was not even the flame would have a long point, smoke, leaving soot deposits on the glass, if the wick was turned too high the mantle turned black and smoked. The Tilley lamp was more satisfactory for general use, apart from giving a slightly better brighter light it could be used outside. A flat base held the paraffin, which was cheaper than oil. A central stem with a knob adjusted the flow to the mantle in a glass globe encased in a metal frame, the mantle was an extremely delicate lacy thing when new, once used they disintegrated if touched. To light, a pad was soaked in meths, after being lit, clipped to the base of the stem, then a pump attached to the base was used to build up pressure till the mantle glowed. As the light faded throughout the evening further pumps were needed. They were highly dangerous things to control correctly. A candle had to suffice to light the way to bed, carried carefully in its holder, called the candlestick; it did not resemble a stick at all. It was made of tin, the size of a saucer, in the middle of which was a short squat tube that held the candle. An attached loop enabled you to carry it, with the other hand shielding to prevent draughts blowing it out. Once in bed you had to wet two fingers with your tongue then pinch the hot wick to put the flame out - or blow it out if you were chicken.

I feel richer for my spartan upbringing, a carefree atmosphere, there were compensations for living in the country, healthy food, fresh unpolluted air, a place of comfort and reliability. While she never had to worry about where the next meal would come from, hard cash was scarce, wages left nothing much to spare. Ours was a household that was self-contained, with no rent to find, no electricity or gas bills the only concern would have been whether the insurance man would get his money. I'm sure it was a struggle to make ends meet but Gran must have been careful with any housekeeping money. Financially poor, it wasn't a question of suffering, it did not trouble us. Our lives were not dominated by the bleep of bar-codes. Nobody went hungry or without clothes, we were not suffering from this itch to possess more and more, not trapped on an unceasing treadmill, that feeds today's consumer society, doomed to shop every day of the year. We fed like kings, we always had plenty to eat from the garden, the orchard, pork came from own pigs, the chickens provided eggs and when finished lying they went in the pot. A young chicken could be spared for roasting occasionally, the wishbone a cherished find, the winner of the pull making a secret wish. What could not be provided ourselves was taken from the countryside around us. Snared rabbits, poached pheasants, hung in the shed for days till maggots appeared, said to enhance the flavour. Hedgerows scoured to provide the blackberries in autumn. A real family outing, each person gathered in small basins, to be tipped into Grans large basket, woe betides if you dropped any, hence the small basin.

These days, our ever changing lifestyles and the introduction of frozen, and fast foods lead us to depend more on the food manufacturer than our skills in the kitchen for the quality of our diet. Cooking was an art form, with only the fire to control the heat. All food was wholesome, plain and simple, cooking done from fresh ingredients, when available, bottled, pickled, or preserved used in scarcity of fresh. A treat to eke out winter diets was delicious mushy peas, made from dried peas bought in a packet; these were then placed to soak overnight with a little tablet, enclosed in the box. Only bought basics, things they could not grow or preserve, custard powder, gravy salt to be mixed with a little flour to thicken, stirred into meat juices (no Bisto). Blocks of salt that needing crushing as needed, added at cooking, seldom added at table. Sugar, camp coffee, butter (Gran no longer made this herself, but did when she lived at the farm).

Who could forget home baked bread made daily, warm from the oven, or the unique aroma, as it sat in the 'pancheon' the huge brown bowl, placed by the fire to aid rising. Pastry baking took place once a week, mouth watering game pie or meat and potato pie, making a little meat go a long way with thick pastry crusts held aloft with an upturned egg cup, trimmed with pastry leaves, *don't ask me why*; corned beef or sausage pasties, bacon and egg tarts, standards for pack-up; baked egg custard; deep-filled fruit pies; treacle tart; and best of all we were allowed to make jam and lemon curd pasties using the last of the cut-offs.

Sunday dinner the only day of the week when dinner was at one o'clock the best meal of the week. You knew the season of the year by the meat and vegetables served. Always Yorkshire pudding, cooked in a large meat tray, risen to touch the top shelf, cut into squares, served first *the idea was to fill you to make the meat go further* with good rich onion gravy made from the juices from the large joint of roasted meat, usually pork, sometimes a chicken or leg of lamb, very, very occasionally a joint of beef. Served with all the trimmings, roast potatoes, apple sauce with pork, mint sauce with lamb, sage and onion stuffing with chicken. Accompanied by lots of vegetables, the remainders along with more than the mashed potatoes needed, were sizzled in rich beef dripping to golden crispness, in the big iron fry-pan, being called 'bubble and squeak' for Mondays dinner, served with the remains of Sundays meat, cold and sliced. Any remaining Yorkshire pudding could be enjoyed with jam, the only day when no other pudding was made. Midweek would see us have 'toad in the hole', *still one of my favourites* a large baking tin of sausages disappearing in mounds of bubbly, crispy, crunchy Yorkshire pudding; or could be Stew accompanied by light fluffy dumplings; Rabbit or Pheasant; the lesser cuts from the pig like Belly Pork; Chicken casserole; Cottage pie, mince topped with mashed potato; boiled Bacon; one of the pies on baking day; Liver and onions; at all times served with potatoes and vegetables. No chips they were a treat enjoyed at the seaside, rice, curries, beef burgers or pasta. No so-called fast food, the nearest we got to that was Saturdays, Luncheon meat fritters served with fried new potatoes; bacon, egg, beans, tomatoes and fried bread or beans on toast. Everyday except Sunday a different home-made pudding was always served first, I'm given to understand it was a hangover from the days when meat was a scarce commodity, served first to take the edge off the men's appetite. Sometimes suet puddings, wrapped in cloth and boiled for what seemed hours; spotted dick; baked apples, the centre filled with mincemeat; jam or treacle sponge pudding or jam roly-poly; rice pudding; fruit pie; bread and butter pudding; all with the accompanying custard. Gran regularly whipped up homemade biscuits; and fruit scones in addition to Cakes which were mainly what was termed cut and come again, ranged from rich fruit cakes; jam sponges; date and walnut cake; (the final joy being to slowly suck the finger savouring every last morsel after wiping around the inside of the bowl of uncooked sweet mixture). In the words of the song these were "just some of my favourite things." Bread and milk, a desired treat when not feeling well. Recipes handed down, ner' a recipe book I ever saw, what good would set temperatures be, with an oven heat dependant on size of fire, a 'damper' used to draw the fire, that took much skill and experience to get and keep to the required heat.

No fizzy pop; cups of tea, - cup and saucer - made in the teapot with loose leaves, then poured through a strainer, a small mesh that rested on your cup - no tea-bags - kept warm, stewed more like, with the knitted tea cosy to keep the pot hot, were drunk from an early age; water drank copiously. I also loved to drink jugs of foamy, still warm fresh milk, thick and creamy, daily fetched in a 'billy can' straight from the farmers cow. The chink of the milk jug dipping into the metal churn, a galvanised can holding ten gallons, with a lid that fitted snuggly in the top rim. Two handles to lift the heavy receptacles onto the roadside platform, to await the collection lorry. Household milk was placed in buckets of cold water, positioned in the coolest available position. I hated, still do, milk that's got the slightest taste of curdling.

It usually fell to me, to walk to the mill at Blyton to fetch fresh ground flour, which came in thin cotton bags printed with the miller's name. I never minded the four-miles walk there and back. The co-op mobile shop came to the house monthly. If we needed something before the next visit, off I went to the Co-op also at Blyton, not just food but paraffin, batteries, cycle parts, the range of things sold in that large double fronted shop was beyond doubt incredible. Stamps were given when spending, resulting in twice a year collecting the 'divi'.

When rationing finally ended, consumers splashed out on foods that had been in short supply --- sugar, chocolate, canned fruit. Sugar intake shot to a record 112lbs per person per year, making Britain one of the highest users in the world. Only half the population now ate cooked breakfast, the new cold cereals were the thing, little toys, in their own bag, some with very tiny parts that needed putting together, (health and safety would not allow it now) often came amongst the cereal. Always at the bottom of the packet, whoa betide you if you tried to rave for it early, the lucky one was the one who tipped it into the dish along with their morning breakfast. Quaker oats taken from the familiar red and blue box with the smiling man dressed in traditional 19thcentury garb, produced a bowl of steaming porridge a great way to start the day in winter. Boiled in water in a pan, the very devil to get clean when washing up, sugar and milk added in your dish. At school cooked dinner was at 12noon, (I had free school dinners, with no stigma attached) men had packed lunches, half taken at 'elevenses' the rest at noon, men came home to cooked dinners, (still called tea) at 5.30pm, and we all sat down at the table together. Us kids had sandwiches, but that didn't stop me sharing another helping of pudding with my dad. Dad and I had a sweet tooth and given a choice much preferred to forgo dinner and have two helpings of pudding.

Sundays were a day of rest as far as possible, always coming home to visit mum, married sons or daughters, bringing their children, only essential cooking and chores were done.

Sunday tea, most likely to be joined by my uncle's girlfriends, was dainty sandwiches. One treat I never got to enjoy was jelly, you were expected to eat bread and butter with fruit, jelly and tinned evaporated milk; the idea being it helped to satisfy those with large appetites, I do not recall ever being hungry but presumably an exception could not be made, so I went without, except when trifles were made, for some unknown reason you did not eat bread and butter with trifle. The meal was finished with cake.

I loved jam sarnie's or sticky condensed milk, thickly spread on bread and butter. In winter the butter turned to liquid if left to long when placed in the oven to be warmed, before attempting spreading on your bread, in summer could be similarly malleable unless placed in the coldest place available. Another childish delight was 'dip' bread dipped in the fat from fried bacon.

Boiled eggs each in our own eggcup, served with rounds of buttered bread cut into fingers, dipped as soldiers into the yolk. When eaten the empty egg shell was turned over in the eggcup to resemble a new boiled egg and I'd offer it to dad or Alan, with the due ceremony of cracking the lid to reveal the empty offer, a known trick but the ritual was observe nevertheless.

Food was never monotonous no out of season produce then, this heightened our appreciation because we set great store on special occasions and seasons, so there was always something to look forward to, food in tins was seldom bought. Peas were freshly podded as used straight from the garden. Mince pies were only eaten during the twelve days of Christmas. Who could forget the tantalising smell of boiling fruits as jam was made in the copper bottomed preserving pan, the endless 'crying' when preparing onions for pickling or that spicy whiff of chutney or piccalilli.

Pigs were purchased as weaners in early spring, or often the 'runt' (tiniest that may die) of the litter was given by the farmer. Expenditure on meal was kept to a minimum, when riddling took place on the farm, potatoes not considered good enough to sell, were called appropriately 'pig potatoes', traditionally brought home, boiled in an old copper stood on a low makeshift wall surrounding a fire, when cool fed to the pigs. When the pig was fattened, the day of execution had to be decided on, two long and extremely busy days began for everyone. In the days before refrigerators everything had to be dealt with quickly. Before it became obligatory to observe humane methods of slaughtering pigs were killed at the cottages. A joint undertaking - one each - with our neighbour, the squealing pigs were killed in a scene of predictable sacrifice on a cold October morning, superstitions said the pig could only be killed when the moon was new for if the pig was killed when the moon was waning it was said the bacon would shrink in cooking. The killing was a noisy, bloody business, next the bristles were burnt off by lighting straw placed all over the carcass. The pig was hoisted to a stout beam, then buckets of water were used to scrub him down, next cut open and the innards, 'offal' removed. Liver, kidney, heart, chittlings, sweetbread could not be preserved. Carried into the kitchen to be used straight away, cut up for dishes of 'fry', casseroled with sliced onion, making a very rich gravy, traditionally topped with sage flavoured dumplings. Then the pig left with its empty belly in the coldest place that it might bleed thoroughly, to preserve the quality of meat. Early next day the carcass was carried on the 'crutch' large, short-legged, wooden rack with four extended handles for the hatchet to begin the chopping up. Some cuts were put to one side for sausages, coarsely minced with just a few bread crumbs, herbs added to handed down recipes. Haslet was also made, sausage meat with a small amount of liver and onion added, moulded into small meat loaves, wrapped in lacy caul fat, roasted in the oven. Coarsely cut meat from the leg and belly, simply seasoned with salt, pepper, nutmeg, but no herbs, surrounded by savoury jelly, set into pastry made with best home-rendered lard produced the finest pork pies. The head, trotters, ears with any oddments of meat and bone were boiled together, strained, meat shredded then placed back in the stock, boiled again to make brawn. Aint nothing you can't use barring his hair and squeal, even fat was rendered down for lard.

The rest of the pork was jointed, salted in an open tub to preserve, the flitch - sides of bacon, the most important meat consumed - carefully wrapped in muslin was hung from strong hooks screwed into the kitchen ceiling beams. Large thick slices of bacon were then cut as needed. A narrow length of 'chine' bones 6"-7" wide down the backbone were removed, put into salting tub for curing. Later scored into the flesh with a pointed knife at ½" intervals, to make deep pockets, these being stuffed with chopped parsley, onions, a little malt vinegar and mustard, then wrapped in an old sheet tied firmly, simmered in the copper (everything had a duel purpose), for 4-5 hours. Sliced and eaten cold carved into very attractive slices, a Lincolnshire delicacy fast disappearing, an acquired taste, but once you get used to it absolutely mouth watering.

Down through the generations, women had been guilty of propagating the traditional way of raising children. Boys had a few outdoor jobs to do, feeding stock, chopping the wood, then free to scuttle away to boys pursuits, girls were always on call just like their mothers, encouraging the idea that men did the real work, women must perform the endless tasks set aside as 'women's work'. I had no such conditioning, I wasn't expected to do chores, Gran maybe because of her own harsh childhood believed children should be children. At that time mothers - or in my case grandma - didn't go out to work, not even in the fields. In her childhood women had needed to, as well as rear families and cope with the drudgery of housework. I did help though, I would shell peas and beans, hull strawberries, top and tail gooseberries (nicknamed goosegogs), throw scraps to the pig. Sometimes I threw a handful of corn to the chickens, while they pecked avidly I collected the eggs, then topped up the water bowl. One job that often did fall to me was making mint sauce. Made fresh in small quantities, first pulling a handful of sprigs, a few added to the boiling new potatoes, strip the leaves from the remaining stalks finely chop them, placed in a dish with vinegar added. Delicious not like today's commercial stuff bought in jars.

I'm sure washday was loathed, it took a full day, always Monday, the battle began as a fire was lit at break of day under the large copper boiler, filled by heaving bucket after bucket of water, then the great circular wooden lid placed on top. First as the steam rose, some water was ladled into the zinc half barrel dolly tub, then the boiler was topped up to be ready for boiling, always the red glow underneath had to be maintained. In summer clouds of steam like a Turkish bath (*not that I knew then what a Turkish bath was*), in winter a pleasant sanctuary of warmth. Starting with whites washing began with grated soap added, then the wooden dolly legs (similar to a three-legged stool with a waist height centre pole, topped by a cross bar to hold with both hands) 'poshed' (agitated) with a left, right, back motion. Next because of the water heat a white dolly (*who was this dolly?*) stick, made of pine and about a foot long, (resembling a policeman's truncheon,) kept for this purpose, was used to lift the washing into the wooden tub, where scrubbing of stains, grubby collars and cuffs using a bar of soap against the glass ridged scrubbing board. Whites were put back into the copper to be stirred, prodded amid the foggy steam in the bubbling boiling soap and soda. All the while with a slippery soap-sudded floor, washing continued with the same dolly tub of water, light colours, dark colours and finally the men's work clothes. Clothes were next lifted into another dolly tub to be rinsed over and over, reckitts blue added for a final rinse. Best things were starched, made from a powder mixed with boiling water, before finally being put through the huge clanking old iron framed mangle with heavy wooden rollers, a very large screw on top allowed adjustment according to the material going through. The rollers operated by turning a large wheel at the side, whilst guiding the items through with the other hand. Fingers beware! As a child Gran had lost her finger end in just such a way whilst helping her mum. Buttons were folded inside garments, broken ones made more work, as they had to be replaced later. Next dragged in a willow clothes basket to the line down the garden, lifted high with the clothes prop, rows and rows of lily white washing billowing on windy days. Back breaking work, although great pride was taken on having a line full of blinding whiteness, and if the line snapped all hell broke loose. With washing done the tubs and copper had to be ladled out, some of the hot suds used to scrub the lavvy, doorstep and surrounding area.

Washday still not finished, as washing was fetched in, things needing ironing were rolled up damp to keep in moisture but if any more were needed water was sprinkled on very deftly with fingers from a bowl. Sheets left in the sunshine as long as possible had to be folded before putting straight in the cupboard, I was often roped in after school to help with this, one each end, both stretching at the same time, then meeting in the middle. Later ironing took place on the table, filling the room with sunshine scented fresh linen or sometimes the smell of scorched cloth. Alternate solid heavy irons heated by swinging on trivets over the fire, had to be replaced frequently, - taken with a holder, an early sewing lesson, usually two knitted squares, stitched together with thick padding in the middle with a little loop to keep handily hung at the side of the fireplace - run over a piece of old cloth to check for smuts, then spat on. Spitting was taboo but an exception had to be made for ironing the only way to test for the correct heat. If the spittle ran quickly into a little ball instantly disappearing the temperature was just right, then plunged onto the garment being pressed, laid upon a piece of old sheet placed over an even older folded blanket with many scorch marks, kept for the purpose. Newly pressed folded carefully, then hung on the wooden clotheshorse to be aired in front of the fire. Washday could spread over several days in bad weather, when clothes with the steaming clamminess of damp linen had to be dried on the clothes horse around the fire, but real effort was made to get everything done and out of the way. Mending was then done as soon as possible, before putting away. With the ever-handy sewing basket, containing your needles, strong thread, wooden cotton reels, differing widths of elastic and tape. Fasteners varied from zips, to differing sizes of silver and black press-studs, and hooks and eyes, finally frogs - a novel looped decorative scroll fastening of braid or cord , one half had a covered button which inserted almost indisquinishable through the other half.

A job could always be found, missing buttons or those squashed in the mangle had to be stitched on, hopefully matching, chosen carefully from the large button tin kept for this purpose. Zips along with buttons were removed to be saved for re-use before anything was finally consigned to the rag bag. The button tin contained an amazing assortment, from odd shoe buttons to heavy coat buttons even regimental buttons from long abandoned uniforms. A source of great joy, I found pleasure in sorting, pretty decorative glass ones leather, wooden, shiny metal, horn or wood toggle duffel-coat buttons, mother of pearl, bone, ceramic, even black glass or jet buttons from mourning clothes, tying each matching clutch together with cotton for instant recognition. Also contained within were cards of linen covered shirt buttons along with spare collar studs. The tin could also be raided for the four primary colours to be substituted for the lost original counters to play tiddly-winks, ludo or snakes and ladders. Evenings were spent forever making do with endless mending, small tears were darned before further damage occurred, worn shirt collars were turned, a wooden 'mushroom' placed in socks to aid darning holes, patched knees on trousers to make them last longer or torn crotches to repair, ripped sheets sewn 'sides to middle', knowing full well that if she did not repair or conjure up bits and pieces the home economy would be the poorer. Gran made clothes, made her own curtains and furnishings, using her Singer sewing machine, right hand turning the handle, left hand guiding material under the foot. Aprons could be made from shirt tails, worn out underwear and old cotton material was used for dusters or rags for window cleaning. My clothes were often other cousins hand-me-downs revamped slightly, thereby making them mine. Alterations could be wrought with trimmings, such as edging with coloured bias binding, ric-rac - a wavy decorative tape, colourful ribbons - often with matching colours in your hair - change of buttons, or a new collar. When you did get anything new it was bought a size to big - to make it last - with the hems and sleeves turned up, let down again when you grew into it. Gran could always be relied on to knock up a costume for fancy dress. Expert at making patchwork quilts from scraps of material; smocking; knitting and rug making. A new jumper; cardigan; socks; bed jackets, to keep those draughts at bay when confined to bed; or mittens, never gloves, fingers being to complicated; from an old woolly unpicked, pulled down with the wool re-used. If wool had to be bought, it came in skein's (long loops) me being the one stood holding wool (imagine holding arms out -bend from elbow, place the skein's over hands between thumb and first finger, far enough apart to keep wool taut), then Gran winding away until my arms felt they were dropping off. Occasionally the skein could be hung from the back of a dining chair, but this was considered unsatisfactory as the right tension could not be maintained. Needles ranged in size to allow very loose chunky knitting to gossamer fine baby clothes, made from wood, bone or steel - which gave the click-clack sound. All these skills I learnt by her side. I recollect once knitting a scarf that went twice around my neck, still almost touching the floor back and front, like 'Joseph's coat of many colours', I wore it with pride. I later knitted jumpers from patterns in teen magazines or bought for a few pence. Very hardwearing rugs were pegged, while sitting in front of the fire listening to the radio; sometimes lovely multi-coloured patterns were made, occasionally just random. Two different types could be made one was done by pulling with a wooden handled peg with hooked needle, small 'snips' about 4" long by 1" wide which had been laboriously cut from old rags, coats, trousers, dresses, through the hessian sacking washed for the backing, then knotting it. The other method was to take long cut strips from old jumpers or blankets and the needle went in and out making loops till the length ran out. nothing was wasted, the word recycling was unheard of but practised unknowingly. All parcels were dispatched and received wrapped in brown paper, tied with string. The brown paper, the past addresses hidden in the folds was kept to re-use, along with the string, the multitude of stubborn knots patiently untied.

Daily work was never done, for all dirty jobs, Gran wore her 'arden' - hard/stiff apron made from a well washed sack - when sacks were hessian not plastic - tied around her waist to protect her, she always wore a full length wrap around pinny underneath. Brass bedstead to polish, heaving of water to fill the jugs in their basins on the bedroom washstands, chamber pots the 'gus unders' used in the night to empty, flock mattress to be shook when making beds. Downstairs, washing up; pans to scour, (no dishwasher then). Well-worn carpets (not fitted) were first sprinkled with damp tealeaves, to slacken the dust before sweeping, the heavy rugs taken outside, to be shook or beaten (no hoover). Cleaning the grate was a thankless daily task, the brass fender had two boxes one at each end, one contained old newspapers, from the other was taken black lead paste, emery paper for the steel, brushes and clothes for polishing. Ashes were put in a metal pail, taken outside, to be sifted. Finally polishing the fender. Furniture was polished (no spray on, only a tin of hard paste and elbow grease) the sun slanting through the window, highlighting the swirling motes of silvery dust in the air that lavender furniture polish failed to capture. Windows cleaned with newspaper dipped in vinegar added to warm water. You could eat your dinner off the doorstep polished with red cardinal. Preparation of bucketfuls of vegetables, straight from the garden, in winter clogged in mud and sludge.

One job done in the evenings with everyone taking part "*Oh No*" was silver and brass polishing. Thankfully not done too often, a messy job. Paper was spread on the table, out came the entire cutlery, (no stainless steel) along with the horse brasses. A wad of rag was soaked, poured from the brasso tin. Rub hard each individual object, now coated in black slime, awaiting a wrist aching polish, till sparkling, a final wash in soapy water for the cutlery completed the loathed job. Badly stained knifes were plunged up to the hilt into the earth overnight, knife handles were bone. These often broke leaving a sharp spike and some knife blades were worn extremely thin from constant sharpening, ground backwards and forwards on the stone doorstep.

In spite of all the intense routine cleaning, an annual major spring-cleaning took place. Lasting about a fortnight this took place around May when no more fires would be needed, starting at the top, working down every crack and cranny was attacked with manic zeal. Preparations were made, everything that could be removed was, all remainders had to be covered in dustsheets.

First came the chimney sweep. He positioned his very dirty well used sacking cloth around the whole fireplace, tucking in to seal as best he could, with his large round bristly brush in the fire grate, the screw end through a pre positioned hole. Further rods were then screwed to the brush, pushing and twisting upwards. Us children were dispatched outside to shout when the brush was protruding, twirling and jigging in a flurry dance from the chimney pot. In reverse the brush was brought down, as the rods were unscrewed. After careful removal of the sacking, soot inches deep filling every nook and cranny had to be scooped up placed in old dustbins outside for later spreading on the garden.

For about two weeks every summer, thunderflies, small black insects living in the crops of fields being harvested, disturbed by the combines, found there way into everything, just 1.5mm long and 0.3mm high, they squeezed into many tight places, especially picture frames, that had to be took apart, cleaned and reassembled.

Flies were a perpetual irritant, inch long tubes were bought, the attached string when pulled revealed a twisting, lengthening sticky tape, hung from ceilings trapped the offending pests; wasps, which loved the sweet things in life could be captured in an almost empty jam jar part full of water, an immediate alternative for either was swatting with rolled up newspaper.

Washing, ironing, cooking, baking, preserving, bread to make, even found time to do her own decorating. If painting and wallpapering, more upheaval followed, colour schemes never got beyond brown and cream. Ceilings were given a new coat of lumpy whitewash that splashed all over. Wallpaper then came with plain strips ½ inch wide, edging each side of the rolls that first had to be removed from as many as fifteen roles per room. Walls were uneven, making it difficult to keep paper straight, corners were a nightmare. Paste was made from flour and water, often lumpy; spreading could be uneven leading to many creases in the finished job.

Decorating time was looked forward to by us children, so many art projects awaited. The edging removed from the rolls could be coiled making various sized circles for sculpted pictures. Carefully pushing the centre from large coil circles, I would attempt to make the longest cone possible before it collapsed. A favourite when paste remained was doing paper mache people or animals. This entailed inflating balloons of differing sizes, then small torn strips of newspaper were pasted to balloon totally covering with many layers. When dry, when the balloons went down you were left with firm globes, which could be used for heads and bodies. A coat of paint completed the assignment.

Next came the washing down of furniture with vinegar added to the water, rugs put on the line and beaten inch by inch with a coiled cane of split bamboo, red cardinal polish on the old red tiles. When completed everything in that house was scrubbed and cleaned till it shone.

Bedrooms were tackled with the same thoroughness, all blankets washed on a breezy drying day.

Last but not least, the privy and wash-house would be lime washed with distemper.

In summer I could be up and out with the lark, but winter I hated getting up. Gran would call me; with porridge ready; from the side boiler take water for a wash, clean socks and school uniform lie warming in front of fire. After putting on my coat and hat, wrapping me snuggly in my scarf sent me on my way. It gave me something more precious than worldly goods.

Always she made time for us, attended school events, took us to church and chapel events, never considered herself fully dressed without wearing a hat when she left home. She taught me so much, good manners, right from wrong, to knit, embroider and sew, I never recall Gran getting cross with me. I inherited her love of flowers she

taught me the names of almost every English wild and garden flowers.
Soothed me when thunderstorms came and the heavens opened, the whole landscape lit by the lightning, was both wonderful and frightening. "It will do us no harm", "its God speaking to us" she quietly reflected. The bubbles formed as the rain hit the path, watched through the open door were "soldiers marching".

It was quite an occasion when the postman came; he did not come very often, but with daily haste on his bright red bicycle if he had mail for you. A telegram was greatly feared; it was almost always bad news. Weekly visitors were the travelling shop, the coalman, as well as insurance man, who collected your shilling to provide for a decent burial, all were from the co-op. It was not unusual for tramps, who in those days frequented the roads everywhere to call, looking to receive a cup of water in addition to a crust of bread before going on their way. A very resourceful lady, with nerves of steel, she once had trouble with one persistent vagrant who would not leave after receiving such charity. Although alone except for Alan and I still in bed, she told the man her son was home furthermore he would be down at any moment. He listened intently for sound of movement, at which point I stirred, thinking it was the son he finally left. A nasty experience but Gran was not afraid, but unfortunately it left me with feelings of fear.
Another caller was the gypsy lady once a year. Gran never turned them away empty handed, a few pegs or flowers bought to help the less fortunate. "After all, she's only trying to earn a little". The pegs were long finger length chips of willow bound with a strip from an old tin can. The flowers, assembled intricate shavings of dyed wood were works of art.

Our doctor was called O'Keefe, a wise man, belonged to the old school, knew each member of the family, remembered illnesses, he never failed to enquire after the health of the rest of the household when visiting.
Always had time to listen to you, had the power to inspire you, did you good just to see him, wasn't writing the prescription before you had described the symptoms. Called out to visit, he always carried his leather bag seldom opened, fresh air and good food cured most things, "I can only give nature a helping hand" he used to say. If medicine was required, recovery was delayed whilst the prescription

was taken to be dispensed at the chemist, difficult and expensive when living in the country, with only buses to get to town. One problem I suffered from was painful stye's, small pus-filled abscesses formed near the inner corner of the eye.

I well remember being confined to bed for weeks, when I had Jaundice. Flu-like symptoms, accompanied by nausea, vomiting, loss of appetite and tenderness in the right upper abdomen. Yellowing of the skin and the whites of eyes, caused by an accumulation of a yellow-brown bile pigment in the blood, a sign of disorders of the liver, which caused me to miss school's visit to the screening of Edmund Hilary and Sherpa Tenzing's conquest on May 29th 1953 of Everest.

The medicine, as recovery progressed was left on the washstand, I, being entrusted to take. Being vile tasting, I avoided this by disposal. Realising the required dose had to be seen to be deplinishing, I could not add it to the 'guzzunder', it would have tainted my urine, if I poured it from the window, a stain would have developed on the grass below. So, cleverly I took the spoon, with the tips of my left finger and thumb holding the tip of the bowl, the handle pointing away from me, trapped between the right thumb underneath and finger over, I proceeded to flick the contents through the open window. Different directions were chosen, to spread the linctus, great fun was had attempting record-breaking distances.

About this time I also suffered from what I recall was cold on my kidneys, whether they were connected and which came first I have no way of calculating. Genuine reasons had to be provided for absences from school; the truant officers visit was greatly feared. One other thing that kept me from school for a while was ringworm. A fungal skin infection, as its name suggests, a ring-shaped reddened, scaly patch on my arm, believed to have been picked up from the cattle.

Home remedies cured most minor ailments. Vegetable soup was all I would eat when ill. In winter daily doses of cod liver oil and malt were habitually taken. A spoonful of syrup of figs was taken if necessary. Chests rubbed with goose grease, revolting yellow fat, at first signs of a cough, fresh lemons sliced into hot water with spoonfuls of honey stirred in, drank as hot as possible. On the whole we were a healthy family, but once Uncle Jeff was confined to bed with bad back, he spent a long time laid on a board in severe pain. As I think about illnesses, accidents come to mind, my cousin John, Aunt Edna's son, once whilst visiting, fell climbing to the sink, with a pencil in his hand, putting it through the roof of his mouth, no telephones, his mum had to flag down a passing motorist to take them to the town hospital. Uncle Bob got shot in his leg whilst poaching, this caused Gran a great deal of worry and stress, not the only thing either, Uncle Bob had to do his two years 'conscription' every male at 18yrs of age was called up for National Service.

Whilst the doctor was a kindly man who visited us at home, (I never recall going to the surgery as a child) he always smiled and made you better. No such affection for the dour dentist, his surgery in a room of clinical superiority was a torture chamber, with gleaming stainless steel instruments, injections, foul smelling gas, blood, and abominable pain. I still have a paranoid fear of the dentists chair and all it represents, the horror never diminishes, even a visit to the place for some-one else brings on the stomach cramps, nausea, hairs standing up on the back of the neck feeling. I tremble, worrying if a hand will reach out, dragging me to the dreaded seat. Needless to say I always found some one else to take my children for treatment.

Whilst I had an idyllic childhood, I have no illusions regarding the hardships of dad's life as a farm worker, under-rated but the finest, the most necessary, and least rewarded job on earth.

Dad, was capable of doing just about everything, a skilled agricultural labourer who sowed; harrowed; harvested; ploughed a furrow as straight as a die, half frozen on an open tractor often in driving snow; no proper protection in frosty weather, in driving rain layering a hedge or clearing a dyke to keep the ditches running free, heads and shoulders under a sacking cowl, with chapped hands all winter, his gloves always drying in the hearth; occasionally milking when the cowman was ill. With the compelling flow of farming, he worked long hours, including Saturday mornings the only holiday with pay being Christmas day and Good Friday. He left home on his bicycle around six forty breeched; gaited and hob-nailed shod; flat cap; thick leather belt held up trousers that did not stay up of their own accord; carrying his snap bag, returning after five thirty in the evening with mud splattered boots, helpless employee of the climate. Working in fields mostly some distance from roads or houses was a lonely life with pack-up, consisting of thick chunks of home-made bread smeared with butter, sandwiched with hunks of cheese or home cured ham; a large slice of home-made cake or apple pie; plus a billycan of tea, sweetened with condensed milk by now cold; taken out in the fields he huddled in the hedge bottom to shelter from winds, rain or snow. If nearby he'd cycle home, or brought the tractor if possible, with an hour, to get home eat dinner, and get back. Many's the time when in a hurry, he drank his cuppa poured into his saucer, then blown on to cool it.

Every Friday night he brought home his wages in a small brown envelope, the outside stating how many hours worked that week, rate per hour, deductions. Inside to the penny the nett amount in cash.

In arable farming, each year the seasons dictated what I watched repeatedly growing in the fields around us. The natural countryside and rural life inseparable.

Harvest memories are the happy ones for me; the sun always seemed to shine. I can picture dad now returning from the hot July fields, soaked with sweat, hayseeds down his shirt making his back itch, but never removing waistcoat, and flannel shirt no matter how hot.

Mr. Anyan had a combine harvester, which cut and thrashed in one operation. Those days it was a new, enormous red monster, that crawled along, hoovering the standing wheat into it's gaping mouth, pouring the thrashed grain into the lorry crawling along side, leaving a trail of straw in its wake. Many miles of companionship followed when I accompanied Dad as he drove the fully loaded lorry to their other farm at Bishopbridge, to be tipped into a hungry funnel, were it proceeded to the huge grain drying sheds. Later the straw was collected by the baler that left compacted oblong moulds at intervals, the length and breath of the field, next, men gathered the bales into interlocking stacks of about a dozen, finally when dry, collected to store in barns for winter bedding for livestock. Harvest time meant four to six weeks of concentrated work, longer days, whole weekends, through lunch and tea break.

Theirs was mixed farming, cattle were kept, cereal crops were grown along with sugar beet and potatoes (I also sometimes accompanied dad on delivery's to the sugar beet factory at Brigg) .

Dad's 'spare' time was used to good effect in the garden, he grew the fruit and vegetables a vital product of the kitchen, contributing to the family economy. Cultivated from the narrow well-trod earth paths threaded between neat rows. Vegetables existed in a tangled web with fragrant flowers, not in special beds surrounding lawns, but interspersed, night-scented stock, with a fence heavy with sweet peas, the more they were cut the more they grew, and my much-loved delicate, fragile peonies. Gran loved a vase of fresh flowers in the house, all her life she told us all, she wanted flowers while she was alive, not when she was dead and could not enjoy them. I loved being with my dad in the garden, in the shed or in the fields. He taught me so much about nature, birds; all things creepy crawly, worms, centipedes, beetles as we disturbed them when digging, gathering firewood (dead twigs were always collected to use for lighting the fire 'kindling') or simply moving a stone to look what might be underneath. Along with survival, what could be taken freely to eat or what to leave alone like magic mushrooms. How to collect seeds to maintain growing things including how to sprout potatoes for the next season, to skin a rabbit or pluck a pheasant.

Only a few rows of very early 'tatties' (potatoes) were grown, main crop potatoes were free and plentiful from Dad's boss. Nothing was wasted, it was drilled into us, "Waste not, want not" it was a sacrilege to throw anything, even the smallest piece of bread, on the fire, there's always animals to feed. Tea leaves, (no tea bags) eggshells, thrown on the compost heap. Potato and vegetable parings, along with anything else eatable was fed to pig. Bones to the dog, bread and cake crumbs thrown to birds. Newspapers could be used for lighting the fire, screwed up tight they could double as emergency sticks.

Ever resourceful, I recall him once repairing the hinges of a sagging wooden gate with old boot soles. Nailing heels to post, soles to gate. Many an old bedstead breached a hole in the hedge.

In the 'bosses' fields, away, up behind us was a derelict farm. The barns had been kept in reasonable state of repair, housing cattle in winter. As a five year old, I loved to climb the crew yard gate and watch the magnificent animals. The old tumbledown house was a place of mystery, creaking stairs led to an upstairs door to nowhere, (parts long since fallen away) many of my best essays and storytelling revolved around that ghostly house and ethereal woods. After autumn gales we went with the tractor borrowed from dads boss, to those same woods and fields, there to collect fallen timber. I drove the tractor, well I sat in the seat with the tractor in low gear crawling along as I steered, whilst dad threw the wood on the accompanying trailer. In the following weeks, thin twigs were bundled together for kindling, pea sticks and bean sticks for the garden were specially selected. Into use came the 'horse', a bench of chunky wood, two X-X joined by a bar, home made to hold thick branches whilst being sawn into suitable sized logs, purgatory after hours of tugging the cross-cut saw backwards and forwards, to me; to you; to me; to you. Extra large logs had to be further split, all stacked under a lean-to cover to keep the home fires burning through winter.

The fowls bought at the Stennets Auction Mart - popped in a hessian sack to bring home - always had to be shut in the hen house at night to be protected from the rats and foxes.

I adored the Rhode island red hens when they hatched their broods of fluffy chicks, dad placed the mother hen, in an old tea chest turned on its side with slats of wood nailed over the front and there she was safe as she called her chicks under her wings. The evocative smells of nostalgia, like the whiff of wood smoke in the garden as autumn bonfires tidied the grounds for winter; the sweet smell of may-blossom; perfumed meadowsweet; rich new mown hay and the gloriously refreshing smell of cooling rain falling onto hot sun parched earth; not like today's choking exhaust fumes in traffic jams or cigarette smoke in a restaurant.

In cages he kept the ferrets to go rabbitting with, bundles of cream fur, a separate cage held the hob (the male) they clawed at the wire for their food of rabbit, bread and milk. I still remember their pungent odour the only animals I did not like. One time we kept pigeons, with one being allocated to me for a pet, but the first time it was released it flew away never to return.

My uncles regarded poaching partly as a craft, partly as sport, real artful poachers, skills learnt of a lifetime of necessity, it weren't just for rabbits neither, they did not leave all the pheasants for the gentry, a twelve bore shotgun, an oversized jacket or coat with extra large inside pockets to conceal the ill gotten gains. The sight of the keeper was the signal to leg it.

The house is now one, still almost unchanged on the outside, times stood still, nothing added and nothing taken away, but still stands as I describe it. Solid and dependable but no pigs in the sty's and no kitchen garden.

I knew every ditch and tree within miles of that house.

When I think of freedom my mind goes back, an enchanting time, my most carefree memories are there. We were children longer in those days, simplicity, inexperienced, purity and uncorrupted innocence; such are my recollections of childhood. Looking back it was purely where and how we lived, in a typical farm workers cottage. It was no easy life, struggling to support Dad, Gran, Uncle Bob, Uncle Jeff, Auntie Annie, cousin Alan plus me, but it was a happy childhood, one filled with love and happiness. I never recall being shouted at or smacked, discipline could be imposed by a look or being sent to bed.(no Television/DVD's, mobile phones to temper the punishment). Raised the proper way, brought up to respect other people as well as self respect, with values and guidance, not formal instruction but a helping, watching, taking part in life skills. Honesty; good manners; commonsense; always ready to help one another. NOT told to "Go away" or " Don't bother me now". Allowed to be in the way, being involved, having a go, making a mess, time for supervising. Respect for people, family, teachers, belongings, churches; consideration for young and old alike; right and wrong clearly distinguished, all learnt by example. A belief you were as good as the next person, maybe others had more money, but wealth didn't make anyone better. Appreciation of what you've got and acceptance of what you couldn't change. The essence of childhood. Throwbacks to a well-mannered, thoughtful Britain. Give your children something they will always remember and be grateful for: your time and knowledge.

Childhood is the best time to 'listen to counsel and receive instruction, that you may be wise in your latter days' (Proverbs 19:20, NKJ).

7. HIGH DAYS AND HOLIDAYS.

Come, climb upon my knee
And I will tell of things that used to be
Of horses and carts, and binders cutting corn,
Of long rows of stooks like wigwams,
Where we used to play
Of long sunny days,
And rivers where we fished all day.
The meadows of butter cups and daises,
The skylarks singing in the blue sky
The smell of new mown hay,
The plough turning the soil,
The sound, of jingling harness,
The plodding faithful horses,
What peace! These things and sounds,
Will never come again.
      P.E. HEWITT

On the day of arrival at Thonock Rd., having looked around inside, I went outside to investigate further and stood in the field at the edge of our boundary was a girl who introduced herself as Linda. She lived in the farmhouse, Beck Farm, with the field dividing us. We became best friends, both being the same age. She had two brothers a lot older who had already left home, so in effect she was probably as lonely as I was. I like to think she was glad we'd come to live there. There were no other children until you got to the village. The field was surrounded by hedges with a portion of high fencing on our boundary, which we climbed when calling for each other. One particular time as I entered the field, the bull was loose, he put his head down to charge me, I turned, not looking back I ran like hell back to the fence, not bothering with the stile I cleared it in one go. I'm sure it would have made the record books at school. Never again did I jump that height.

Beyond were further fields and further still was the woods, a huge expanse to explore then play in, it was absolute paradise to a child with a vivid imagination. We knew every inch and had specific places for specific games. A small stream ran behind the farmhouse. We spent hours throwing different woods of varying lengths from one side of the bridge which spanned the main road and waiting the opposite side to see whose was first through, it was a very competitive game to see who could find the 'best' and 'fastest' boat.

The road was never very busy, the buses came along regularly the motor car was the exception rather than the rule, and intermittent sit up and beg cycles with guards to protect your dresses and trouser legs came along almost empty roads. From the top of a haystack we'd watch Tab Hunter, so called because he was always looking in the gutter for cigarette ends known as the *'tab'* end. He was a cripple with a wooden leg, so his bike was adapted with a fixed peddle enabling him to cycle along with one foot. We also wrote down the registration numbers of passing vehicles, but for the life of me I know not why.

I was quite a tomboy, one stretch of the stream had trees we loved to climb, all sizes and shapes ripe with age lining its banks. Many had branches that met overhead forming bowers, romantic fairytale land. Our circus the very miss-shaped long branches, some split with age lain across the stream where we balanced and swung. Two low dumpy branches which responded to every movement, fixed with string made reins for good horses in cowboy and indian games, with cap-guns along with bows made from suitable, flexible hazel sticks and arrows imaginatively dipped in deadly poison, (cow pats). Fort Knox with suitable shaped lengths of wood crudely carved into rifles. An old sheet and discarded wheel we sailed our fishing boats as they met the North Sea swell; this locality was our den, fairground, the backdrop lending itself to many other backgrounds with our fertile imaginations. Plus there was no shortage of chestnut trees to provide our conkers.

One area had been the dump long ago, before there were dustbin men, it was a rich source of finds and treasures, mainly beautiful pieces of broken pottery in addition to coloured glass we were always trying to piece together. A huge tree, nearest the road, with a suitable branch overhanging the field, had a stout rope fastened around it to become our swing. Hide and seek in the hay lofts, stables or stack yards; a slide down the straw rick; endless steps and old wooden ladders seeing who dare jump from the highest rung. A veritable paradise for adventurous kids.

Corn, the general name covering wheat, barley, and oats was harvested differently at smaller farms. Mr. Wray's, harvest was cut by reaper, with its slender rotating arms, its musical whirr carrying across still air, the binder then gathered small amounts into bundles tying neatly with string , then spat them back onto the field. Next, the workers stacked these 'sheaves' upright, grouped together in neat

rows about four at a time to form wigwam stooks (pronounced 'stowks'). These were left to be dried in the sun, before being collected to the stacks for thrashing. As many tractors and trailers as possible were sent to the fields for pitching and loading, the rope was thrown over the hay, hitched to the hooks on the sides of the trailers to secure the loads then brought back to the yard, arranged in huge stacks, these were then thatched - a way of keeping them dry until thrashing.
The visit from the threshing machine caused great excitement, such fun to watch for us children, with it's noise, steam and spinning wheels but not so pleasant for the workers. Arriving in the grey light of early morning, it was a long dusty, sweaty day of endless toil. All available men attended, it took at least seven people, (often women were called upon to help). One end of the stack the tractor stood, attached to the threshing drum by an endless crackling 'drive'-belt to keep the shuddering monster running. Like clockwork figures, men often in bib and brace overalls, tossed down the sheaves with pitchforks, to the man who cut the bands, next fed into the huge, ear-splitting, clattering, shuddering machine. The water butt had to be kept full, used to keep the belt on pulleys, delays cost money. Corn grains emerged collected in sacks, to be wheeled away to the granary. The remorseless machine, shunted back and forth in rapid motion, chewed, swallowed and spat out chaff and straw, pouring from the pulse hole, the bowels of the machine, often referred to as the black hole, the clouds of dust whipping into every pore, eye and nostril, filling eyes and throats, repeatedly raked, removed as far away as possible. The men held up their trousers by braces and tied at the calf with binder twine to stop the ever-present rats that ran from the stack, running up the legs before the dogs could catch them. As dusk fell the rhythmic clattering, pulsating beat of machinery slowed down, then stopped, bringing a returning welcome silence, the men washed under the cold water pump, then enjoyed a substantial meal provided by the farmers wife.

When I look back summers were long and hot, the sun always shone, bedtime was agony when it was still so bright outside. As the heavy curtains were drawn we could only await, Mr. Sandman drifting in as you planned for the dawn.
Winters were extremely harsh. As I sit her typing my memories I drift to another world *shivering I breath on the glass, rub hard to make a peephole to peer through the window frozen inside and out,*

revealing a world beyond unseen except for a blanket of snow several feet deep, magically sparkling on a glittering landscape of fields, the hedges wave with high curving crests, garden completely out of sight, all other objects transformed into grotesque shapes. Thick icicles up to five feet long, like long pointed witches fingers hang from the roofs of sheds. The winter wonderland of my childhood,
But this is January 2010, as I look through the window, after twenty two days of snow, today's view is quite different. Firstly I am toasty warm in the study of my central heated house, the double glazed windows do not freeze over. It is as nothing compared to my childhood. Although still living in the country, unfortunately I donot have the benefit of isolation. The houses in the street have the odd roof tiles showing minute amounts of snow, poor insulation *in this day and age*. No grotesque shapes, no icicles, no curving crests, just lightly dusted as if sprinkled with icing sugar. A layer of snow covers the street, not even as deep as the paths, along with the paths (no-ones heard of shovels), dangerously icy. No gritting in our village (the councils are even struggling to grit main roads). A bit of snow, (admitted some of the country has more than others, but nothing like 1947, 1962/3) and the papers tell of a country nearly at a standstill. The brilliant white has turned to dirty grey as cars slither away to work and shops, the exception the intact lustrous playing field. Where are the children? Not a snowmen to be seen, no children sliding, snowballing, sledging or skating on the frozen pond. To cold, to dangerous, to lazy or to much trouble for mum with all that wet washing?
Returning to my childhood, I loved to run out onto the sheet of unsullied whiteness stretching as far as the eyes could see, writing my name in large letters with a stick. With clouds of breath like dragons fire, we skated on the frozen pond and snowballed. We became budding architects as we drew plans of our future mansions in sweeping strokes with a brush in the field of virgin snow. Plunging our boots deep into the crunchy frozen snow we built snowmen placing a carrot for his nose, two lumps of coal for eyes, tied a scarf around his neck, to stand on parade lonely and forlorn. It must have been a nightmare for Gran, all those wet clothes and no dryers then, but I never heard a complaint. Outside night time prowlers could be identified by their paw prints. Overnight snow drifted high, remaining frozen statuesque as the door was opened, milk frozen in the bottles, rose inches high above the tops, the water

butt outside the door has an impenetrable foot of ice crust.

I once read that Britain had the coldest day since 1895 on February 1st 1956, but the winters of my childhood were as nothing compared to the older family members. I have been told the 1939/40 winter was particularly severe. It began to snow on boxing day and continued to snow and freeze for several weeks, covering the fields to a great depth, intensely cold, frozen points on railways caused long delays, roads impassable, blizzard conditions cut houses off for several weeks isolated, people ran short of food, men and snow ploughs worked long hours. Tales were told of sheep buried in the snow, looking for signs in tell tale holes, searches taking place with dogs. During one blizzard, an old man had died in his cottage, any approach along the roads was impossible, so the coffin was carried over fields, supported by a ladder on strong shoulders.

But at last spring came, icy cold winds no longer blew across the fields, the snow melted, until next time goodbye to freezing cold hands with icy feet, birds sang sweetly or raucous calls could be heard in the open fields, by the stream, in the wood. The roadsides, meadows and hedgerows were rich in wildflowers, butterflies to catch, streams to wade. We found the rabbits who lived in their holts in the banks of the ditches.

"We're bored" was never heard. We free ranged all the fields and woods, the wind blowing through our hair, sun warming our backs or soaked to the skin by rain, we were true children of the countryside. Whatever the season, wherever we walked there were things to delight. We grew to know the cycle of the four seasons, noting the changes taking place of plants and trees, birds, butterflies, dragonflies, and insects, a source of joy and wonder to a country child. How well I remember intricate cobweb patterns on the hedges early in the mornings.

In the middle of the field between the houses was a pond we were very attracted to, providing hours of fun, catching tadpoles, sticklebacks or collecting frogspawn in jam jars. Primroses; rosehips; violets; cowslips; wild roses plus honeysuckle grew in profusion, gathered in their season for vases at home, also pressed between the pages of books, weighed down with anything heavy we could find, in winter to be mounted in our scrap-books. Poppies occurred frequently in cornfields, wafting their scarlet heads in the breeze. Daisies in abundance, we picked, split the stalks with our fingernails threaded one through another and made long, long daisy chains. Our shoes yellow with pollen dust of massed buttercups we held them under each other's chins to see who liked butter, dandelion seeds were blown in the wind, how many puffs taken to extinguish was supposed to indicate the time. In May we celebrated the passing of winter, the new life of springtime. One of us with blossom garlanded around our hair, sat on a throne in a decorated bower, presiding over the other, with great pink-striped bindweed flowers on trails of snaking stalks and leaves, weaved around her body to pirouette in royal robes. We had picnics, of jam sandwiches with a bottle of water. If we wanted to 'spend a penny' when out, we had to retire to ditches or behind hedges to answer the call of nature, you risked being tickled by long grass, or if really unlucky stung by nettles, the remedy being to rub the affected area with dock leaves. We went to the woods collecting bluebells by the arms full, from the carpet of blue under springtime trees, in the morning dew the stalks of plants were woven with spider's gossamer threads, the cobwebs glistening like mirard diamonds in early morning Sun. We never got lost when going deep into the cool, dark, amazing, mysterious, secret world, we just tied a rope to the first tree, allowing us to retrace our way out. We enjoyed a freedom of the countryside you'll never know. Brought up as I was close to the workings of the British countryside, I have retained the mental images of tilled fields, green trees, clear running water, abundant wildlife in the midst of wide skies. I am keenly aware of the debt I owe to my country upbringing. Will you hear the birds singing or the wind blowing in the trees, with your ever-present mobile phone and MP3 player permantly attached to your ear.

We were allowed to roam the fields going anywhere we liked, taught to respect the countryside. Close all gates, don't damage crops or property, leave no litter, protect all wildlife, and starting fires never crossed our minds. Gran never knew for sure were we where, until mealtimes when rumbling tums always brought us home, I once brought visitors with me, I came back complaining of itching, Gran must have heard the murmuring or spotted them hovering, speedily removing my clothing on the doorstep to reveal scores of wasps crawling all over me, how I don't know, but I escaped without a sting. Often coming home wet to the waist from playing in long wet grass, with permanently grazed knees, I was a mix of tom boy also a shy reserved girl who would not say boo to a mouse, always in dresses in summer or skirts and jumpers in winter, girls never wore trousers or jeans.

Linda's parents had a large level front lawn, well maintained amid sheltered bushes of all shapes, sizes and colours, providing delightful settings for our plays and concerts. I viewed myself as rather plain and timid; but in pretending I could be anyone but myself, from elegant lady to wicked wolf; exquisite butterfly to ugly duckling. Entry through the front door also provided direct access on the left hand side to Linda's playroom, with a dressing up box full of adult clothes with wonderful high heel shoes, to hobble around in, along with a tall cupboard full of dolls, teddies, soldiers etc. that also could take part in our make believe world. There was also a gramophone, which you laboriously wound up, carefully lifting a sizeable arm to lower the needle into the first groove of records providing music to sing along or dance to with suitable actions. How I loved 'How much is that doggie in the window'; 'Daisy, Daisy'; 'I'm Shy Mary Ellen I'm Shy'; 'Any old iron' and the rousing 'Roll out the barrel'. A clothes horse with an old blanket thrown over made a perfect tent in which to take tea out of the sun, on rainy days a playhouse could be found under the table.

A drainpipe grate was the perfect place to play marbles. There was never a shortage of large blank walls to play ball games, or hard surfaces for skipping. A game called Snobs, called for dexterity, five metal crosses or small pebbles, were scattered in front of you, using only your right hand you repeatedly tossed a wooden cube slightly in the air, before catching it again, the aim being to move your snobs close enough together in order to pick them up in one go with the same hand, continuing to throw and catch your wood you attempted to turn the hand over catching them all on the back of the hand. Variations followed, you could continue turning the hand, catching alternate palm and reverse or you could arch your left hand, with the right hand the snobs had to be pushed between spreading fingers into the centre, picking up the set again to complete, whilst throwing the wood in the air. At any point if you failed to catch your wood, you had to start again,

Dad once had a scrap car in our yard, it provided endless fun, no battery but I had the key, I suspect I drove twice around the world. A curved corrugated roofing sheets, one standing each end made a great sea- saw. Dad also made me trolleys from old pram wheels, and planks of wood, sledges when the snow came, stilts made longer as you grew.

When on my own our apple trees were climbed, perched in the branches a place of quietness, opening the door to sensitive pleasures, like listening to the birds, a place to read a book in peace, or just watch the clouds float by.

Whilst working in the fields bordering the golf course, dad often found golf balls, hurled out of range. These treasures he brought home for me, one day he returned with the star prize, a discarded broken golf club. Placed in the fire, to burn out the wood, a new shaft inserted, a new game emerged. When enough family members gathered we played rounders or cricket

We were happier I'm sure than they are today, simple pleasures we no longer understand, that cost little or nothing, before the television, computer, Internet age. I feel sorry for today's children --so much artificial amusement created for them, in the drive to give them an array of gadgets, gimmicks and extravagance with relentless pressure to purchase more than we really need and often beyond the means. I'm not against progress but children are subjected to the adult world to soon, I believe we were better for being children first, what's the bored child of today going to do tomorrow. My life was blessed with certainty and belief. A safe world, life then was idyllic.

On long, dark winter evenings which I hated and still do, the whole family played games, designed to keep us amused in the long dark evenings, pass the time with a strong educational purpose, encouraging reading, spelling, geography, history and maths skills. Learning never was such tremendous fun, all good character building stuff, training memories, giving us an enormous fund of information and general knowledge.

Many games were played with pencil and paper. Noughts and crosses, squares, (make any sized square of dots, anywhere on the square take alternate turns to join two dots together, the object being to make a square which you put your initial in, whilst preventing your opponents from completing squares. The winner is the one with the most complete squares). Lists, was played by choosing a subject, a time was set, a category was chosen, names of birds, towns, countries of the world, food (or narrowed down to vegetables, fruit), animals, etc. a point was awarded for each item on your list that no-one else had acquired. Boys or girls names, was slightly different, going through each letter of the alphabet in turn, as many as possible names of the chosen letter were wrote in the allotted time. Again each name you had that your opponents had not, gave you a one-point score. (A game that can be adapted to play in your head, when you can't get to sleep, beats counting elusive sheep). 'Words within words' example Constantinople, contains Police, Tin, Scone, Stop etc.

Hangmen, draw the gallows, upturned L, choose a word in your head, substitute the correct amount of _ _ _ _ for your chosen word. The guesser chooses letters from the alphabet, if correct it's added in the appropriate position, each wrong guess an appendage of body is drawn until you've hung the opposition.

A beetle drive is great entertainment for any number of players. Taking it in turns to throw the dice, allowing you to draw your beetle a six giving you a body, must be thrown before you can commence. Next drawing parts that correspond with the number thrown, 5 head - can proceed without, 4 giving tail, three legs each side of body- 3 each, must wait patiently to throw again if no head, 2 each for two feelers to place upon head - finally 1 each for two eyes. First to complete shouts "beetle", stopping the game, totalling each persons score, the game restarts, after a pre-arranged number of rounds, say ten, the person with the highest score wins.

Various games, - snakes and ladders, ludo, tiddlywinks, came complete with spinner (you cut out and inserted a matchstick in the centre), (no dice) - on the backs of selection boxes at Christmas, buttons provided the counters. We had many packs of cards, including snapdragon and old maid, a tin of dominoes and draughts with board (I still have them). We were never just allowed to win, that didn't teach you how to develop your logic, if you were always given in to. You had to think for yourself and try harder.

Books have played a large part in my life, I have a voracious appetite for reading, I still devour books, and have collected an extensive library of fact and fiction books. I hate parting with my books, experience has made me reluctant to loan any out, as people are careless about retuning them. Aunts and Uncle's supplied me with books for Christmas presents, they kindly gratified my appetite for reading. 'Rupert Bear' annuals, Enid Blyton's 'Famous Five', 'What Katy Did' 'Black Beauty' now long gone having reached the scruffy stage after being enjoyed by three generations. Alan who enjoyed me reading to him every night very much-favoured 'Millie Mollie Mandy'. One very special book 'A Childs Book Of Ballet' that has survived, all be it discoloured by age, a bit dog-eared, with sellotape binding the pages together, was given me at Christmas 1955 by my Aunt Edna. To me it's priceless and evokes recollections of high aspirations, reading by candlelight or torch under the bedclothes when I had batteries. Always money was found to buy me Dandy or Beano comic, later Musical Express.

I was one of those kids who was always making things, never ever throwing scraps away, a real hoarder, you never knew what you might want, always a challenge to see what you could make, I always had a project on the go. I had very few bought toys; after all I had no need. I had a Golliwog, together with Rupert bear; they sat on a chair at my bedside. Those dolls I did have served a purpose, acted out roles, or were for the skill of making. Dad produced soundly made masterpieces, the most fantastic wooden dolls house, it had a kitchen, sitting room, with central stairs to two bedrooms. He painted bricks on the outside, the front slid away for access, and best of all it had real lights, tiny bulbs working from a car battery. Together we made all the furniture from matchboxes. Gran gave me left over wallpaper to paper the rooms, scraps of material made curtains. Pipe cleaners were extremely useful, just twisted to make outlines of dolls shortening of pipe cleaners produced varying sizes. Buttons were used for feet, body's bound in pink bias binding, with heads made of pink felt. Animals too could be made, or the arms for peg dolls, (the old split pegs) tiny faces painted on the knob. With wool for hair, tiny scraps of material, ribbon, lace for clothes provided hours of pleasure.

I made myself theatres in many forms, one from a shoebox. A series of pictures were drawn and coloured on a reel of paper almost the width of your shoebox, to make your film. Two holes, in line were made at one end of your shoebox, place your pencil through one hole, wind the film onto pencil and then push pencil through second hole. Make a viewing hole at opposite end, place lid on top and turn pencil. Another theatre was more the traditional stage, made from a cardboard box on its side. Home made curtains, painted scenery with paper dolls in various outfits completed the effect. Old socks suitably adorned with patches made hand puppets for Punch and Judy shows, if no striped material available for the traditional showcase you just painted stripes on your chosen box.

Christmas and birthday cards made wonderful peep shows. Cut a window in the lid of a shoebox, cover the box with pretty paper, make a pin hole in one end. Mount a scene inside the box, carefully cut from your cards with a little bit extra left at the base of each, trees for forests, flowers for gardens, leaving a winding road down the middle. Imagination knew no bounds, add robins and stagecoaches, the sun or rainbow, painted if no suitable picture.

Bend your excess, glue them in standing positions, finish by fastening down your lid. Held up to the light, to shine through the 'window', peep through the pin-hole.

With the light behind you, a magical show could be achieved by using various interwoven interlocking hands and fingers placed in strategic positions making moving shadows on the walls. Birds, butterflies floated silently, while giraffes, elephants prowled by.

I was very arty always having plenty of pencils and crayons; odd rolls of wallpaper cut into squares provided lots of drawing material. Patterns could be made by even the least artistic person, drawn around your own hands or different size coppers (coinage) repeatedly drawn overlapping into original and effective arrangements. Even pencil lines imaginatively looped, twisted, spiralling across a sheet of paper made the basis for ingenious colouring pictures. Tissue paper could be used for tracing, placed over picture to be reproduced, copy the image, scribble heavily on the reverse side, place on clean sheet and trace over again, the picture is transferred. Two copies of your writing or drawings could be produced by placing a wonderful thing called carbon paper between two sheets of paper. Likewise coins placed under thin paper could be rubbed across with a lead pencil to reproduce the image. Paper provided endless possibilities, strips could be folded carefully in concertina style, a half doll drawn on one fold, cut, leaving hands joining, unfold for strip of dancing dolls, also applied to father Christmas's, elf's, fairies, endless possibilities the imagination conjured. We practised the art of paper folding long before we knew it was called origami. Newspaper made Robin Hood, pirates or witches hats, boats, an amazing bird with flapping wings, and who could make the plane that whizzed across the room. Flowers were made with coloured paper. A sheet of square paper could be used to play a game long gone 'fortune teller'. Taking the corners of your sheet, fold to the centre point, turn over paper and repeat, taking hold carefully meet corners to middle, pulling out edges to insert thumb and finger of each hand. Placing edges down gently unfold, under each folded point write a forfeit i.e. 'stand on one leg for 1min.' or love notes, like 'I love you' or 'meet me tonight', "you will meet a tall dark stranger" closing put names on folded point, finally turn over and put any numbers on edges under which thumb and fingers go. Object of this conundrum, ask your chosen friend to pick a number, thumb and fingers work the chosen number of required movements till two of the four folds are visible, again ask your friend to choose, making the necessary moves to spell the chosen name, finally lifting the last fold of the chosen name reveals the message.

Collecting things was something everyone was driven to do, then as now, a kind of standing amongst your peers, confidence in ownership. A scrap book was one such early treasure made from sheets of small, perforated, glossy vibrant pictures, mostly children, flowers and country scenes, bought for a few pennies when the chance arose, eagerly collected, then stuck them into a scrapbook with flour and water paste. Oh how I wish I had those beautiful scrapbooks now. I also wish I had my much prized collection of *empty* cigarette packets. I recall having Woodbine and Park-Drive, the most common then smoked; Dad had a work-mate who knew some-one in the Navy who sent me others from around the world but I can only remember the names, Players Weights; Players Navy Cut; Capstons; Senior Service; Camels.

Other than singing my only musical ability was playing a comb with tissue paper over it. I often wished I could play the piano that stood sentinel in the front room, in my daydreaming I danced my fingers over those white notes thrilling audiences around the world.

Happy hours were spent with Alan when we made and raced tanks. Make a notch on the rim of empty cotton bobbins, stick a bit of broken pencil (*see, nothing was wasted*) through the central hole, then wind them up with an elastic band, away they went, but many snapped elastic bands.

Another favourite thing to make was silver cups. Cigarette packets when opened contained silver paper, this we wound around one finger, twisting to make a stem, then flatten the end for a base. Then came the star attraction, with a little spittle added to the base, the cup was thrown at the ceiling with the intention of it sticking there. Great skill was needed, much hilarity followed, with competition fierce, sometimes numerous cups could be hung there attached to the ceiling for many weeks.

Coloured silver paper (from chocolate, Easter eggs) was collected throughout the year, torn into tiny pieces and wound around the individual oats on the stalks gathered at harvest-time. Decorated they were displayed in a vase for winter flowers , a kaleidoscope of colour shimmering in the evening light.

Wool or string approximately two foot in length, knotted to join, held between thumb and first finger on both hands woven to make assorted cats cradles, produced hours of enjoyment as we wove it, in, out and around, twisting, turning making intricate patterns, until you came back to where you started. Finger games were played by cupping fingers together, "Here's the church, here's the steeple, open the doors' and here's the people".

My hobbies were in order of preference drawing, painting, reading, dancing, acting then sewing. The colour Red; banana's; rose's; in the words of the song "These were some of my favourite things". Nothing's changed but with the addition of, a love of motor sports; watching show jumping; crosswords; family and local history; sixties and country music.

Dad was a great one for teaching us tricks. Middle finger nail on each hand were covered in a small piece of tissue paper and danced in front of you, saying "Two little dicky birds sitting on a tree, this one's Peter this one's Paul, fly away Peter, fly away Paul" (at which point the hands were thrown alternately over the shoulder) clever switching revealed the missing birds then "Come back Peter, come back Paul" reproduced the birds. .

A ritual never tired of, until outgrown, was observed when eating boiled eggs, when finished, the empty eggshell was turned over in the egg-cup and offered to someone else "would you like another egg", when cracked open to discover nothing there, all present erupted in laughter.

Mealtimes when the whole family sat together, we learnt the hugely importantart art of conversation, so sadly often missing today.

Today's children learn slogans and catchphrases from television, we were taught tongue twisters like, "She sells sea shells by the sea shore," "Peter Piper picked a pickled pepper," "Red lorry, yellow lorry".

What about this one, "Constantinople is a very hard word spell it", reply "C-O-N-S-T- A- N -T-I-N"

"Stop, hold it right there, I said Constantinople is a very hard word spell IT"

With no car to go out in, no television to distract, no money for outside entertainments, we had that precious thing ___ time for each other, time to laugh, time to play, time to talk.

In the evenings the family gathered around the fireside, tales were told, ghost stories, tales of long ago or best of all true or false, (tales told, were they true or simply invented web of fantasy?).

Out in the countryside, in the kitchen, in the garden, in town always explaining, pointing things out, all presented the opportunity to talk about what we saw and did. Despite growing up in a house with three men plus all the visiting uncles, today's automatically recurrent swear words were not heard, no-one swore in our house or in our presence.

On the whole we were encouraged to speak correctly, not in local dialect, but adults often had comical replies to questions. Asked their age, replied "As old as my tongue and a bit older than my teeth";

"Where you going", "There and back to see how far it is";

"What's for tea" "Bread and if it"; (countered with "if we've got it, you can have it").

"Ours not to reason why"

Some things had family pet names as in *spuds* -- potatoes, the *Gus under*, walking anywhere was known as going by *shank's pony*.

Odd phrases used were

"I'll have your guts for garters" a light-hearted threat, if you so much as thought of doing anything wrong.

"Where is????" "What's this????" "Don't know nowt (nothing) about it."

"Will he manage to complete it?" "Willy Eckerslike" (will he heck as like) "he certainly will not"

"Finders keepers, weepers losers"

"Cross my heart and hope to die - if I tell a lie.

"Throw t nother log on ta fire lass"

"Never cast a clout till May's out" or "no you can't take your vest off until the sun shines both sides the hedges".

"Look after the pennies and the pounds will take care of themselves." which should now be "take care of the pounds, they are soon spent"

Dad would often say to me "I would not trade you for all the tea in China"

One not meant literally " Pull your socks up" (try harder).

"Like a bull in a china shop" (some one careless, barging about).

"Butterfingers" (when you dropped something).

Of the basics needed to buy, Sunlight soap, Tide washing powder, box Soda crystals, Reckitts blue bags, Robin starch, Vim scouring powder, tins Harpic, or Brasso, as much as possible was bought from the Co-op Van that visited the house on his rounds, because being a member you shared in the profits made by the society. Affectionately known as the 'divi', correctly called dividend, was calculated from check slips containing the members share number and amount spent. Paid out twice a year, from the office upstairs in Bridge Street. Long queues formed on the steps, I never tired of watching the swirling, brooding, murky, shadowy, winding river, from the large windows overlooking the Trent.

Occasionally Gran, when leaving the house always wearing a hat, did make trips to town (Gainsborough), at all times taking a shopping bag with her, carrier bags weren't provided then. I was always pleased to accompany her, with so much to observe and people to see. The Tuesday weekly market - held since at least 1281 - was a tradition, her mum and mothers mum would have visited the local market where for generations (when shops would have been unheard of) many smallholdings, farmers wife's and gardeners had stalls from which they sold their surplus, at bargain prices, nothing exotic, hadn't yet seen such fruits. Greengrocers in winter struggling to weigh things with freezing hands in fingerless mitts, once weighed their 'spuds' were tipped from the big silver scoop directly into the customers own held out bags. Best vegetables for regulars picked from the carefully arranged front display, no such service for the casual customer, theirs came from nearest the trader. Shopping never failed to fascinate me, no self-service then, no assistants gossiping instead of serving, service meant service, with a smile a cheery and cheeky greeting "how's the old legs to today mi duck, still playing you up", "you're late today, was the old man laid on your nightie". In most cases knowing the customer by name, if not a "good morning/afternoon mi darling". A wonder to behold, the many stalls packed tightly together, filling the Market Square and sprawling down Silver Street. The noise reverberating from the traders, all-contending for a slice of the action, women jostling among the stalls trying to find the best deal, in cold weather heads covered in headscarves bent into the wind and sleet. In summer stopping to chat with friends and neighbours. The hustle and bustle of traders from far and wide competing for your money, offering a wide selection of wares doing a brisk trade, all booming their prices to the old ladies, often tempting them to spend a little more "got a nice bit of 'something', especially saved for you' or 'special price today".

Inside the old Town Hall, out of the sun the cool Butter Market, imagine the dairyman with fresh farm hen, duck, bantam or goose eggs stacked in cardboard trays, round English cheeses, butter straight from the farmhouse kitchens, grooved wooden hand paddles 'pats', making a perfect half pound rectangle often with each farmers own crest imprinted; smell the Fishmongers, fish resplendent in rows of chunky crushed ice. All wrapped in greaseproof paper then a final wrap of newspaper.

The public buildings were stately and imposing, the following selection of shops were full of activity, but still the proprietor or manager seemingly installed for a lifetime provided a service second to none. **Inskips** in Market Place, on the pavement clothes baskets temptingly displaying tea and dinner services, the kind of shop that could find in the depths an odd cup, saucer or plate to replace a broken one. **Bomers** and Co. Waterloo house, the clothes shop for women who didn't make their own, in addition the supplier of school uniform. **Bunster's** Chemist, in Church St. the window occupied by large car-boys with glass stoppers containing brightly coloured liquids of red, green and amber, brilliant as jewels. Inside counters and fitments gleaming mahogany and brass with cut glass etched with advertising. Rows and rows of blue and white Delft jars on display labelled in Latin, beneath which sat little drawers with brass knobs holding powders and dry goods, every one had its contents inscribed upon it in curly gilt lettering. Wooden medicine cabinets, apothecary scales, pestle and mortar, along with grooved boards used for making and counting pills. **Scotts Bazaar** the ironmongers, the window displaying household articles, cooking utensils either copper or brass, neither aluminium nor stainless steel available then. Here you could purchase large tins, then popularly ornamented with Chinese scenes, used for storing tea at that time bought loose and weighed out in the shop, when packaging was unknown. Where you could buy nails by the ounce, screws loose as many or few as needed, segs and pre cut leather soles and heels for mending shoes or boots, or patches to mend aluminium bowls, pots and pans. This was done by screwing a metal washer, pressing a rubber disc, either side of the hole. Cheaper than new equipment, no cheap throw away plastic replacements at that time. Under the town hall clock stood **Barnes** the jewellers where they took in broken watches to be mended. **Woolworths** store with doors onto Market Place and Silver street, sold Cuthbert's garden seeds, once planted you stuck a stick through the bottom of the empty packet to mark what you had planted. They also sold broken biscuits at a fraction of the cost of the whole ones. **Cooper and Baumber's** in Market street, a drapery shop a treasure trove of needles and pins, cotton on stout wooden reels, hooks and eyes, press -studs in silver or black; ribbon, tape, bias binding, lace, elastic in all widths; all to be bought as much or as little as needed, no pre-packs. Embroidery silks in hundreds of shades, to find just the right hue, not to mention that elusive button you wanted to match up, dropped into small brown paper bag. Material was unfurled from bales of cloth, to be measured over mahogany counters by a yardstick with shiny brass ferule at each end. To reach the large brown storage boxes stacked upon high shelves a small wooden step-ladder was procured from the depths of organised dis-order. Opened out, teetering precariously climbing to the top step, with a triumphant smile and customers relief, make their way down with the obscure commodity. Purchases complete, payment made into long wooden drawer cash register that opened with a pleasing 'ping'.

Mr. **Stovin , Butcher,** Lord street, whole pigs, half sides of beef hung from stout hooks in the ceiling, feathered pheasants and unskinned rabbits hanging outside from the tops of windows. Irresistible haslets, polony, pork-pies, potted meat, local hams, sausages, pigs fry and tripe all prepared on the premises, the appetizing smell wafting across town.

Today in empty streets, as all the local shops disappear one by one, boarded up against the vandals, everywhere looks like you have just missed a terrible exodus. You now buy everything under one roof in a large anonymous, brightly lit space from people who have never seen you before and would not remember your name if they had, with the manager an unseen face, just a name on a board.

Tuesday afternoons Vero Barker stood on bank corner calling "news", billboards announcing the latest headlines. the Gainsborough Evening News could be bought for 2d. The other local newspaper The Retford, Isle of Axholme and Gainsborough News, *what a mouth full,* was on sale Friday's price 4d.

Dad would be asked, "if he wanted anything bringing" his answer was always "a rubber hammer with half a dozen glass nails"

If caught short on these outings, when shopping and socialising took up a large part of the day, there was always the town hall toilets in flag alley, one of the last remaining areas of York stone flag streets. A crumbling Victorian edifice with green tiles completely covering walls. An ever present (lady in the ladies) lavatory attendant with cheerful banter, bustled in the midst keeping them scrupulously clean. The six-foot high revolving iron gates forbid admission to

anyone not putting one penny in the brass slots to gain entry. .
I often had to wait patiently while Gran chatted with her best friend Miss Hilda (never married) who managed sweet shop/ tobacconists in Lord St., occasionally we called at her house in Little Church Lane.
The bus drivers and conductress had their own canteen in a one storey building once the old stables, attached to the rear of Black Bull on the corner of Lord street/Parnell street, windows and door though bricked up still visible. Weary from shopping Gran and I often slipped in to join them in a cuppa, before catching the bus home; Gran was always made welcome she knew them all by name.

Gran loved a bargain; probably her favourite pastime was the saleroom. These auctions took place in the redundant Methodist Church on the corner of Hickman Street/ Heaton Street. Off we went early with sandwiches and flask of tea, the anticipation almost too much to bear, to claim a seat in easy chairs, that lined the front row, Mr. Harrison auctioned these too later. But Gran was only interested in the smalls anything from pots to bedding, Trays or boxes viewed before the start, watching closely for the chosen lots - the name given to individual or collective items offered for sale by the auctioneer - to come under the hammer. A single lot would be an item worthy of commanding a high price, examples being antiques. Mixed lots would consist of the trivia of the sale, the bargains could be found here, going for the sparse shillings, hoping yours would be the highest bid.
There is something about auctions that still continues to draw me, the buzz of seeking out a bargain. Dad got an old red, flat nosed van, with sliding doors (no seat belts) I sat on the engine placed between the only two seats when he also took me along with him to different auctions; mostly these would be farm sales, a sale on the premises. Every so often a farmer would be retiring, going to live in a nice new bungalow. At the auction saleroom attended with Gran, the buyers, mainly women, sat in rows of chairs, standing at the back when these were taken, the lots were held aloft at the front by burly porters. Whereas at farm sales, mainly attended by men, lots were laid out in rows, with his trusty clerk by his side recording transactions, everyone crowded around the auctioneer, who was continually shouting "move back, move back" as they moved along. As the sale progressed, each completed sheet was hurried by a runner back to a commandeered shed or room in the house used as

an office, for the cashiers to tally the receipts, each customers purchases, also the sellers pay-out each with commission deducted. Starting with the excess contents of the 'big' house, displayed on the lawn for all to view. Many times dad would buy a mixed 'lot', in my childhood dad gave me many nik knacks from these, I never lost or broke them, in fact as a child I took great care of my possessions, when I left home for employment my trinkets stayed behind, what became of them I know not. Moving on the whole contents of a brick lean-to (those things the farmer saved that may come in useful one day) would often be sold in one lot. Next would come wooden sheds from small chicken coops to larger ones that wanted dismantling before removal (often past their best). As in everything bought at auction 'buyer beware' when the hammer fell it was your responsibility. If it was rotten or your chicken died - tough, it still had to be paid for. Often a pile or piles of wood could be bought from firewood to stakes to planks or mixed lots the farmer was always 'just saving' in case he wanted to mend something or build something. In the rows could be anything from a tractor seat to a pig trough, small hand tools like spades, scythes, rakes, buckets or rolls of wire. Invariably there was a pile of scrap, years of accumulated old tin buckets with holes, old bed springs, old broken pig troughs, wrecked machinery. Next came the stock, finishing with the 'best, working' machinery. The auctioneer gets to know the regulars and old hands who simply nod, wink or twitch their fingers to catch his attention, the buyers he can glance at when the bidding slows or he needs someone to make an opening bid. Dad was always on the lookout for things he knew others wanted, or he would buy something at a knockdown price knowing he could find a buyer to make a profit. Throughout his life he joked he'd bought and sold everything but an elephant.

A different type of auction were farmers gathered in groups, discussing the sale of their stock, with an overriding odour of dung, sweaty old men, and bad breath was the cattle markets. A bustling, raucous, rowdy, echoing atmosphere, the animals arriving in anything from small vans, the boot of a car to huge cattle trucks. Like all auctions there was a complex support service, with an intricate back-up, the drovers ushering animals into and out of rings, cattle, squealing pigs and bleating sheep stood awaiting their fate; aiding the penning of stock in differing size squares of metal railings, according to the animal size; clerks to record transactions - who brought what in, allotting numbers to animals, then as the sale progresses who buys what; with cashiers to receive from purchasers and pay out to vendors (sellers); maintenance staff; huge metal weigh machines; lorry wash points; with constantly patrolling security men.

The auctioneer 'on the planks' raised catwalk above the boisterous, crushing crowds gave him a good view of stock and bidders. In rapid monotone with telepathic understanding of clients secret signs, they did not want to miss a raised hand, a wave of catalogue, slight nod or wink, the higher the sale price the happier his seller and more commission for himself. At Doncaster many auctioneers would be selling at the same time, different animals, in separate areas of the market. One would be seated in his box behind a ring, his allocation of animals ushered in and out as the hammer fell. Horses of every type, shape and colour were shown by running them up and down the street, much bartering and arguing over the price, but once clapped hands the sale was made.

A large brass bell shaken by a clerk, heralded the start of Stennets busy poultry market at The Mart - once more an auction - under a make-shift lean-to tables laden with moulded cardboard trays of eggs; sacks and boxes of vegetables, freshly dug earth still clinging; fertile eggs for hatching, (if you had a broody hen, given pot eggs to sit on until your return); dressed poultry and game, trussed up ready for the oven; flowers and plants. Dead rabbits and pheasants usually sold in pairs strung by the neck from racks.

All live poultry, point of lay pullets, cockerels, capons and hens that had finished laying; different breeds of rabbits; pigeons; in wire cages, tiny fluffy day old chicks carried home in their cardboard box with many holes in the lid. Buses and trains were cheap, plentiful and ran on time, so we enjoyed numerous outings, especially memorable, tremendously looked forward to because there was almost no entertainment available in the villages. The park, pantomimes, cinema and circus never lost there appeal. Connections could be made for a day at the seaside or visiting relatives.

Many hot summer days were spent at Richmond Park, opened in 1947. Approached through the metal entrance gates, with the name in cut out letters, with the dinky caretakers cottage still on the right-hand side. It had been the home, then named "The Hollies" of Mr. C.F. Richmond who made a gift of it to the town. Hours of fun and adventure provided by the tall slide, in summer the metal scorching hot bare legs; the sea-saws; a wooden roundabout, propelled by running with the metal arms, then jumping as fast as possible onto the encircling low running boards, to launch yourself onto the seating area; (youngest ones pre-seated); the witches hat, as named, a cone of bars connected to a circle of seating, that pivoted and swivelled as it rotated; long rocking horses with seats for eight, but boys given chance dominated, with many more standing, the object being to rock hard and fast enough to touch the concrete with the front and rear ends; swings again mistreated when the patrolling park warden wasn't looking, attempts were made to swing until the highest possible point before jumping off, the clanking chains then proceeded to wrap around the topmost bar, the (usually) boys then fell about laughing watching whilst these were untangled. Harmless fun, just high spirits, respect was given to other parents or the warden, no swearing when chastised, never any harm to younger children - in fact great care was shown to little ones. Along with the paddling pool, all were packed to capacity creating a summer sound that still echoes in the minds ear. All that remains of our playground are the sandpit, and the shelter were the accompanying parents and grandparents sat to watch over the children. Horses grazed in the field beyond now the extensive Springfields Estate. A green painted converted railway van served cups of teas and ice creams *a real treat then, only enjoyed here or the seaside, an enduring love affair with the cold, soft stuff began, today my weakness,* these being the block of vanilla, (no multi flavours) you unwrapped and placed between two wafers or an oblong cone, refreshing cold water was available from ornate drinking fountains. The big house contained a reading room on one side of the front door, the room the other-side where old men gathered to play cards and dominoes. Before catching the bus home a woodland walk around the greenhouses and gardens, perfectly laid out with flowering trees, trim lawns, rose garden, classically English herbaceous borders wherein stood the old horse trough that once stood outside The Elm Cottage. Today's park still has swings; a roundabout, just handles on a low slung frame; see saws now with handles; the modern equivalent of our witches hat is two tyres swinging from a cap, notice announcing it's a swing, see saw and merry go round all in one, a notice declaring only two people at a time admitted to the fenced off area, all supposedly removed or improved in the name of safety, to take away the responsibility of care from parent's, who now let their children go alone. So tame that youngster's turn to railway lines and building sites for thrills. Nice to see the old clock still in its position and still working. Credit must go to today's wardens, the grounds are still a picture, with the house been put to good use as the Registry Office, a beautiful setting for civil weddings.

As I recall images as vivid as if they'd happened yesterday, my first visit to the State Cinema in Church Street also springs to mind. Dad took me to see Norman Wisdom in "When I'm cleaning windows", a distinctive character, so comical, seemingly a simpleton in his scruffy undersized suit along with his peaked cap. A mesmerising experience, usherettes in smart uniforms having checked your ticket, showed you to your place as your eyes adjusted to the dimmed lights with their torches casting an eerie flicker in near darkness. Everyone had to stand for people to pass to seats further along the row. As the curtains opened the vast single screen dominated the auditorium , first came the supporting B movie, then before the main feature, came one of the most endearing images, the cockerel crowed heralding Pathe News. In the days before satellite link-ups, the only organisation that had the resources, and the skill, to cover events. Whenever, wherever, a story was breaking, pathe cameras would be there, to capture the events at the heart of the nation, bringing exclusive news footage to the cinemagoer in the days before mass televisions.

As the credits rolled on the last sequence it was all right to make a beeline for the exit, but once the National Anthem was played at the end of the night, great respect was shown, everyone stood like soldiers, not a movement made, until the last note faded.

The years fall away as I'm a child again, now old enough to catch the bus to be transported to another world to visit alone the Gaumont cinema in Market Place where for a few pennies you could wile away Saturday morning, Being a member of the club guaranteed you received a card in the post on your birthday. The anticipation was tense as children met, joining the long queue. We eagerly awaited the doors opening, then a mad dash for the best seats (not allocated like at adult pictures). In the darkness I tried to avoid, sensing something amiss, the horrible man that collected your ticket. A treat not to be missed, the scene of great excitement, sweet bags on laps, hankies at the ready for the sad bits. The ushers stood at the back during the films and didn't hesitate to put a stop to unruly behaviour, in the interval usherettes sold popcorn and ice cream from a tray suspended around their neck. Feature films like 'Roy Rogers', 'The Greatest Show on Earth', 'Ivanhoe', 'Hopalong Cassidy' or 'Robin

Hood', the list is endless, Huckleberry Finn, Tom Sawyer, Laurel and Hardy cheering our heroes who upheld the law and justice against the baddies, preceded the serial. Would the heroine be rescued in time? highwaymen, pirates, bandits cowboys riding with the wind on palomino horses, either chasing after or fleeing from painted Red Indians, with mounting tension came the dreaded message "continued next week" . With not a minute to waste as the end neared came the frenzied stampede for the exit.

The majestic Kings Theatre crowned with the lion, was the venue for a traditional yearly ritual, of endless interest and delight. Inside the palatial extravaganza, I still recall the red velour seats, the Wurlitzer that used to rise from its small dark place below front of stage. With mounting anticipation, never afraid, we knew the characters were just familiar favourites based on legendary characters from storybooks, spectacular, laugh-packed Pantomimes, brought vibrantly to life in creative imaginations.
The productions always produced a 'winner', brought to us by the wonderful, indomitable Bert Ward, who always played a dame. Cinderella with magnificent illuminated crystal coach drawn by white horses with princes in long scarlet robes trimmed with ermine, wearing coronets.
Red Riding Hood with the wicked wolf, whose appearance brought forth screams of "look behind you"
Dick Whittington, leading male always played by tall, long-legged beauties, finds himself in Morocco at the sumptuous Emperors Palace, falling in love with the beautiful princess, before returning to London to become Lord Mayor.
I loved the audience participation, boos and hisses, the catching of sweets thrown into the audience, repetition of the traditional cries of "oh yes it is" and "oh no its isn't" as the audience argues with the villain. The organist played loud or soft whatever the pace, the audience sang along with gusto from oversized song sheets held aloft with the words of the song, pointed at with a small thin stick, bouncing from word to word,

The Circus was an annual event into an exotic world, with their dazzling colours, the splendour of the sawdust ring received you. The excitement began when Linda and I would espy Bertrum Mills or Billy Smarts wagons rolling past the farmhouse en route to town. Countdown began until the evening arrived we were taken to visit, the only chance we had to see live animals. It was a tradition for a parade to take place through the town of more than 200 animals and acts from around the world before opening night. I have been told this harked back to the days when the circus arrived by train and walked to the show ground. Only once was I privileged to see this spectacle as thousands lined the streets.

The scarlet uniformed doorman, greeted you at the entrance of the vibrant 6,000 seater striped canopy big-top as the pungent smell of sawdust assaulted your nostrils, the excited buzz from the waiting audience assailed your senses. Every age of man forgot themselves in the thrills, excitement and laughter as the drum rolled for the opening fanfare, the show began to tumultuous cheers the ringmaster splendid in pink coat, with top hat takes centre stage, followed by one act after another in a kaleidoscope of colour, sound and movement.

Clowns abounded with a mixture of slapstick and conjuring in which the larger than life harlequin costumed clown, assisted by the thin, silent, pasty white one, hand each other eggs breaking one or two on the way, often all over the face, put them into a pan, pour on inflammable liquid, light it, clap on the lid children squealed with anticipation, as a live duck appeared. Or the red mouthed, bulbous nosed one, with baggy trousers, big boots with long toes, bowler hat and huge fur coat which when taken off, the clown said "out" and away it would go apparently of its own accord. A boy would be summoned to volunteer, a funnel held under his ear, after his arm had been pumped up and down a bit, water would start trickling out of the side of his head.

Slow motion slapstick where two at either end of an extremely long table attempted wallpapering they plastered each other in white wash, paste and water.

Shouts of "big 'ead" rang around the ring when, huge paper mache heads of a monster coal-black head with swivelling eyes, or a gigantic Chinese face, on the face of it, all bodiless, all grotesque, above dwarf's legs entered the ring. Outwardly unable to see huge laughter erupted when the character collided with everything around and once down was unable to get up without help.

There was the long narrow 'coffin' which someone was shut inside and swords passed through with blood curdling screams being emitted as though the person were being sliced to pieces, but of course after the swords were withdrawn the pretty girl stepped out unscathed

The stilt walker towering many, many feet above, has a larks eye view of life as he straddles many of the animals, but earlier still managed to bend down to talk to the children in the queues.//
A fine lady rides a white horse. The horse wearing his plumed head-dress seemingly dancing on his toes, with his shimmering, bejewelled ballerina riding bareback. Clad in fish-net tights, shimmering costume tassels swishing she smiled down from her domain performing dangerous acts, with precision balance and timing she vaulted on and off his back, did handstands on his back, rolled under his belly all while galloping around the ring, before being joined by a second horse to stand with a leg on each horses back without losing balance, it made you feel quite dizzy. Big chief eagle eye with his covered wagon led in the troupe of Indians whooping with pride and joy as they leapt in various formations on and off two black stallions, finishing with a perfect stance on shouldered pyramid.

The only place to see the exquisite white polar bears, graceful giraffes, splendid zebras, and performing sea-lions other than in books. The chimps, girls in frilly skirts, boys in posh trousers with dickie bows at the neck, sat on dinky chairs at a miniature table with pocket-sized teaset to have a captivating tea party.

The elephants entered trumpeting, walking in perfect line, with tails entwined around each others trunks, in colourful head-dresses, they twirled, stood on immense multi-coloured tubs, front feet raising their bulky body's and rear legs into the air. Two wee folk (clowns) would make a trunk call the one with a telephone, the other using the elephant's trunk. As they left the arena, one exotic girl rode high on the neck of the lead elephant whilst it balanced two scantily clad girls each end of a bar in its trunk.

Quivers of terror ran through audience as the big cats roared down the tunnel to sit atop their pedestals. Wild animal trainers risking their life need to gain the trust of lions and tigers, would you put your head in its mouth? Or wait for the great beast to place its head between your legs to ride it's back.

The fire-eater, throwing spectacular flames into the air, impressive tight ropewalkers in tight silver trousers, glided on thin razor sharp wires.

Jugglers, tumblers, acrobats that walked on their hands, then lie flat on their back and come to their feet in one swift movement; or the balancing of cups and saucers on his head, or another man standing on his shoulders, or juggling increasing amounts of balls, all whilst riding a uni-cycle; another one kept plates spinning on a row of canes.

Holding your breath as the sequined trapeze artistes fly suspended only by the feet, gracefully swinging high, then performing daring somersaults from one roof high trapeze to another.

The clever fortune telling pony trained to easily answer questions, for telling the time, or counting the pony would bang its forefoot on a board, with an all but invisible signal from the handler, half the fun of the performance was the patter.

Before half the public were out of their seats at the last performance, the workforce start to dismantle, intense packing following, speed and precision was everything in the almost pitch dark. The troupe had their own vets, chefs, police and fire services. Everyone having their own job, the 250 staff knowing exactly what to do, from labourers to wardrobe mistress in charge of the thousand plus changes of costume. With 'clean up' of the 3-acre site complete, the midnight move began, ready for the build-up at the new day's destination.

Nowadays in the world of TV etc. it's hard to imagine the imprinted thrill it left.

The most special occasion of a recurring nature was traditional Christmas's, symbolism of a strange mixture of pagan tree, the Yule fire plus the story of God personified, born in a stable. We enjoy the customs we have inherited from the past. Preparations began early with the baking of the substantial cake. Marzipan, then artistically iced with pointed peaks, capturing a winter wonderland complete with miniature snow laden trees, Santa in his present loaded sledge. Followed by periodical piercing from beneath with a knitting needle and brandy poured in to soak. The making of the puddings, with children having a lucky stir. Days before Christmas the tantalising smell of mince pies with homemade mincemeat, jam and lemon curd tarts, cooking, when cool, hidden, due to possible raids by the sweet tooth brigade.

Decorating took place a few nights before Christmas Eve. First trimmings were suspended from each corner to meet in the centre of the ceiling with a large paper bell. Paper lanterns, decorated days earlier with crayoned patterns were placed at intervals. Christmas cards were hung over string strung across the wall fastened with drawing pins, In the front room we always had a real tree, brought home by one or other of the men from the forest. Then the fragile spun-glass multi-coloured ornaments saved carefully, wrapped in tissue paper from the previous year, were brought out to decorate. Bags of chocolate coins were added, these taken down and handed round on Boxing Day. No fairy lights then, silver tinsel shivered in the firelight with an illuminated glow. Topped by the old faded white fairy looking down with a satisfied smile on a job well done. Holly was attached to the mantelpiece, wedged on mirror and picture frames. Primitive people hung evergreens on buildings so that seeds in the frozen ground could know that there was still life to be found, believing it was necessary to do all they could to encourage nature to wake up and start all over again. Superstition dictated that decorations be taken down 12days after Christmas.

Before going to bed we left Santa his customary mince pie, then hung our pillowcases on the bottom bedposts. Waking early next morning before light, rushing to investigate the bulging sack, to find the contents had a certain delightful sameness, at the bottom of the sack would always be an orange; a pink sugar mouse with string tail; a tin of toffees. This is my first recollection of sweets, (not until 1951 could sweets be bought without ration tokens) sweets were never bought on visits to town and not until about ten years old was a few pence found for the sweet shop on the way to school, even then only intermittently. Always a book could be found with lots of small objects which gave an exciting bumpy feel, my memory recalls these simple much played with presents. Knitting Nancy, sometimes called French knitting set, or dolly bobbin, this was a wooden doll with exaggerated painted face, about three inches long, in her head was a circle of small round-headed pins. Oddments of wool were knitted by hooking each stitch over the preceding one, long rolls of colours disappearing down the hollow body in snake like profusions. (a free version could be assembled with a cotton bobbin and small nails). Another 'craft' box I once received contained a weaving loom, although spending tedious hours on these activities, I have no recollection of ever doing anything with resultant products, other than comparing the length you had achieved against friends and family. A more useful 'make it yourself' box contained two small cardboard circles without centres, with small amounts of wool. By working evenly around, threading over and over the circles, knotting off at the centre, snipping between the two circles you produced a pom-pom. It only took one for me to realise I could a) make my own, b) make any size I wanted. Was this the beginning of the excessive use of plastic and cardboard packaging so prevalent today?

A book with cardboard doll including many outfits, each joined by tiny paper strips, you tore to separate the little tabs to hook onto dolly. Pages of highly prized, colourful pictures to add to your scrap book, or stamps to add to your collections (what did happen to these things). One of my favourites, a kaleidoscope, multi coloured crystals viewed through a telescopic panorama in ever changing patterns as you turned the end. As a very young child early presents that stand out clearly in my mind, are a jack in the box, plus a pulsating, gyrating, colourful, humming, spinning top along with magic painting books, where the beautiful picture emerged before your eyes with only a brush and pot of water. Each year one large present would be included, often these represented something to mimic the real world, a Post-office; a bus conductors set; sweet shop; a blackboard with easel including rubber and coloured chalks. Other presents I recall were a typewriter, not keys like the real thing but a dial turned produced the requisite letters; a potato men set, this consisted of arms, legs, tiny hats, eyes, lips, noses, ears, even over the top eyebrows and moustaches all that was needed to complete the picture was a potato, hence the name. Large cardboard boxes acted as props, the shops, the school, the bus, the imagination knew no bounds. Through the years Alan got home made garage, castle, and farmyard, made by my Dad to the same standard as he'd made my doll's house. Matchbox cars, animals, soldiers, he could collect further each year. Sometimes he received a smoking set, complete with liquorice pipe, (but never smoked as an adult). As he got older he received a Meccano set which gave pleasure to all of us. Many the hour we spent improving our engineering prowess constructing cranes, lorries, bridges and buildings with small spanners or screwdrivers to tighten fiddly nuts and bolts.

One year, he received a train set, I guess that wasn't his favourite, he never got past the one train and circular track, whereas the garage must have fired his imagination, he became a mechanic. My toys do not appear to give any indication of my future, I spent a large part of my working life in catering, but do not recall ever having a tea set, likewise I did not have a doll or teddy bear, I was not a cuddly kind of child, I saved all my loving for my real family.

Christmas 1956, should have been one of the best Why? It was a white Christmas, but I was confined to my bed. The doctor had to make a visit on Christmas Day, it turned out to be Mumps. I awoke at four a.m. feeling quite ill, I managed to drift off again until eight o'clock when I had some porridge, the only other thing I had that day was soup, not even bothering with my presents until Boxing Day. That year I received a new coat, shoes and watch from dad; hand bag from auntie Joan; train-case from auntie vi; 2 books from auntie Annie; crayons with colouring books from auntie Mary; whilst auntie Alice had given me a work-box; grandma had got me a bracelet and autograph book, unfortunately only the latter has survived. Presents I'm sure that took more foresight in planning than when purchased on a credit card, love not bought by the latest most expensive must have. In today's fractured society were adults try to win the affection of their confused children with expensive presents, it should be remembered children really need love, routine and stability. At thirteen I received my first camera, a box brownie. The very first photo I took was of Alan stood by the peony bush, to my knowledge the only photo still surviving from that camera.

As we grew older we made presents for aunties, things like padded coat hangers and embroidered handkerchiefs. This rich tapestry of life has today been replaced by buying goods, a poor substitute for interacting with others.

In this modern selfish society the traditional bonds and rhythms of festive periods that held us together in my childhood are evaporating in a mood of apathy, replaced by a preference to be left in peace to watch the television, or play with the latest gadget. Always a very close knit family, sons and daughters came home for the festivities, bringing husbands, wife's and cousins many stayed over, I have no idea were the adults slept, - no guest bedrooms then - perhaps in the chairs were they sat, us kids didn't get much sleep either, we were all in one bed, head to toe.

A huge log chosen as the "Yule log" was placed on the open fire in the best room, to burn continuously throughout the period, (during which people remembered their dead and believed that they were sharing in the festival) a symbol of good luck if it could be kept burning for twelve days, also perfect for 'roasting chestnuts by the open fire'. The dresser groaning with the best cut glass fruit bowls full of nuts, apples and oranges.

Turkey or goose - only afforded once a year, was packed with chestnut stuffing then put in the oven overnight to cook, next morning sausages wrapped around the bacon were placed around the base, the chosen vegetables were always parsnips and Brussels sprouts, with roast and mashed potatoes, bread sauce, cranberry , or in the case of goose, gooseberry sauce to accompany. Xmas pudding followed, everyone hoping to find the hidden silver sixpences, served with white sauce a spoonful of brandy stirred in, no mean achievement all cooked on the range.

A very large pork pie was purchased each year and this was customarily for breakfast on Christmas day.

Great effort went into setting of tables, the best china used, with a cracker placed on each plate, compulsory wearing of paper hats, much laughter as the jokes were read aloud adding to the merriment. Much bartering swapping and frustration of minute trinkets, compasses, yo-yo's, Chinese puzzles (interlocking metal shapes, that had a special way of separating - you just had to find the right way), mazes (a circle of cardboard wall, containing a ball, you tipped and tilted, until you settled it into a sunken hole). Teatime the table groaned under the weight of, pork pie, the large leg of cooked ham ready to slice, with the remaining turkey. Cheese, pickles, hard-boiled eggs, followed by warm mince pies, tarts, or bowls of trifles to tempt.

Whilst the men traditionally, the once and only time each year, washed -up, children were dispatched to the front room to play card games such as "Happy Families" the pack consisting of sets of four composed of Mr Bun the baker, Mr. Soot the sweep, etc, their wives and two children, Miss and Master. The object was to make up as many complete sets as possible until all the cards were used up. Each player when their turn came, asked for some character in one of their own potential sets in the traditional words, "Is Mr. Bun at home?" from the player they guessed might have it, to maybe receive the answer "No Mr. Bun is not at home." In a favourable response the card had to be handed over and the enquirer got another turn repeatedly until he ask unsuccessfully. By a process of elimination and deduction the players soon got to know where the wanted cards where, but one mistake could cost you all your partially completed sets. Chores complete everyone now retreated to the best room for the rest of the day, first to sit in silence to hear the Queen's speech, then while women rested, men helped assemble new toys, or organise the games that needed supervision, games like 'Hunt the thimble', the seeker leaves the room, whilst the thimble is hidden, on return wandering about the room, to shouts of "cold, cold, warmer, freezing, warmer, hot, hotter" until holding the elusive object; another was 'pin the tail on the donkey', picture of donkey minus his tail was stuck on the wall, all taking turns, blindfold and spun three times, you tried to pin the tail in the right place. Another favourite being 'Blind Man's Bluff', usually starting with a blindfolded grown up who made a great play of trying to guess by the feel whom they had caught, prolonging the suspense by guessing wrong a few times. After tea, everyone sat in a circle; the well-loved family games were played. 'Spinning the plate' The 'breadboard' was spun, as slow as you possibly could, to make it difficult for the name you call to catch it before falling, miss it a forfeit had to be paid, i.e. Stand on one leg turning three times without falling, that sort of thing; 'Whisperers tell lies' something is whispered in the ear of the next person, continue likewise around the circle, the last person says the sentence aloud, the first person says what they actually said, the two prove to be nothing like the same; 'Poor pussy' in the middle of the circle pussy imitating a cats movements crawls around meowing, each person visited must stroke pussy saying "poor pussy", the point being pussy has to make the chosen one laugh or move on to the next victim. When a casualty has been found they become pussy; musical chairs; 'Charades', actors played little scenes in which each syllable of the chosen word, and finally the whole of it, were worked into the conversation for the audience to spot; 'Black jack' the game strictly to catch the newcomer out. Dad sitting strategically next to the fire, the prey is encouraged to sit next to him, instructions are given "everything I do, you must do to the person sitting next to you, repeating "I touch you there" dad begins, a touch on the forehead, all the way around the circle this is repeated, continuing small dabs are placed upon the face, as progression is made children begin to laugh, the greenhorn unaware of what is really taking place sits in silence until realisation dawns, the perpetrator had been secretly placing sooty marks upon his face; good sports, laugh, we thought we'd never stop, never a tear was shed, simple pleasures, Happiness, Fun and Frivolity with capital letters. Later children gave solo performances, "I Saw Mummy Kissing Santa Claus"; "Twelve Days of Christmas"; "Rudolph the Red Nosed Reindeer"; "When Santa got stuck up the Chimney". Ending the only night we were allowed to stay up late with recitations, old time music hall, then carols, before a final sing-a-long, accompanied by aunt Annie on the piano.

Boxing day uncle John would entertain us with his pole vaults, using the clothes prop, cleanly clearing the clothesline.

My earliest recollection of Christmas was whilst we were at H.B.B. Cottages, it would have probably been Christmas 1950, the year

Father Christmas visited during the party, I was so upset Dad wasn't there, on asking where he had gone, it was explained "he'd had to go to work to do the milking", being just five I fell for the explanation hook, line and sinker when he returned I had so much to tell him, I forgot to be cross with him, it was many years later before I learnt the truth.

Most people had to work next day, New Years Day wasn't a holiday then, so few stayed up for the witching hour. On New Years Eve. superstitions were upheld rigidly, to ensure plenty for the new year, a piece of bread, so the family would not go hungry, lump of coal for warmth throughout the winter and silver for wealth; a piece of wood to prevent a death in the family; all were placed outside in a hidden spot, all but the wood recovered first thing next morning, it was believed if the wood was brought in you would take wood out again before the year was out in the form of a coffin.

Every one wanted the 'first footer' (first person to cross the threshold on New Years Day) to be a tall, dark and handsome man, if it should be some one with ginger-hair it was considered a real bad omen. This day people reflected on the past year to try to make amends for anything that was wrong and resolved to make the new year better by making their New Year Resolutions.

It was considered bad luck to throw any muck out, or you threw your luck out, "out with the muck, out with the luck"; not to visit the doctor or you would be ill all year; not to spend money before 12 noon or finances would be stretched even further; never, ever do any washing or you ran the risk of washing one of your family away.

My mind evokes memories of 1st April, how hard you worked to trick someone, the simple "you're shoelace is undone" to changing the time on the clock - whereupon when the victim looked down or got anxious over the time, a shout went up of "April Fool", if after noon you were the fool.

My earliest memories of Cleethorpes begin when Gran took Alan and I. After an early start, still rubbing Mr. Sandman from the eyes, we would stand impatiently on the platform, mesmerised by the vastness, excitedly awaiting the steam train, fascinated but a little fearful of the hot hissing monster when it came to a stop along side. The Gainsborough Central, station was a magnificent Victorian iron edifice once a source of pride for the town, an important stop on the country's main east to west line of the Great Central Railway, with as many as 60 trains a week, a gentler time, extra carriages added in times of need, everyone got a seat, the golden age of travel. An object of great beauty, now so sadly, all that remains is the bricked up arch of crumbling brickwork.

Upon arrival, entry was through four imposing stone columns; tickets were purchased at the little office window kiosk inside the foyer, before proceeding to the platform, appearing to a child to be so high above the rails. A noisy, boisterous, bustling, atmosphere. Each side had scrolled, wrought iron benches, waiting rooms with fireplaces for winter, a lofty iron bridge with intricate mouldings for crossing between the two. The 'buffet' sold sandwiches with dry curling crusts along with strong, sweet tea. The W. H. Smith kiosk sold a vast array of daily papers, books, magazines, and comics, along with confectionary. Porters in smart uniforms were in attendance to assist with enquiries or help with enormous trunks piled high on clattering trolleys. Joining throngs of smartly dressed travellers carrying leather suitcases, often covered in stickers of interesting places, not the modern things on wheels today's traveller possess, alongside multitude's of families, children happily swinging buckets and spades, hungrily waiting the joys ahead, in a frenzy of anticipation almost too much to bear, adults fraught, with bags bulging with the swimming costumes, towels, all the paraphernalia needed, for us like most, the only trip of the year to the sea-side. Everyone impatiently keeping a watch on the large, old round wooden clock with its roman numerals *what happened to that beautiful clock and old gas lamps* suspended from the girders, with ears tuned to the announcer with his heavy nasal voice echoing "the train now standing on platform ----calling at -----". Finally the train with its grinding wheels, shuddered and inched forward in a cloud of steam coming to a standstill, in the cab, shovelling coal into the furnace were two black-faced men, wearing faded navy-blue dungarees, with peaked caps thick with grease and tar. The scramble to board now began, down the corridor to find a dark wood panelled compartment, stowing your belongings on the overhead knitted string luggage nets. A cloud of dust glinting in the shafts of sunlight were released as you sat down with a bounce upon the plush upholstered springy seats. With white clouds of hissing steam billowing from the engine onto the platform, the door of the carriage slammed shut, far down the platform a whistle blows, station master having checked all doors were closed, waved his green flag to the engine driver to signal alls well to get underway, the train with a sudden jolt chugs slowly out of the station, with trails of smoke floating past the window the platform began sliding away.

With a clickety-clack sound the train gathered speed through the beautiful Lincolnshire countryside, with my nose pressed to the large, damp carriage window, I watched the changing scenery flashing by. The hustle and bustle as the train stopped at other stations along the route, reunions, people hugging, greetings, partings, laughter, sorrows. Place-names that became familiar, waving to people waiting at level crossings. Sitting staring expectantly into the distance in an atmosphere of quiet reflection, watching meadows full of buttercups and daises, the moment shattered as another train thundered by on the parallel track. Watched the wires linking telegraph poles dip and rise, or ripening cornfields splashed with red poppies flashing past or read books without disturbing mobiles or bleeping electronic equipment, only the inspector with the words "tickets please" breaking the silence. It was the most perfect place for people watching, fantasizing about my fellow passengers, all those anonymous men and women going somewhere - cheery faces - troubled faces - ambitious faces - different expressions, some totally blank and mesmerised by routine, others full of expectation, what were their hopes, ambitions, fears? where did they work? what were their homes like? who's the man and women whispering conspiredly in the corner? is that a spy, his eyes watching everything whilst pretending to read a newspaper the whole journey? why is he sat a distance from her - why does she look so sad - have they had a lovers tiff? All my life I have been fascinated by people. When interest had waned a visit into the corridor which ran the length of the carriages, where the top half of the doors had a leather strap to sliding down the window, watching the miles whizzing past in a blur, listening to the rhythm of the clattering wheels, minding heads as the whistle signalled an approaching tunnel. Exploring further down the train brought you to first class were the restaurant car was found, out of our league, a glimpse of another world. Each place setting had it's own plates engraved with the line motifs, complete with dainty salt 'n' pepper shakers, heavy knives and forks, proper linen napkins, uniformed waiters serving coffee from silver pots.

On arrival a competition to see who would catch the first tempting preview of the distant sea. Leaving the busy station amid the sounds of coupling and uncoupling, shunting and whistling swift progress was made for the miles of sea and sand stretched out in front of us, bright with breezy east coast wind making childish cheeks glow, with the fresh clean salty tang of the sea-air in my nostrils, dragging Gran by the arm. Towels to sit on, secured a piece of sand to call your own for a few hours, pulling off our socks and shoes, experiencing the sensation of sand between our toes, at the waterline leaving cool, damp footprints in our wake. Deck chairs for adults, hired if economy allowed. Bags disgorged for the buckets and spades, frantic building of sandcastles began, the sands searched for shells to decorate our creations complete with moats, and then a few pennies were found to purchase a dozen tiny paper flags, to crown the masterpiece. Sometimes we carved out a boat then dug tombs burying one another. A jug of steaming hot tea was fetched from the booth on the sands, deposit paid, ensuring return, to wash down our sandwiches, by now penetrated with sand. Children's clothes were discarded, as the day got warmer, revealing swimming costumes, a mad dash made to frolic in the icy cold waves. Women would discreetly tuck the hem of skirts into their knicker legs to manage a paddle. A ride on the donkeys, with their jingle-jangle bells, round cornets with soft ice cream melting into sandy fists (unlike the ones at the park), the punch and Judy show, finally a ride on the helter skelter, then swing boats completed our day on the sands. Buckets of water fetched to swill bodies before drying and redressing behind strategically placed towels. Now and again a stroll was taken along the pier, viewing faraway ships through the telescopes placed along the elaborate cast iron and wooden structure. Then a walk along the immaculate gardens, here was the famous statue of the boy with the leaking boot, now sadly removed, because he was stolen. To draw to a close we sat on the wall and enjoyed our candyfloss watching the world go by, before catching the train for the return journey. The joy never dimmed, a happy, contented boy and girl fell asleep dreaming of the next time.

A day at the seaside with Dad was a difficult thing to achieve; harvestime on the land meant labour was needed to make hay while the sun shone. The first time I recall going with dad was after I had received my first bike. We first cycled to the station, meeting Bet who spent the day with us. Were Gran always spent the day on the sands with us, Dad wasn't a great lover of water, his idea of sunbathing was to peel off boots then socks, roll up trouser legs, handkerchief knotted at all four corners, placed on the head, seldom venturing into the sea, so after about an hour a bit more active day followed. With his bit of overtime money saved, whilst still on the sands came a ride on the big wheel, a birds eye view of the surrounding area with people appearing like little ants. Not my favourite ride, I still have no head for heights, but sitting in the swinging chairs, whilst rising slowly as the wheel loads is perhaps the scariest thing I have endured. *A few years ago, now a big brave adult, I thought I could conquer my fear, but before the thing was fully loaded I had to beg the operator to let me off. The same qualms haunt me if I climb a castle etc. the enclosed climb is OK but I can't get close to the edge and look over, un-railed high walkways, as in the surrounding walls of Lincoln Castle produce the same terrors. Recently I tried to walk across the Pontcysyllte Aqueduct, 121ft above the river Dee, which has railings one side of the path that runs alongside the canal, but despite not having a fear of water, could I do it could I eckerslike.* Following a walk along the promenade often chewing a bar of nougat we made our way to the amusement arcades, the slot machines vied for your attention, (some things never change*)*. With precious pennies early lessons in money management were learnt, decisions had to be made what to spend and where from the myriad of attractions on offer. First passing the vendors who for a price guessed your weight, giving you cheap gaudy trinkets if wrong (could not lose could he). The mechanical laughing policeman in his little box was not to be missed; if crafty you could chuckle along at some-one else's expense. Sound and illuminations drew you down to 'Wonderland' some things are long gone like the big dipper, screaming as it plummeted its way around the whole site, plunged into the edge, of the central boating lake, splashing all, next rising, soaring to the stars, coming suddenly to an abrupt end. Balls could be thrown into mechanical laughing clowns as the gaping mouth moved incessantly right to left and back again, a hit, the ball then rolled down numbered partitions, prize dependant on score; yet another side-stall a chosen string from a tangled web, pulled, gave a prize every time. A favourite of mine was the horse racing. Along a wall was stretched in lanes, numbered motorized horses complete with multi-coloured jockeys. Your horse chosen, you provided the power, turning your own wheel placed in front of your seat, the nags galloped to the winning post, instinct made you want to hurry, but the secret lay in going easy, the slower you turned the faster your stead went. The dodgems; the boating lake were further contenders for your funds. Spent up, the music still ringing in your ears, it was time to wend your weary way back towards the station, but not without supper. Who can forget the taste of your first fish and chips? sitting on the wall, eaten straight from the paper, a greaseproof envelope sitting in a folded sheet of newspaper, salted to taste, swilled with vinegar, the rowdy seagulls awaiting a tasty morsel. Sometimes a rare treat, advantage was taken of the sea front café's all-inclusive offer, fish and chips, bread and butter and a pot of tea for a fixed price. On the last leg of the return, Dad often having to give his weary daughter, a push-shove holding the saddle at the rear.

Only a few people owned their own car, I still see in my minds eye even today, the excitement when Dad got his first car, an old rattling Ford with running boards - step running the length of car, below the doors, orange indicators on the sides between the front and rear doors, to signal directions. Hand signals had to be made in the event of them refusing to work. A straight arm extended out of the lowered window for a right turn, to be circled for a left turn, slowly raising and lowering for slowing down. A wedge was inserted in the event of a failure on the part of the window winding mechanism, enough force used to hold up the rattling pane, whipped out smartish if necessary for the afore mentioned signalling, subsequent wind chill factor being likened to north pole until such times as it could be wedged again. Cars were idiosyncratic, many is the time I watched him start it manually, cranking it with a long handle, inserted in the middle of the front bumper positioned for this purpose, swung vigorously it connected to the crank pulley. A special knack was required, at best severe bruising to the thumb, at worst a broken wrist or arm could easily result if the handle backfired. A ratchet arrangement on the steering column produced gear changes.

Oh what fun we had and what freedom it gave us. There was no yellow lines, no traffic wardens. On journeys involving a long pull uphill like Caister drag, dad being one for jokes often made out we would all have to get out and push. With a sigh of relief we always managed to reach the summit to a round of applause.

On what appeared to be long journeys, approx. 40 miles to Cleethorpes. (Mablethorpe or Skegness out of the question), with no services, a stop would be made half way for the ritual picnic, out came the primus stove to make a nice cup of tea., On the way home Dad always called at Bishopbridge for half a pint of beer. Lemonade and packet of crisps (only plain available containing a blue screw of salt you shook on yourself) for me. Now trips to West Country or Scotland are made without a second thought but old bangers (second hand cars) being less reliable travelled less miles and much slower then. Car games helped to passed the time on journeys that seemed to take forever. The journey often began with a number-plate game, passing registration plate letters were made into sentences, like STA could be 'some take all'. Tiring of that, waiting for cars few and far between, I spy would be enjoyed. On return journeys rousing songs were sung, '4 Wheels on my Wagon'; 'Ten Green Bottles'; 'Ten Men Went To Mow'; Daddy Wouldn't Buy Me A Bow-wow'; 'I Do Like To Be Beside The Seaside'; 'Don't Dilly Dally on the Way'; were some of the more popular ones.

Garages at that time were small affairs with a couple of pumps at the roadside, the proprietor worked by hand, swinging the pipes out to fill up the tank. Children could request badges; constantly appeals were made to visit garages with different brands of fuel to swell the collection (would children today like to collect them). I still can't resist mumbling "The Es-so sign means hap-py mo-tor-ing, call at the Es-so sign" when passing Esso garages. I recollect the curtailment of trips, when strict rationing had to be introduced between December 1956 and May 1957. Applications were made for a ration book people being issued with tokens to be exchanged for petrol according to requirements, ours were deemed negligible, so decisions had to be made regarding the most needful journeys.

I was christened, and confirmed as a conventional Church of England girl, we never questioned the existence of god. When visiting cousins, I attended Sunday school with them. Church or Chapel, there was only one God the universal provider as far as our family were concerned, wherever he was in residence. The chosen story from the Bible each week was read aloud, there was texts to be learned, and often-longer passages or psalms, offer prayers, praise God, listen to sermons. Older children helping the younger ones.

Religion played a large part in our lives, The church and chapel with ancient traditions was the natural hub, an important part of any community, but especially a farming one, an opportunity to share one another's joys, there was a special communion with God in his Holy House. The appeal of religion lay in its relevance to life, a combination of fun, frivolity with solemnity and dedication, the test of religion is not righteousness but love. I loved the peal of bells carried over the air calling homes near and far, the splendour, pomp and ceremony of church, the strict formality of its ritual, the vaulted roof, stained glass windows. The cross a constant reminder of the fundamental teaching of his faith, water for cleansing, candles are lit as a reminder of Jesus, who came to bring light into the dark world. The vestments worn intended to transform the wearer from the everyday world to 'holy' time in the procession of sumptuous colours of purple, gold and white robed clergy along with surpliced choir.

On the other hand I also loved the informality of chapel, the lustier singing and sincerity.

The Sunday School Anniversary, brings faded memories of the Chapel children's own day, we children in Sunday best, sat in ranks facing the congregation the wee ones on the front row to the big boys and girls at the rear, all on our best behaviour. Between the hymns, some sang collectively, some in pairs, with the occasional angelic solo, when it came to your turn it was a terrible ordeal to say your 'piece', which for weeks you had been learning and practising for recitation.

Festivals each with its own customs and traditions, many of which go back to the ancient times of darkness, fear and superstition, play an important role in the life of any religion. Serving as a seasonal calendar, annual reminders of the familiar yet important stories that need to be remembered. A mixture of folklore, tradition and belief. Public occasions when people share their feelings, something special broke down barriers of reserve and prejudice.

For hundreds of years as soon as Christmas festivities are over farmers begin to plough the land preparing the ground for sowing of crops. Before the work began, there used to be a special ritual when people ask Gods blessing on their work, the day was Plough Monday. Times have changed, instead of the plough decorated with ribbons, being pulled through the village with the accompanying dancing and noise, intended to drive out evil spirits so the land would produce a good harvest, the farm workers attended a special service to ask Gods blessing for those who worked on the land.

Lent, the period of forty days before Easter - at one time kept very strictly as a period of prayer, penance, fasting and self denial. Starting on Ash Wednesday, commemorates the forty days that Jesus Christ spent fasting in the wilderness. Today many have forgotten or simply not learnt the reasons for so many of our celebrations. The day before the restrictions, Shrove Tuesday, became Pancake Day as people used up their fat and eggs (forbidden foods) to make pancakes. We had our pancakes, cooked in the big, black, heavy frying pan over the hot flames, as many as six a piece never savoury, always with lemon juice and sugar, jam or golden syrup. Never since did pancakes taste so good.

At the end of Lent, Easter marked the resurrection of Jesus Christ. Hot cross buns for breakfast, the warm smell of the baking buns (not available any other day of the year, kept as a special symbol of Good Friday), making the mouth water in anticipation, sheer temptation, the hot squishiness was steamy-sweet pure bliss. The bun, in pagan times, represented the moon and the cross served as a reminder of the crucifixion, divided it into four quarters. Fish for dinner, no one would dream of eating meat on this day. No washing allowed on that day, an old superstition.

On Easter Sunday, it became customary for people to give dyed eggs, (regarded as the ancient symbol of new life) usually decorated, as presents. Nowadays real eggs replaced by chocolate ones. Our chocolate Easter egg hidden, to be searched for on Sunday morning, but not allowed to be eaten until breakfast was over, a boiled egg, dyed red with a little cochineal added to the water or cooked in onion skins to produce intricate patterns. Afternoon visit to church to sing that joyous song "There is a green hill far away". An occasion for a new homemade summer frock, new white ankle socks, white sandals, topped with Easter bonnets. The perfect end to the celebration of each new year a visit to or from relatives for Easter tea, with delicious Simnel Cake. Originally this cake was baked for Mothering Sunday, an old legend says that a brother and sister were going to make a cake for their mother. They had an argument as to whether to bake or boil the cake (which was then quite a usual method of cooking a cake) in the end they baked one and boiled the other sticking both together, giving the characteristic division through the centre. Almond paste was made into small balls - eleven was the traditional number - placed around the edge of the cake for decoration a tiny model chicken placed top centre.

A hundred years ago many more workers were needed to gather the harvest with everyone giving a hand. Harvest Home was the celebration for the safe completion. It was believed that the last of the corn contained the corn spirit, therefore the last of the corn was gathered and twisted to produce the corn dolly. Taken into church for the special harvest service before being hung in the barn, kept during the winter to be sown with the new corn, ensuring another good harvest. The last wagons were often decorated with ribbons and garlands of flowers. That night the farmer and his wife gave a thank-you supper in the farmhouse for all those who had helped. Today the role of harvest supper's is played by the church.

Marking the end of harvest was the much loved Harvest Festival, thanking God for the man-made bounty of crops and all those who helped to bring them in. A riot of colour with sheaves of wheat and oats weaved into corn dollies, among the autumn flowers stacked round pillars, windows, pulpit and pew ends. The locally grown offerings of fruit, giant marrows, home made cakes and jams the scents filling the church (later distributed to the needy of the parish). Profusion of apples, baskets of eggs, pyramids of potatoes, carrots with their feathery tops, clusters of beetroot cabbages, and turnips all solemnly carried up the aisle while singing at the tops of our voices,

"All good gifts around us
are sent from heaven above
then thank the lord,
o thank the lord,
for all thy love"

were arranged in front of the alter, were the outsized harvest loaf took pride of place.

As I recall those halcyon days long ago, nostalgic images of Church garden parties on the vicarage lawn drift through my thoughts. A local dignitary would open the proceedings, through a badly crackling microphone. Ladies with big floppy hats in pretty summer dresses tip-toed across the grass, fancy dress competitions; various stalls and games; lucky dips, as hand dived into sawdust to retrieve a surprise package; skittles/bowling for the pig (usually a joint of pork) with the heavy wooden saucer shapes to knock over the equally heavy nine pins; bowling for children meant rolling a ball towards arched openings with differing values in a castle wall; dancing displays, tea from the huge aluminium teapot, poured into china cups and saucers accompanied by cream scones served by willing volunteers.

Remembrance day was revered, always the eleventh day of the eleventh month at the first stroke of the eleventh hour, it produced a moving effect. The cars ceased to cough and fume, gliding to stillness. Everyone stood to attention, the hush deepened, the spirit of memory brooded over all, for two minutes silence.

The new Religion is consumerism, our Saints are our entrepreneurs, our Cathedrals are the great supermarkets, and the 20th century may come to be seen as the century when man realized he did not need God. The only afterlife we have is through our genetic posterity, tradition which we as a nation are largely ignoring, from birth until death, each one of us is vulnerable, needs guidance, direction and sanctuary, if not continued must eventually die, to our cost. If the present trends in fall off of church attendance continues our churches will be empty by 2020.

Halloween is a real mixture of ancient pagan ideas, folklore and religion. Long ago 31st October was the end of the Celtic year with its ceremonial extinguishing and lighting of fires. The old day of darkness became a time of mystery, when ghosts, witches and evil spirits needed to be driven away. Times change people are no longer afraid of evil spirits, today pumpkins, horrid masks and 'spooky' atmosphere have transformed this festival we did not celebrated.
Bonfire night so delightful a tradition (its roots go back to the ancient Celts who believed that huge bonfires would help the sun to keep its strength as it became weaker at the end of October) was always on 5th November. The anniversary of the day Guy Fawkes' plot to blow up the British Parliament was discovered. With no large organised displays it was a family affair in your own back garden, taking place when darkness closed in. A guy was made with an old jacket or jumper, trousers, both stuffed with straw, tied with string at arm and legs, if one could be spared topped with a hat. Sat atop the fire in a broken old chair if available. As soon as it was dark enough the fireworks were taken outside in a tin box, dad taking control, lighting the blue touch paper, retiring a safe distance away, setting them off one by one. None of the monstrosities manufactured today, we were happy with our Silver Fountains; Starburst; Falling Rain; Serpents; Roman Candles; Rainbow Showers; Roman Candles; Moonshine; Shimmering Stars; Sparkling Dust; all in red and blue wrappers, covered with stars or magic signs, promising a rain of fire or golden cascades to illuminate the sky. Sparklers to wave in increasing, decreasing circles; Catherine wheels nailed to a stout post, spinning and sparkling; hop around to avoid jumping jacks; couple of rockets soaring into the night sky, launched from old tin cans; hands on ears for a few Thunder Flash, firecrackers/bangers.

Hot jacket tatties, with crispy skins straight from the oven, then toffee apples to finish the night.

In 1956, Linda, who had gone to a different primary school to me, passed her 'eleven plus' exam and went to High School. Finding she had a lot more homework than me, combined with a whole new set of friends met at senior school we saw less of each other, the process of growing up had begun, leaving childhood behind.

I was not good at saving. As a small child I was encouraged to save pennies given by aunts and uncles in a miniature replica post box savings tin. Deeply etched in my memory I call back, using a table knife with practised skill, to make withdrawals. Worse to my utter shame, between 1956 -1957 when I was at Ropery school, dad or Gran was probably struggling to provide me weekly with 2/6d to buy stamps in the national savings scheme, although I did at first do this, I discovered the temptations of the post office next door to the school. Instead of taking my money into school on Monday morning, covetousness overtook my better judgement. I started to buy the things I thought I needed. My greed for new pencils, crayons, protractor, set square, books etc lead me not only to spend the money intended for saving but I slowly withdrew the money already saved. I appallingly regret my inexcusable actions, that one indiscretion made me the more conscientious person I am today.

In 1959 I joined the 1st Scotter Girl Guides. I joined and enjoyed my time in the 'forget me not' company, receiving my Tenderfoot Test Card. First test was knowing the motto "Be Prepared"; along with a Guide does a good turn for somebody every day; finally the threefold promise, I promise on my honour that I will do my best, to do my duty to God and the Queen, to help other people at all times, to obey the Guide Law. Further tests were complete understanding of the composition of the union jack, the right way to fly it, along with some of the stories and legends connected with it; the salute and greeting sign, shaking hands with the left; whistle signals, tracking signs, hand and flag signals. Understanding of knots came next, being able to whip the end of a rope, tie the following knots, knowing their uses: - reef, sheetbend, clove hitch, double overhand, fisherman's. The origin of the guide movement, the meaning of tenderfoot and world badges; before the final hurdle The Guide Law, once learnt never forgotten. 1. A Guide's honour is to be trusted. 2. A Guide is loyal. 3. A Guide's duty is to be useful and to help others. 4. A Guide is a friend to all, and a sister to every other Guide. 5. A Guide is courteous. 6. A Guide is a friend to animals. 7. A Guide obeys orders. 8. A Guide smiles and sings under all difficulties. 9. A Guide is thrifty. 10. A Guide is pure in thought, word and deed. Some of the village girls were not very good Guides, not paying much attention to number four, the lack of acceptance made it difficult to continue, so with regret I left before being enrolled.

The town, village and countryside of my childhood have gone forever.

LINKS IN THE CHAIN

Being such a close knit family I now find it strange we had no contact with any of Gran's siblings or their descendants, I now know many of her brothers and sisters were not living a million miles away. So many questions and no-one to answer.
One of my greatest and most remembered pleasures was the frequent family re-unions. Most of my life revolved around my closest relations who all lived within a 30 mile radius, so holidays staying with aunts, uncles and my cousins, mostly accompanied by Gran and Alan, but occasionally alone was a captivating time for me., It made school holidays so exciting in those far-off days, I'm sure Gran would equally have enjoyed these breaks away from the monotonous routine of running a house for four other adults plus us two children, I like to think it gave her a respite from total responsibility with a much needed rest.
After Gran left in 1958, when the wicked stepmother *although I never called her mother* came to live with us, my holidays changed. I now went every weekend as well as holidays to stay with loved ones, although I continued to enjoyed these times, the balance and reasons had changed, I went because I couldn't spend a moment longer with Bet than I had too.

Of Gran's step children - *but I did not know then she was a step-daughter* - I only knew Aunt Alice who was married to my uncle Bert. They lived in Messingham at the bottom of Wells Street the house then was three separate homes. Trying to catapult my mind back to scenes long ago, I find it difficult to recall as much as I would like of the happy holidays I did spend with them. Aunt Alice and uncle Bert, who then lived in the bottom house now demolished, with my cousins, twins Daphne and Derek with an older sister Pam. The old house could not have been very big perhaps only two bedrooms because Derek had a bed on the landing which wasn't that unusual in those days. In the huge living room - the only downstairs room other than the small kitchen - was a television, although I do not remember watching it a lot. The one exception was when Dad picked me up on Sunday night he would arrive in time to watch "Sunday Night at the London Palladium" I would sit on his knee enthralled as we all gathered round to watch this variety show. As I write memories stir of seeing differing artistic mediums for the first time, my encounters with ventriloquism, Lord Charles a talking dummy, sat on Ray Allen's knee, the human not appearing to be the one doing the talking I was mesmerised. Tap-dancing, the power to increase or develop steps at an ever growing pace, the rhythmic sound magnified by the metal tipped shoes. Minstrels, entertainers who wore curly black wigs, black suits, black facial make-up, with very distinctive whitened eyes and lips, white gloves worn to complete the look, unfortunately now considered racist. Magicians performing conjuring tricks and illusions so pleasingly performed as to appear supernaturally created.

I recall little of how I spent my days, I did not play in the streets and make friends - if indeed any children lived nearby - although I had other cousins also in Messingham they were at that time living too far away from the village. Pam, Derek and Daphne who were considerably older than me, must have been at work all day. One specific occasion stands out in my mind, the time Daphne with her then boyfriend took me to a club in Scunthorpe. Clearly like a picture in a book I can see a large room in which stood a row - perhaps half a dozen - of large snooker tables supported by fat bulbous legs - much bigger than the pool tables in today's pubs. Each illuminated by their own overhanging light nearly as large as the table, suspended to within a few feet by long chains from the ceiling. The brilliant green baize of each table - so soft to the touch - in dazzling contrast to the dark panelling of the walls. Rows of cues were neatly held in racks upon the wall, with a small chunky wooden oblong for each table, upon which was a knob like arrow to slide along to mark the scoring. Grandma paid the occasional visit for a few hours presumably walking from aunt VI's, but one visit still haunts me. No sooner had she walked through the door than an almighty quarrel broke out - I never discovered the reason, but all these years later sat writing this, words haunt me - "you did" - "they said" - "you are" - "she's my responsibility" - "your dad would turn in his grave" - I wonder were aunt Vi and aunt Alice friends for I never recall the one visiting the other. Did something happen or was something said that Gran took aunt Vi's side, blood being thicker than water. After a period of shouting, I was called from the corner were I was cowering *I'd never heard raised voices before,* I was told to gather my clothes, then Gran took me away, we walked all the way to aunt Vi's in silence, it was never to my knowledge discussed.

Years later uncle Bert had an accident at work and bought the whole block with his compensation, they moved up to the front, Derek lived in the middle when he got married and Pam had a bungalow built in the garden. I did visit them once after I got married. Uncle Bert was overjoyed to see me, making a great fuss of me and baby Jacqueline, but aunt Alice had had a stroke and I found that very difficult to deal with seeing her like that, loping in a chair, dribbling from the side of her mouth, unable to communicate. Combined with what I thought of as my betrayal of Gran *although I still knew not why they quarrelled* also my own movements around the country, sadly I never got to see either again. Fond memories remain of the love I had for them both.

15 Walkeringham Rd Beckingham lived Aunt Mary, Uncle Jack, with cousins Jean, John, and Janet. At that time the main road passed the last house on its way out of the village. The row of council houses stood a little way back from the road with trim rectangular front lawns - cut with a clanking side wheeled lawnmower laboriously pushed up and down making attractive stripes - bordered by an equally neat border of flowers without a weed to be seen, no drive or parking places, a path led to the back door, having also branched off to the front door. The rear garden was given over to growing fruit and vegetables in uniform rows. On one visit Aunt Mary made a raspberry pie none of us could eat, after picking the raspberries it was standard practise to place them in a bowl of salted water to rid them of the little insects that lurked, but in her haste she forgot to rinse them. Here my cousins ate bread and dripping at tea times but I never could stand the stuff so a tin of Golden syrup was purchased for me to enjoy bread and treacle.

I loved visiting Aunt Mary, but I soon learnt to avoid cousin John who had a cruel, tormentative streak. How well I remember one of our many visits to the playing fields, John found a grass snake *I did not know that then*, he insisted it was poisonous, curled around a length of wood he repeatedly brought it within inches of me taunting me unmercifully. To this day I won't go anywhere near snakes, not even at Zoo's were they are behind glass. Another time he sneaked up behind me, whilst we were on the swings, he pushed me higher and higher, petrified I screamed for him to stop. I can still sense the fear of those days fifty years later. Jean and Janet seemed powerless to intervene or perhaps they too, in the way only kids do, thought it was funny.

They moved to Sandbeck, Blyton in 1957, where I continued to spend weekends with them. The huge farmhouse, about three quarters mile out of the village had many rooms, some not used, when Jean married, she and her husband had one front room for their own sitting room, I could visit her as well having two bites of the cake. Because of the size aunt Mary often had my cousin Colin - aunt Edna's son - over at the same time. The extensive land around as the name suggests was gorse covered sandy hummocks with a bubbling 'beck', an ideal playground. We often walked for miles, back up the road to the village or continuing along farm tracks reaching Laughton Woods. Three years later *by now we'd all grown out of childhood* they came to live in the other chalet next door to us at Scotter. I remained close to aunt Mary until sadly she died only 44yrs old in 1963.

Aunt Vi and uncle Bert also lived at Messingham, - cousins Anne, Jennifer *(Jenny the closest in age at one year younger than me, we were best friends and shared so many childish pleasures, I was devastated when she died recently at only 62yrs old)*, last but not least David. But if I thought we lived in the country, this really was isolated. Now due to extensive quarrying the whole area for mile upon mile is flooded.

The bus to Scunthorpe was caught outside the house, through Blyton it then left the main road for a detour around Laughton, Northorpe, Scotton, before rejoining the A159 at Scotter. After arrival at Messingham we alighted at the Green Tree Inn, crossed the road, leaving all signs of life behind we had to walk behind the pub along little more than a track, four miles down fields, only passing one farmhouse about halfway. Alan and I were responsible for carrying our own small suitcases, but once about half way Gran realized Alan wasn't carrying his, we had to retrace our steps, using the public phone-box (by the way telephone exchanges in those days were still local defined by names not numbers ex. Gainsborough 4872, not (01427). Gran rang the bus-station but the case was already missing when the bus arrived at the station terminal.

Of all the houses I have been in I remember virtually nothing of the inside of this one. What I do recall most vividly was being unable to have fresh milk daily, bottles of pasteurised, capped with a metal top was bought, I would not drink milk when visiting I hated it, I will never forget the taste, even today I shudder just thinking about it.

Outside was a kids paradise acres of clover fields with sandy hills and hollows, childhood here only registered idyllic sunny days. If there was rainy days and I'm sure there was, I can't recall them. We discovered our bodies playing doctors and nurses; we made wild rose petal perfume. In games of hide and seek, the person 'on' leant against a post, closed their eyes and counted to hundred, then called "coming ready or not". Never leaving base far they attempted to find the others as they attempted to return to base before being seen. If spotted the post had to be touched to shouts of "blocko, one, two three out". The old tumble-down walled garden well overgrown, and meadow fields all provided good cover for returning to base, to gleefully touch the post enabling you to stay 'in'. The barns, along with the hayloft above the carts were dens where you could stay hidden, causing frustration for the seeker.

Jenny taught me to ride a bike, she held the saddle of her old boneshaker *or was it the unmade roads* as I peddled away, when I realised she'd let go I promptly stopped pedalling and collapsed in a heap. Dusting myself down, and starting again, concentrating on peddling and balancing I succeeded on my first wobbly attempts. I did not get my own bike until my birthday in 1959, my greatest treat, it must have taken considerable effort to save to afford it, second hand it may have been but it gave me more freedom and greater pleasure for many years, than any youngster today gets from their brand new one's or multitude of expensive presents. My cousins and I were often sent to the village to fetch groceries, everything had to be carried down them fields, or perhaps sometimes the local farmer helped out with his tractor, the only vehicle that could have reached the house.

Aunt Vi. Uncle Bert and Gran used to think nothing of walking to the village pub, well they walked there, but many times they staggered home tipsy, after one particular merry night uncle Bert had

to support one drunk lady part of the way leaving her singing on the grass, returning for the other, so it continued in relays.
When walking to the village, away off to the left was the quarry, which was on the side of the road that went to Brigg. Gran and aunt Vi often made trips to scour the tip along this road, taking us with them to help carry the discovered booty home, its surprising how one persons junk was another persons treasure.

Around 1956 they moved into the village so many firsts followed. The new home was the old vicarage, long since demolished; it stood were the Rix garage now stands. It was a rambling old house with lots of character, more than once I heard aunt Vi complain of bumpy walls with sunken floor tiles, which made the floor very uneven. The back door around the back of the house led into the small kitchen, next came the largest living room I have ever seen, I recall three large comfortable squashy settee's, numerous easy chairs, large dining table with dining chairs, sideboard and still spacious. Passing the front door - opening up onto the side of the house - seldom used, the front room - window overlooking the main road - mainly used for storage was virtually unusable, being extremely expensive to heat due to the cold and damp. Upstairs were two good-sized bedrooms, but still not enough. Anne and Jenny had two double beds in the back bedroom, doubling up when Gran and I visited - Alan was by now living at Doncaster with his mum, now married - aunt Vi and uncle Bert had the other one, David had a double bed on the huge landing.
Although we'd had fish and chips at a café in Cleethorpes the village takeaway fish and chip shop - now a gent's barbers - became a novelty. For a special treat on Friday dinner Aunt Vi would send us for 'one of each' - years later I found them known as fish lot down south - one fish and bag of chips each for however many of us were present, with salt and vinegar added there and then to be soaking in, wrapped in greaseproof paper with outer covering of newspaper to keep contents hot. A cheap and popular meal, the queue could be several yards long, the aroma was enticing, the appetite wetted a hasty return was ensured. In an age when standards were still maintained it was still compulsory to sit at the table, however a concession was made to eat directly from the wrapping with, aghast! fingers, two reasons I suspect, to eat while still hot in the days before microwaves and to save on washing up. It wasn't long before we children realised for a few pennies; or when in short

supply discarded newspapers could be exchanged for a bag of chips, usually claimed in the early evening with some scraps (the batter bits - for free), then eaten walking down the street. One first was the taste of fizzy pop, ice cream soda; cherryade; or dandelion and burdock. It was the practise for shops to put a premium on soft drinks - a deposit to ensure the return of glass bottles, this being refunded - empties saved produced a tidy sum on return.

My first introduction to collecting for reward came with paper golly's carefully peeled from labels on Robertson's jam jars, saved, stuck to a card, then exchanged by sending away for miniature sets of golliwog statues.

Another treat eagerly awaited each year was the Works Gala, held in a great park in Scunthorpe for the children of workers at Froddingham Steel Works - uncle Steve had thoughtfully added me to his children - after an afternoon of races plus games, at four o'clock we sat on the grass to enjoy our tea of dainty sandwiches, crisps and cake we'd queued to collect neatly packed in little brown bags. Entertainment like Punch and Judy would follow, before collecting our commemorative mugs, then wending our weary way home.

There was no Halloween nights then, but mischief night was fun, things like garden ornaments would be moved, doorknobs would be smeared with syrup, knock on doors then run and hide, letter-boxes rattled or metal dust-bin lids rolled down the path (once only and never where you knew old or lonely people lived) gates unhooked from posts, no graffiti, not late at night, no vandalism, just that, mischief.

Children then were well behaved, there was great respect for parents, a pleasurable feeling of care for one another for friends and neighbours too. We mostly did as we were told, the threat of a sharp, swift smack was enough deterrent and we never, never answered back. Teachers, bus conductors, school teachers, shop-keepers, park-keepers even lavatory attendants were respected, bikes left unlocked were untouched. The church, graveyard too was sacrosanct, not a place to play, if reason to visit, never, never tread upon a grave. We were taught not to take anything you could lay your hands on, under no circumstances lie, steal or cheat, nor betray people for your own advancement. The highly visible presence of the uniformed local bobby in traditional tunic wearing his helmet, and cape in cold weather, offered reassurance , constantly patrolling the beat had considerable preventive value.

The only other shopping trip, a Saturday delight was a trip to Scunthorpe market, it would be many years before I visited Lincoln, Doncaster or Sheffield. Its hard for people now to realise how far away even places now considered fairly nearby were. The highlight being watching in awe the man on the crockery stall. He held aloft a clothes basket containing a tea or dinner service, taking a selection he showed the transparency of china by holding items to the light; performed complicated juggling acts, deftly cascading plates from one hand to another; knocked glasses together all without chips or breakages. Then came the sales patter, starting with "these are priced £? at ? (some local shop), I'm not asking ?£, not even ? bob (shillings)", reducing the price until he ask "who'll give me ? the lot" whereupon a frenzy followed of eager housewife's holding aloft arms, from all directions his assistants handed out the goods and grabbed the money, throwing loose change into a chamber pot, as they called out, "one over here Charlie". I heard it said, some unfortunate women were taken in, discovering when they got home, only half the goods were china, the rest earthenware or items were missing from supposedly complete sets.

Jenny took an evening paper round to earn some money. She had a bicycle to cover the large area. She'd pull a paper from her heavy canvas bag slung across her chest, neatly fold it and pass it to me to 'help' her deliver quicker. Only once did I fall for this con. Trotting along-side her, I realized I'd done the work walking, sometimes running down varying lengths of paths, pushing newspapers through assorted letterboxes, discovering they came in all shapes and sizes, high ones, low ones, small ones, those with tight springs, those with snarling dogs waiting on the other side waiting to snap unwary fingers, then *she got the money.*

I became quite good at roller skating, the pavement outside the house fell away downhill, which gave us many a tumble, many a bruise, but we just would not quit. Heaven forbid, you would not allow your children to roller skate along side a busy main *not so busy back* then road these days.

A time for rejoicing, my life long love affair with the fair began at Messingham. Swarthy showmen arrived with their exquisite chrome, glass and mirrored caravans, towing extremely long trailers, some that miraculously unfurled into rides all ready complete with coloured light bulbs to connect to pounding generators, to erect the latest picturesque, flamboyant painted novelties along with coils of oily cable snaking around the field. Uncle Bert earned good wages, so money was always found for us to go.

As you approached the field behind The Horn Inn the excitement rose to a crescendo your toes tingled, your heart raced with excitement as the music from many different rides blared at an unprecedented level with the brilliant blaze of fairy lights, drawing you into a magic land that always captivated me. Popular tunes from the hurdy - gurdies that echoed for miles and went on all afternoon till late into the evening, laid in our beds the music thrilled me. The residents probably cursed the volume of sound, but everyone looked forward to its advent, and would have been the first to fight with jealous pride, if anything were done to stop the arrival of the annual carnival.

The elaboration and richness of fairground carving, mirrors reflecting the glitter and illusion. Awaiting your delight, the carousel began to turn, slowly but surely rotating more rapidly , the garishly painted galloping wooden horses and cockerels waved up and down, everyone squealed as the music increased to a crescendo with a speed that seemed geared to the melody, the trick being to lean a little and ride with it, not fight it. The 'gallopers' carved horses rose and fell as they circled to the music of the built in organ. The thrilling, stomach churning 'Walzer' each car revolving madly whilst the whole twirled in ever faster circles. Sit on the seat in the massive head of the dragon and look out through the creatures eyes, up and down round and round in a sea of vibrant colour. Dodgem cars, with sparks igniting as contact made, when everyone's intention was not to dodge, but to notch up how many you could collide with. Toddlers with mum or dad, to teenagers climbing the narrow steps with your coir mat to reach the top of the Helter Skelter, to reappear again feet first, at the bottom of the corkscrew chute

For babies roundabouts with miniature buses, aeroplanes and magical coaches pulled by two white horses, speed determined by the power of the man turning a handle. Unlike the swing boats powered by yourselves pulling on the multicoloured plaited ropes.

Games of skill ranged from rifle shooting galleries, how many static or moving targets could you hit; or darts, could you hit any playing card let alone enough for the high score needed.

Feats of strength, coconut shies, with six small hard wooden balls, could you topple the coconut from its perch; you were implored to try your luck at the tall thermometer shaped pole, could you strike a peg with a wooden mallet flashed down hard enough to knock the arrow enough to clang the bell high above at the top of the pole, securing your cheap garish reward.

Games of chance, roll a penny, down grooved slopes, if landing in clearly defined squares, rewarded with varying set amounts; Hoopla, hard enough to throw your hoop a fair distance over the desired object, but it had to also land flat on the table; hook a duck, floating almost out of reach, various values found on the underside; ping pong balls aimed at goldfish bowls, to win the ultimate prize of a goldfish carried away in a little plastic bag, parents cursing because no proper bowl being available the poor little thing never stood a chance housed hastily in the glass trifle dish, from which he invariably jumped committing hari kari.

Prizes were never up to much but it was the joy of winning, huge cuddly soft toys hung temptingly from stalls, that no-one seemed to win; the most likely prizes tawdry tin brooches; be-feathered celluloid dolls; lustre-ware dishes, jugs or vases; doo-dahs, a coiled up paper tube attached to a mouth-piece, which as you blew into it a feather on the end tickled the targets nose, as the air left the mouth-piece whistled; brightly coloured bouncing ball on elastic that concealed sawdust to shatter asunder when hit; or a bat with ball attached by elastic.

Penny slot machines, that you never got the better of, if you had a win you fed it back in your childish desire to win more.

Throughout the visit enough toffee apples, candyfloss, hot-dogs, were consumed to leave you feeling queasy.

A night at the fair in 1957, ending with fish and chips cost me seven shillings four pennies, how do I know? I wrote about it in my school essay. I started with three pence on the 'roll a penny', with my winnings of a shilling I had sixpen'oth of skittles, with my six balls I knocked down three having three pence returned. A ride on the dodgems, a hot-dog, proceeding to 'roll a ball' I scored enough to win an ash tray, the round-a-bout followed, finally buying myself a bouncing ball.

All schoolchildren were allowed the day off to visit the major event in the county's farming calendar - not until an adult, did this become part of my yearly visits - the Lincolnshire Agricultural Show.

But for our family the Messingham show held at the bottom of

Church St. was more important, at an early age my Gran took me, but for Jenny and I our first visits without adults took place when they moved up to the village, I was to continue with this pilgrimage until I left Lincolnshire. An opportunity for farmers, breeders to get together to exhibit their products, an exhibition and celebration which typified all the best of British farming. A fine day out for all the family, villagers gathered to sit in rapped attention on the straw bales arranged around the arena. The great shire horses, those gentle giants, immaculately groomed, decorated with eye-catching plaited manes and tails, intertwined with coloured ribbon, highly polished harness with dazzling brasses glistening in the sun, led by equally immaculate grooms, paraded around the ring for judging of the finest animals of each class. For years Uncles Jeff and Robert paraded some of these magnificent beasts belonging to James Forrest. *Later going on to exhibit their own cattle at other shows including The Royal as well as Yorkshire winning cups and rosettes many times.* Pedigree livestock competing for best of show, sparking friendly rivalry between farmers and stockbreeders. Top class show jumping with the country's best known riders competing; children on fat little pony's participating in pony club events; culminating in the grand parade, proudly sporting winning rosettes and trophies.

Inside a giant marquee everything that could be grown, cooked or sewn, ardently competed over. The judges walked meditatively, with their notebooks and wrinkled brows, cutting, tasting, smelling, giving every vegetable, preserve, flower, cheese, handicraft the benefit of their wisdom and experience. Many anxious adults and school children awaiting their emergence, having unquestionably placed their chosen 1st, 2nd, 3rd and commended tickets upon exhibits. Around the edge, the traders with their fine array of expensive horsey / farm ware goods for sale, demonstrations of rural crafts, farmers wearing tweeds and bowler hats with their shooting sticks, munched their gourmet luncheons from picnic hampers at the rear of land rovers, stockmen boiling the kettle on a primas stove near the horse box.

Soon after moving to the village, at a party playing a game appropriately called boyfriends, I met Michael Davies the boy who was to be my first boyfriend. One person - in this case Michael - goes out of sight behind a curtain, while those sat at the table write down a name of someone of the opposite sex, who's present in the room. If different names emerge the one behind the curtain, depending how they see it either has a lucky escape or if one or more chose the same name the boy and girl have to kiss. From twelve years old, a poignant puppy love developed, the most daring thing we did was hold hands, with a goodnight kiss. For two years we were inseparable when I was visiting Messingham, always with Jenny tagging along, we visited the fair and the show together, he was always welcome at the house, waiting for me when I arrived. During the day we would go for walks or hang out at the park, in the early evenings - always had to be in by nine p.m. - we gathered around the phone box, (our old red telephone box is still there) were we could dial for free the speaking clock "on the third stroke the time will be -----and ---seconds precisely". When we all had bikes to use, we went on cycle rides down Scotter bottom road for picnics, we'd lay in the sand dunes, sinking into the yielding grains arms entwined, staring at the deep blue sky, it seemed as if we had left the ordinary world altogether, talking about life, hopes and dreamed our dreams. Some weekends when I could not get over to Messingham Michael would cycle over for the day (we were living on Thonock Road, by now I had my own cycle) we'd go further along the road to a suitable spot, we kissed a lot, but never even got warmed up. When we'd moved to Scotter I was unable to go to Messingham as often, we exchanged love letters for a while, but gradually drifted apart. I often wonder were he is now and if he thinks of me, his first innocent love.

On 5th July 1958 I went on my first ever holiday, *and only one other than stays with relatives, until 1963,* with aunt Vi, uncle Bert, Anne, Jenny, and David, staying a week in G8 caravan on Limekiln Lane Camp, Bridlington. The night before I had gone to Messingham on the half past five bus. The day of departure we had to rise and shine at four a.m., leaving Scunthorpe by coach at 5a.m., arriving at destination at five minutes past nine a.m. On our fifty-five mile journey, the furthest I'd ever been. I took my savings of £2. 10s, with half a crown each day to spend, half a crown for postcards, the remainder for presents and ten sticks of rock. Memories are so still so vivid of my holiday, Aunt vi and uncle Bert gave me a terrific time. We had beautiful weather all week, Jenny and I made frequent visits to swim, more accurately romp *I did not learn to swim until 1973* in the sea. We strolled around Sewerby Park seeing wallaby's for the first time, picnicked on the grass, had a game of croquet that cost 6d.before making our weary way back to the caravan.
A visit I still picture in my mind was the 96ft high Flamborough

lighthouse, climbing all 139 spiralling steps. When the guide had explained the workings of the incredibly radiant lamp, he started to say "the quickest way down..." quick as a flash our Ann chipped in "jump", after much laughter the keeper went on to explain he was saying "turn around and go down backwards" it was considered safer. Whilst Uncle Bert fished from the harbour wall, not having much luck, we went for a ride on the trip boat 'Boys Own', with music while you sailed, a boat owned and sailed by local fishermen. The harbour was also visited at night to see the illuminations, with a fish and chip supper, sat on the wall. *Memories not to be forgotten.*

In April 1954 uncle Jeff married Joan Steadman at St. Lawrence's Church Corringham. Dad borrowed his bosses Land Rover so we could attend the wedding. This was a new experience in travel, only room for two in the front, so relegated to the rear, I sat trying to steady myself, with my back to the cab, under a temporary canvas awning placed over the pick-up body designed to keep off the worst of the weather.

They went to live in Aisby a small hamlet with few houses in a little cottage - now called Eversley House, much extended. With a door straight into the kitchen, a walk-in pantry off to the rear and sitting room to the left, two bedrooms if I recall correctly. Dad would drop me off Friday nights, collecting me Sunday (he had by now got an old van). I spent many a weekend with them whilst their only daughter Susan was a toddler. There was a lovely old couple at the end of the road that sold a few things from the room immediately inside the back door. Aunt Joan was always generous with a few pennies for sweets or pop. My favourite bars for many years were Fry's 5 boys, a thin chocolate slab with boys faces imprinted on the squares, or Fry's Crunch, crispies enclosed in chocolate. We - I recall two other girls, formed our own secret society, with no serious purpose and probably short lived, but great fun. Collecting the pop bottle tops which had to be levered off the bottle, we scratched them with our names, the cork lining was carefully prised out intact, then the top placed on the outer side of cardigans, the cork carefully replaced inside the top to hold the 'badge' in place. We also had a password, dens in the hedgerows, coded writing adding to the mystery. Aunt Joan's mum and dad lived in Corringham, where we visited often. I would set off with Susan in the pushchair walking there just over a mile, most of it a long section, stretched ahead like eternity, aunt Joan would leave a little while later on her bicycle passing us about half way. Uncle Jeff would collect us at teatime when he left work.

In my life I have been influenced and encouraged most by my aunt Edna. At only sixteen years of age not long out of school, for four years she'd given up paid employment to look after me.
Aunt Edna, as well as uncle John, have a very special bond with me, giving me unconditional love, even to this day. Throughout those difficult transitional years of childhood to adulthood and beyond, the good times and the bad, watching out for me, always treating me as one of the family.
Sharing   they have seven children of their own, John born 1952, Colin born 1954, Yasmin born 1956, Vanessa born 1958, Lila born 1960, William born 1963, last but not least Gaynor born 1967. I have been privileged to love like brothers and sisters, each of them remaining very special.
My salvation   allowing me a refuge from the hated Bet.
She taught me many things   *to read*: I could read before I went to school, it was one of those things that came easily and the advantages were enormous, a constant and abiding joy we share which has never waned. *to cook*: using a recipe book and gas oven, scones I never managed to get light and fluffy but I was a dab hand at rich jam cake. Mix 8ozs flour and ½ teaspoon salt, rub in 2ozs lard and 2ozs margarine, then stir in 2ozs sugar. Mix to stiff paste with a beaten egg. Divide into two parts, rolling out thinly, both same size. Place one piece on a greased baking sheet, spread with jam. Place the other piece on top and nip together. Bake in a moderately hot oven for about 15-20 minutes. When cool cut into squares. *to iron* (now electric iron with an ironing board): and boy did I iron thereafter, I did it all every weekend, but I'm not complaining I enjoyed it *(then)*, seeing the finished pile all pressed.
Explaining things   At thirteen I knew nothing of the workings of the women's body, or the men's for that matter., I'd gone to the toilet to discover spots of blood on my knickers, having no idea what was happening, I changed and went back out to play. On returning Bet with no explanation, gave me some old white rag to be folded in a pad, held in place with two safety pins, attached to a thin elastic belt around the waist, and matter of factly called it the women's monthly curse, and that was it. She then washed these rags each month to reuse. I hated it, it was cumbersome, messy and I felt unclean. Fortunately when I was next at Aunt Edna's, she gave me a booklet

to explain things. She bought sanitary towels for me whenever I was visiting, the purchasing of which was a furtive business - with no supermarkets to pick them off the shelves, only women shop-keepers would be approached. Childhood had ended.

To believe in myself   A shoulder to cry on when things have gone wrong, loving, giving, keeping me on the straight and narrow we have laughed together, cried together, worked together, she picked me up, dusted me down, then sent me out to start all over again

In September 1954, houses were in short supply; the war had prevented new ones being built. Previously having to live in bedsits and rooms, aunt Edna and uncle John got their first home of their own, on Bankside, Lea Rd. I understand these long, single storey, with high windows in the round roofed, corrugated Nissan huts were relics of an army camp, brought into use to ease the chronic shortage of housing. But they had electricity, which is the first time I came across a home without paraffin lamps. Entry was into a spacious kitchen, a small very cold bathroom to the right-hand side. A large living area with coal fire, directly off to the end three bedrooms. Despite my love of the countryside, and town life being very different I still wanted to spend weekend's and school holidays with them whenever I could. Fleeting thoughts and images return, like when the sun used to become too much for me, then I had to lie down in the cool bedroom. I walked a lot taking young John with Colin in the pram, sometimes to Lea Green one mile each way, passing the houses I'd make up stories for them about the people who lived there, thinking one day I'm going to own a house like that. Other times we'd go in the direction of Lea Road station, where we'd watch the people coming and going imaging them travelling to distant places. I'd tell the lads tales of countries far away, my imagination knew no bounds. I would guess there were about twenty families, although there must have been other girls I only recollect playing boys games, cricket, cowboys and indians; robin hood and his merry men; knights in armour; water pistol fights. The children had toy trucks, trains, tractors, trailers, small chunky things made of wood, we'd take outside into the gritty, sandy area of the communal yard getting very grubby especially when we added water. Aunt Edna never seemed to mind, a bath soon had us clean, smelling nice again ready for bed. When the boys were tucked up, I'd be allowed to watch television, the first - a small screen in a bulky cabinet - I ever saw. On the news that year we saw Roger Bannister become the first man ever to run a mile in less than four minutes, when he broke the record by completing in 3 minutes 59.4 seconds. The only channel was BBC - which then used to stop broadcasting between 6.00 and 7.00pm. On 22nd September 1955 Independent Television arrived. Just half an hour into the evening's programming, a picture of a tube of Gibbs SR toothpaste in a block of ice, became the first advertisement shown. Guinness - a poster ad of a sea-lion balancing a glass of Guinness on its snout - was another of twenty three shown that night promoting products from Cadburys chocolate to Esso petrol.

From 1956 when she got a brand new state of the art council house in Baines Rd. I walked most holidays and week-ends across from school on Fri night, and back on Monday mornings, with my uniform washed and neatly pressed. Three, yes three entry doors, front, side and back, with interior flush doors throughout. The front door seldom used, was at the bottom of the stairs, no old-fashioned stair spindles, neatly boxed in, leading upstairs to a toilet separate to the bathroom, *nice one*, three bedrooms - husband and wife in one, boys in one, girls in one. The side door in constant use, then safe to leave unlocked during the day, opened into a small area we nicknamed the shed, but handy for wet clothes, dirty boots, hanging coats, storage. Straight on was the kitchen with sink-unit, with hot *no less*, and cold water on tap, very small pantry under the stairs, gas cooker, table with the third door leading into a square garden. Apart from hanging washing out, not much use as the rear gardens of the four rows of houses met as a block. Turning back to the front, passing the bottom of the stairs you came to the sitting room. A long room (depth of house) with a nicely tiled fireplace (still no central heating), above the mantle piece hung a bevel-edged mirror with painted flowers, under a tree stood a lady in crinoline dress. Furnished with settee and wooden armed chairs, square dining table with chairs, the television plus radiogram.

Life was busy always something to do, but pleasurable, with a house full (by 1958, two adults, four children plus me when there - the two youngest were born after I had started work) cooking and baking for hungry mouths; cleaning, all those muddy feet; washing, no modern automatic and no tumble dryer in wet weather - clothes line or clothes horse around the fire.
Uncle John had allotments, he had a motorbike and I loved to go

with him, bringing back the home-grown vegetables and fruit. Aunt Edna *unlike Bet* continuing to bottle, bake, make her own jam.

Life wasn't all work and no play. We often went to the playground, as always youngest in pram or pushchair. One was over on Danes Road, (*another coincidence Derek at that time lived in Danes Road, its highly likely we met as Derek as told me he was often over there, favourite places in those days*) the other was at the top of Pingle Hill, although not as well equipped as Richmond Park, with swings, slide and friends still enjoyable places to be.

As the lads got older, with the girls in pushchair we went for long walks down Heapham Road, then just a lane beyond the end of our street, we roamed the fields and by-ways down into the countryside to Park Springs farm, then turning back. As there little legs got stronger we thought nothing of continuing in a huge circle via, Foxby Lane, Middlefield Lane, taking Thurlby Road to return. This was long before the building of Morrisons, Thorndike way and the Park Springs Estate.

One favourite treat was being allowed to have the photos out, I derived great pleasure from seeing Gran, aunts and uncles when they were younger, photos of my great grandma and great grandfather Rudkin whom I never knew, a couple of myself as a toddler, plus the bridesmaid photo.

For relaxation we watched television with absorbing interest, Ward Bond in 'Wagon Train' featured stories of the journeys of a wagon train from Missouri to California through the plains and Rockies; 'Take your Pick' the first Friday night game show, contestants chosen from the audience played for cash prizes, answering quick fired questions without saying the words yes or no; When In 1957 the Russians launched the first satellite called Sputnik, eyes turned to the heavens, as the exploration of space at last seemed possible; On October 11th 1957 the largest radio telescope in the world went into operation at Jodrell Bank. I was extremely proud that my uncle John was one of the contractors that painted the massive bowl, photos show the men appearing no bigger than ants; By 1960 we enjoyed Richard Greene in the adventures of Robin Hood; Juke Box Jury; Blackpool Tower Circus on Saturday night's; Sunday's, Wells Fargo; finishing with the Palladium Show.

For the youngest one's, safe, maternal, homely programmes like Muffin the Mule *not noticing the strings*; Flowerpot men , Bill and Ben; Andy Pandy with his enduringly jerky walk, Teddy and Looby

Loo, at the close singing along "Time to go home, Andy is waving goodbye, goodbye"; Sooty who brings to mind, "I'm sooty the pirate, I fly the Jolly Roger, a-sailing on the sea. Chasing all the other ships, as fierce as fierce can be, make 'em walk the plank and if P.C. Nab should ask you, just tell him it's a prank.

Saturday tea-time absolute silence reined as uncle John checked the television football results given in a monotonous voice against his pools coupon. I selfishly hoped he would never win big money has I'd heard a conversation stating if he won a substantial amount they would emigrate to Australia, I couldn't bare the thought of them all leaving me.

Another love was the 78rpm records (these easily breakable or worse, when the edge got chipped), played on the radiogram, electric record player and radio in a long, low cabinet regarded as a piece of furniture, on lifting the lid half contained the turntable, now records could be loaded four or five at a time held in place with an arm, as one record finished another dropped and played automatic. The other half was storage for the records, the wonderful Paul Robeson; Pat Boones 'April love';, Debbie Reynolds, 'Tammy'; Black Hills of Dakota; We'll Meet Again; A Nightingale Sang In Berkeley Square; The White Cliffs of Dover; all these and more aunt Edna had quite a collection. It later became the craze to mould old records - made from a material called shellac - into any shape required by placing over a heatproof bowl, placed in a warm oven, until soft and pliable many an old record became bowls for fruit. Another use was miniature gardens, insertion in hot water made them bendy, shaping the sides, when cool they turned into a wavy edged pots complete with drainage hole in base.

We all went to Sunday School at St Georges Church, later, John and Colin became choir boys. I took confirmation classes, indicating that I had decided to follow the Christian way, confirming the promises made by my godparents at the time of baptism, and affirming my beliefs in the words of the Apostles' Creed. After confirmation, at All Saints Parish Church on Sunday 6th December 1959, by the Bishop of Grimsby, who placed his hand on my head and prayed that Gods spirit would work in me. I took the bread and wine symbolic of the body and blood of Jesus Christ at my first Holy Communion with our vicar Rev Stanley, on 6th March 1960.

Although my faith has been severely tested, today I am happier alone in prayer than being part of any church. God is everywhere, religion for me is not a question of dutifully attending religious services, it's a secret affair very personal, I do not believe I would be a better person if I attend communion, although occasional attendance gives me confirmation of my beliefs. To this day it is the prop that holds me up when I falter. For me religion is really simple, like doing unto others what you want them to do unto you. With no rules laid down other than we do right, question our conscience. No one structure - no science - no philosophy - no religion has all the answers.

When Gran came to live with us in 1951 uncle Bob was 17yrs old and aunt Annie 18yrs old. Both were at work, Annie worked at the wig factory in Gainsborough, Bob despite Gran leaving, still worked on the farm for James Forrest. I did not enjoy the closeness with this aunt and uncle that I did with the others. I suppose as a 6year old I was probably more of an nuisance to them. I found interaction with aunt Annie difficult. I have always been under the impression that there was no love lost between Dad and his sister, therefore she didn't like me by association. She married around 1955/6, then went to live in a village outside Doncaster, a difficult place to visit, before private motoring. I was totally devastated, because she took Alan with her, I missed him dreadfully, although he did come to stay with us occasionally as he grew older. I only visited her home once with Gran for a couple of hours. Although Alan remained living in Doncaster we became devoted again after we had both married and had our own means of transport.

Uncle Bob married Maureen Roberts in 1956 at Misterton, I stayed with them occasional weekends at Misterton but as explained before the wide spread use of private vehicles, it was more difficult to visit anyone not on a direct bus route.

A short while later they came to live at Wharton. First at the bottom of the hill, then at the top on the outskirts of Blyton. Until we moved to Scotter I could visit regularly in the evenings on my bicycle and always enjoyed doing so.

Will you know and regularly see your aunts, uncles, cousins, have large family gatherings and parties

8. POOR SUBSTITUTE

**Trouble is a tunnel though which we must pass
Not a brick wall against which we have to break our heads.**

During the 1958 school summer holidays, Dad suddenly started to take me on picnics, not the bottle of water with jam butties that Linda and I took to the fields. Not posh enough to own a picnic hamper, our picnic was carried in a shopping basket, hard boiled eggs complete with shell, the dainty sandwich's wrapped in greaseproof paper, with a flask of tea, the whole covered with a checked tea-towel. This women called Bet would come too. Not long after, a combination of factors conspired to change my life and not for the best.
With my uncles and Auntie Annie - who also took Alan with her - now married, leaving home, my whole world crumbled when Gran, getting older, becoming ill, having to take things easier, went to live with Aunt Edna. Bet moved in, my whole existence was threatened.
Life was never the same, I hated her. What's more she had a son a proper mummy's boy. He could not, and never did replace Alan. When dad was not around, she would treat us differently, things like he could have a second biscuit, I could only have one. He could go out to play while I had to do some chore. He was taken to town with her, but "I was old enough to stay behind" this I hated more than anything. I was always on edge until she came back. I was afraid of being on my own. If Linda (my friend) wasn't around to play with, I much preferred to hang around outside, outside I could see what or who was about, thinking (almost certainly mis-guided) I could out-run them if I felt threatened. If I had to stay indoors, bad weather for instance, I would lock the door and sit in the front bedroom window (*never admitting this to her of course*) until I saw the bus. I locked the door very precisely, the key had to be kept turning as far as it would go, I'd read in a book were if the key was straight in the hole, it could be pushed out onto a piece of paper slid under the door, and pulled towards the intruder. All very over-the-top, an overactive mind derived from reading to many stories.
Looking back on it now I was perhaps jealous, I'd got into bed with dad when I was frightened and wanted a cuddle, I'd sat on dads knee at tea time and shared his dinner even though I'd had a dinner at school, now there was someone else in his affections, although I knew my dad still loved me, I had to share him, this women meant

something to him.

When I could not do something for myself, on utterance of "I can't", instead of helping "there's no such word as can't only won't and shan't " was chanted. To this day I fail to see the connection between cannot, - - -will-not - - - shall-not. She was always accusing me of being 'mardy' (miserable). I hated her.

I wanted to be somewhere else, anywhere other than with her, I became rebellious. I hid behind the hedge till the school bus passed, then went inside and said it hadn't come or I must have missed it, I know not why because I certainly did not want to be with her.

They had the front bedroom. I had the back bedroom, I loved this room, except I'd had to share with her son Barry until we moved house. I had a single bed to myself for the first time. Dad shelved the old wardrobe for me; always encouraged to be tidy "a place for everything, everything in its place", methodically I neatly stacked my precious belongings. Clothes folded neatly on the largest shelf. An avid collector from early childhood, I had cardboard, silver paper, acorns, feathers, pebbles anything I thought would be useful bits, saved for making things, nice and tidy in small cardboard boxes along with my drawing book, pencil, crayons. . My comic's, never thrown away and books took pride of place on another shelf in perfect piles. A large cardboard box on the floor contained my tin of marbles, whip and top, rubber balls and rope for skipping.

If bedroom doors were left open the occasional passing car headlights circled the room in a profusion of sinister shadows as the car travelled down the road, further fuel for my fertile imagination.

When it rained I discovered a new sensation, the water could be heard gurgling down the pipes from the gutter into the rainwater butt outside the back door, a very hypnotic sound.

Around this time, gripped by strange insecurities my senses became heightened. I started having dreams, lent on the gate as I became wont to do, waiting for dad to return from the days toil, I would lose myself in daydreams. Worse was the recurring nightmare images of Alan and I out for a walk, Alan lent on a bridge that collapsed, he fell into the raging waters below, I was unable to save him, this haunted me for years.

I also started seeing abstract images in trees or clouds, certain places on the wallpaper patterns would reveal pictures that no one else could see. An ability never lost, makes it easy for me to see the hidden picture within a picture. In my own world I started calling myself Christobel, I scrawled it all over my books. Until the day I left school, this was the beginning of the most unhappiest time of my life, I'm sure a Psychiatrist would have had a field day. I found some relief in being able to spend the weekends and holidays with my beloved Aunt Edna. I have her to thank for saving my sanity.

1958 - 1960
Because we only had two bedrooms, or maybe because they wanted a new start, or maybe even because dad wanted a better job, I don't know, but we were soon on the move. This coincided with my move to Castle Hills School.
Scotter, four miles nearer to Scunthorpe, not a bad place to be. Down Sands Lane, a dusty, rough, bumpy, uneven dirt track - nothings changed - a mile out of the village, one of two pebble dashed seaside chalets, placed in the country - now replaced with a lovely brick built bungalow - but boy, to say the new home was small was an understatement, like a Wendy house. I was never truly happy there, despite having my own bedroom.
When we first arrived it consisted of four, square, empty rooms except the first one which had the one and only fireplace; a door off to the right was to be my bedroom - just big enough to hold the single bed plus a set of drawers; in front of you was a door to the front room to be used as Barry's bedroom; and off that room a further bedroom for Dad and Bet. No hallways, straight from room to room. Dad improved things by building what would now be called a ramshackle lean to. He divided it into a kitchen with a calor gas cooker, big enough to hold table and chairs. Freeing the other one to form a small sitting room, just big enough to hold two arm chairs, and two smaller fireside chairs. He joined his 'building' providing a entrance area to the outside shed containing the "pan", to make it now an inside lavatory -still an earth closet though. I still have nightmares about the whole business, finding it perplexing, frightening and totally unhygienic, the old copper providing a wash and washing area. The whole being an improvement in terms of size, being larger than the existing structure. But did we have problems when it rained; we had our very own shower, also we had to go outside to the standpipe tap shared between the two of us. Dad's skills did not extend to plumbing.
I was the only child in school who had no electricity at home, ours probably one of the last households in Britain to live without electric, today of course homes without electricity are unknown.

The only redeeming feature of this place for me was an even larger, longer garden. Quite a way out of the village, with no one my age nearby, I became solitary and withdrawn, but not unhappy, in my own company. I enjoyed the company of my dog Dad had given me. A gorgeous golden Labrador I'd named Faith, being young and innocent I had so named him for the future. At first light he would be waiting, greeting me with yelps of delight, watching me with bright intense eyes. When I left for school in the morning, it was heartbreaking to see his now miserable head hang rejected, but on return in the evening he would bound up the lane to greet me with frantic wagging tail, running along- side my bicycle, as he did anywhere else we wandered. When I reached the bungalow I speedily leant my cycle against the gate whereupon Faith leapt into my arms, snuggling me into his fur, nuzzling my neck.

At the bottom of the garden was the Beck, bounded by old gnarled trees; I often paddled the clear gurgling, babbling brook carrying my shoes by their laces. About a mile along I found a perfect secret hiding place, were no-one ever went, one tree in particular was overhanging with a hollow middle amidst the branches, a perfect retreat. They say running away, or in my case hiding is never the answer, but I say it can be a perfectly good answer at times. It became my sanctuary hour after hour when at home my dog and I escaped to our spot, I read, wrote, drew, or did my homework with Faith cuddled up close. A dog shares those qualities which are best in one's character, I embraced my true best friend, my soul mate, a patient listener in periods of distress, I whispered my secrets, my hopes and fears. He listened, he sympathized, he did not sit in judgement, he loved me for who I was. We sat drinking in the peace, beauty, whilst observing the wildlife or watched the clouds through clear blue skies, returning when the sun went down. He alone shared my secret ; no one ever found me, no one ever knew where I was.

Looking back it was probably this move that shaped the rest of my life, to make me the shy, loner, nervous, anxious, introverted, reserved person with inferiority complex I became. I found it difficult to make friends in or out of school, it was impossible to interact with the village children whom had all grown up together, gone to the village school together appearing to resent an outsider. In school, groups of friends formed clique's they had known each other most of their life's, also enjoying a town, street, estate life when school was out. At school I was fortunate to form a friendship with Jacky Cook, but living so far apart, lots of things we could not share, like after school hours and holidays. I missed Alan, my oldest friend Linda, with no Gran to take me, going for my stays with cousins at Messingham, and my sweetheart. Perhaps that's why dad had given me my first very own dog, I was more in tune with animals than humans.

For the first time this place had the advantage of being rented, giving dad the chance to seek and secure higher paid, independent employment with the river board. But he missed the independence that farm work had provided, there had been no one breathing down his neck day in day out. Dad always short -tempered, it didn't take long before he had a fight with the foreman and threatened to throw him in the river, thankfully he did not he walked away, never to return.

With no job life became harsh for a while. Rent to find, both heavy smokers, and Bet did not have the skills that Gran had, no well-stocked larder. Dad no longer grew vegetables. More now had to be bought and a weekly shopping trip to town was necessary, but no wages were coming in. Things were getting desperate; Tea had little stamps on the packets, to be stuck on cards, to convert to cash. These were redeemed. Day's now became intolerable, coming to a crunch with no cigarettes and no bread. Dad begged me to take my dog to sell to Mrs. Bayes.

Mrs. Bayes had a shop in the village that could have come straight out of a 'Dickens' novel. As you pushed open the door a bell on bendy metal tinkled above you head. As you descended down the step, hollowed with a century of use, you stepped down into what had once been the front room of the tiniest two up, two down cottage to enter this tiny dim cave of delights. Almost immediately you were confronted by the large mahogany counter, closing off the sales area, leaving the customer - more than two was a crowd - a few square feet of floor space to stand in. As ones eyes became accustomed to the gloom, with little natural light - the tiny paned window screened with more treasures to make the most of every conceivable inch - rows of shelves could be seen sagging beneath tall glass jars with screw top lids, crammed with delights. Boiled sweets like strawberry and cream; rhubarb and custard; toasted mushrooms; pear drops; peppermints; aniseed balls; sugared almonds; black and white striped or mint humbugs; lime drops; cough drops; coconut ice; the list was endless, screamed out to be bought, the jars reached down, scooped out, weighed before placing in white paper bags. Undoubtedly my favourites were sherbet limes, suck them and patience was rewarded when the centre taste of lemon sherbet released fizzing onto your tongue. On higher shelves, temptingly displayed boxes of 'Bertie Bassett' liquorice allsorts; large and fancy boxes, of luxuriant dairy milk or evocative black magic, to be bought and enjoyed as much for the scenic beauty or adorable animals gracing the picture fronts as the chocolates they contained. The counter restricted to a small area of serving space barely seen under an array of boxes containing penny assortments of every conceivable kind, counted out then wrapped in a poke of twisted paper. Trays with slabs of toffee, plain, treacle, nut, cinder toffee, broken up with a little silver hammer. I had always found this a magical place, with a character and atmosphere not found in shops today. From behind a curtain suspended on brass rings, sliding along a thick mahogany rail, Mrs. Bayes a delightful little old lady with grey hair would appear from her back parlour. Mrs. Bayes had taken a shine to my dog, always wanting to buy him. Today she was going to get her wish. I took my much-loved pet for our last walk together, tears streaming down my face, trading him in for a packet of tea, 20 woodbines and 2 bread loaves. As I walked away Faith watched me with piteous eyes that burned into my soul. I walked home in a daze, my heart breaking. I never went in that shop again, and it was to be another sixteen years before I could allow another dog to share my affections.

Along with his lifelong wheeler dealing, Dad ever ingenious erected an extensive series of what could only be described as shacks, *the original re-cycler,* telegraph poles, odd assortment of old doors and windows, wood, wire, tin sheets, if it filled a hole he found a use for it. Over a period of time enclosing the whole, including a self attempt at a wall with breeze blocks bought cheap, into a area larger than our living quarters. Keeping chickens, he tried his hand at making a living from selling eggs at the market; ducks along with geese were bought young, fattened up selling for the Christmas dinner table. He bought a couple of old sows, borrowed a boar to put to them, when the piglets were born fattening them, before taking them back to market. He semi-successfully built up stocks, trading with other small-holders. One day a buyer came, he liked the look of one of the sows and was eager to buy it. Dad was reluctant to complete the deal, as the man a poor payer already owed him some money. Unfortunately within a few days for some reason the sow died over night. Dad rang from the telephone box, the chap who had been interested saying he had decided to sell after all on condition the man brought the money, he duly arrived, paid a deposit and cleared his debt, checked 'his' sow laid bedded in straw in the corner of the sty, left promising to collect paying the balance the next day. Dad had to be on the phone early to inform the poor guy his sow had died overnight. He had took a gamble that paid off, he returned the deposit, but had received his dues, the man never bothered him again. *I wonder why?*

Things were tough but then he had chance to turn what he knew best to his advantage, he became a 'ganger' now a widespread practise, then one of the first in the country. Farmers didn't employ the quantity of full-time manpower any more, so he found farmers that wanted land work doing, negotiated a price, word spread and he became in demand all over Lincolnshire and Westwoodside. He set off in his van Monday to Fridays to pick-up from their own doorsteps and deliver home at the end of the day, ladies who could work between school hours. He paid them a good pre- arranged hourly wage (but rained off, no pay) and pocked the difference.

He had a small band of women that he managed to find work for most of the year, additional labour - often college youths on summer vacation - was engaged as seasonal work necessitated.

You couldn't have too many for Potato picking. Machines had been made to hoover potatoes from the ground, but they were far from dependable, those days there was no reliable substitute for women with a wire basket, moving as fast as possible, bent double, along the seemingly endless rows - the length of the field was divided, according to how many workers were present each day, working in pairs, in measured 'stints', moved across the field as the day progressed. Each round of the spinner turned up freshly spun spuds, when the basket was full, you lugged it over to the sacks placed at intervals, heaved the spuds in, and away again. More labour mostly provided by the farmer, if not, - highly prized tasks usually going to the core workers - weighed and tied the bags before stacking. When the lorry arrived, usually at the end of the day, all hands to the task of loading, for speedy departure to the factories.

Many hands made light work of rhubarbing, singling beet, pulling oats or chopping mangles all involved a person in each row, walking the length of the field. The first three were done at the height of summer, under a blazing sun, the sweltering heat burning shoulders and arms. Under school age children and in school holidays sun-baked children played contentedly. Once, Jacky (about four years old) holding in her hands played with a harvest mouse for a couple of hours, just before home-time it nipped her, in shock she released it, then cried all evening because she'd wanted to take it home.

Sugar beet was planted by machine, at that time quite unable to set one at a time. When at a height of approximately four inches the rows were walked with a hoe, spacing the plants, the theory being you only left one at intervals of a foot apart. Manys the time with a slip of the hoe, the farmer would have had large gaps, as individuals struggled to keep up, mechanical failure taking the blame.

All day walking shoulder to shoulder, making a broad sweep of the current cereal crop, the self-set oats from a previous harvest had to be pulled out, carried to the end of the row then deposited at the headlands to be collected later. A doddle of a job, but resulting in scratched, itching arms.

Inside my head an odd word triggers a rare event, one such, was the time while cutting rhubarb, after pulling the stalks from the ground, the leaves were chopped off leaving them were they fell to be ploughed back into the soil. When arms were full, stacking them carefully in huge boxes, later loaded on lorries for deliverance to factories. A very roguish child had took the petrol cap off, filling the tank with soil. Needless to say the van would not start and we were all stranded until alternative arrangements could be made, a costly repair for Dad.

Jobs using lesser manpower included bringing the hay and straw home to the stackyard. By now modern machinery had replaced the sheaves. The bales, left at intervals around the field were assembled in groups of - perhaps sixteen, four at base by four high with oblong bales. The chosen tractor driver, usually taken in turns - circuited the field, while three to four persons using pitchforks tossed the bales each about maximum weight the average women could lift - to the person responsible for loading - a skilled job, wrongly done the load would not make it back to the farmyard. Driving the tractor back to the farm was not entrusted to me again, after one time turning into the yard too sharply. I upskittled the trailer spilling women and bales - everyone rode the load back - thankfully I broke no bones with only minimum damage but I was not popular. On arrival at the farm unloading began, man-handled again, straw bales were made into large outdoor stacks, hay bales were stored undercover, feeding an elevator aided the highest reaches.

Potato picking was back breaking toil, by the end of the day it was difficult to tell which part of your body ached the most, but riddling potatoes was finger numbing, bone chilling, toe freezing labour, always taking place in the depths of winter. After the earlies, later crops of potatoes were gathered from the fields, to the 'tattie pies'. Tipped making a long tunnel then protected under a mound of earth and straw against the severe winter weather. As the price according to scarcity, rose, the pie was opened. One person scooped the potatoes onto a long, narrow bone shaking wooden and iron contraption worked by a diesel engine. After rising up the rotating iron slatted stairs, the potatoes past over a length of strong squared wire frame, under which was another similar wire frame, moving at cross-purposes. The 'riddle', grading the size - set by the buyer - according to the dimension of squares chosen, those considered too small along with soil fell through the wire. Two to four according to that day's workforce picked off rotten potatoes, clods of earth not shaken through along with any stones, all the while keeping the waste chute area free. The 'perfect' selection now passed into the two awaiting paper sacks. One capable worker could manage both, alternate sacks filling while the full one was taken off and weighed. To complete the job a wire with two loops was placed around the neck of the bag, a plunger twisted the wire tying securely to be finally stacked on pallets. That was the right way to do it, things could go spectacularly wrong. If there was only one available end worker the potatoes coming to quick resulted in the sack being filled, overflowing; the same mountain quickly grew if the sack was not hooked on correctly causing it to cave in. The weight of each sack did not leave much room for the tying, the wire if not twisted just right, often came off as the completed sack was hoisted onto the pallet, if too tight it would snap.

Another winter job - keeping the money coming in - was hedging and dyking. The dykes (ditches) needing to be kept free running, clean of fallen debris, maintained at a certain depth, in order that thawing snow, ice or rainwater drains effectively off the fields, spades were the answer. Likewise hedges were trimmed back with thin bladed knifes on long wooden shafts. Many hands made light work. Today with mechanical technology more readily available moreover affordable, one man and his machine does most of these tasks.

I worked for him in late 1969 until 1972, the wage then was 30s a day. When the sun shone *which seemed most of the time in summer* it was grand, we got as brown as berries, the birds singing with lots of banter and comradeship but my Dad was a hard taskmaster; he always said he couldn't be seen to favour a daughter. Many's the time I walked home, following a quarrel and swore I'd never work for him again... Till next time.

9. CAN I BE OF SERVICE

If there was nothing to strive for,
There would be nothing to win.
If there was nought at the finish,
There'd be no need to begin.

Leaving school, April 1960 at 15 years of age, meant leaving any vestiges of childhood behind, suddenly venturing out into the frightening world of adult life. I did not feel grown up and did not want to leave the security and routine behind.

One day you were at school, then the minute you were legally able to it was out into the world and fend for yourself, earn your keep, enter the daily grind and reality of everyday life you had to grow up quick.

For us 'practical' outcasts, no work experience to pave the way, no forethought, One visit only was made by an employment officer with the sole intention of attaining you a job for a while, no feeling of job being important, after all girls did not need advice on careers, girls gave up jobs on marriage and raised families. That was the way it had always been then, the way it was always going to be.

If only I had been able to see all the choices, If only I'd known there were choices. My life would have taken a different direction at this junction. Being a Pisces, a life on the ocean waves in catering would have appealed, but I knew nothing of opportunities in this field. I had no ambitions which were set in reality, with nobody to help me formulate any. I seem to remember it was more practical to aim at being good rather than imagine riches or fame.

I couldn't work in a factory , being shackled at a bench , deprived of fresh air; I wasn't cut out to be a typist, much needed then before the computer generation. Shop work in the age of £. s. d. (Pounds, Shillings and Pennies) as known before decimalisation was out of the question, No automatic tills or calculators shop work then called for accuracy, speedily.

Give me pen and paper and I could work out the most complicated maths, but my mental arithmetic wasn't up to it. I had limited choice, at this point I was destined for drudgery, a job had to be found. Gran knowing how unhappy I was living at home with the hated Bet's presence had found me a position, she took me for an interview, to become a live-in home help, at Grinley on the Hill. This was a totally different world to ours this house had electricity, was large and stood in equally large gardens. we approached for the first time, from Finkle Street , passing through an arch into the cobbled courtyard. to the left was an old door I later learnt was into a room, then called the scullery, now would be called the utility room, with access to the kitchen. Used mainly for storage of eggs, it had a sink for workmen to wash their hands. Vegetables came in daily with earth on them and all birds were hung then plucked and drawn hares and rabbits skinned and gutted, no place for the squeamish.

directly in front of us was the back door, w e were greeted, by the lady of the house, Mrs Arquile and followed down the hallway, to the sitting room at the front of the house.

Gran and I were sitting on a chunky sofa that devoured me, with two matching armchairs set at right angles to the vast marble fireplace. Not really paying attention, I was hearing snatches of details of my employment "Mr. Arguile is a farmer", "only one child , a daughter, eighteen month old Sarah", after all it wasn't going to make any difference, Gran would decide if this job was suitable, anything was going to be better than being around the hated Bet. I was admiring a little of this beautiful farmhouse, a comfortable, lofty room with the sun streaming in the large bay window. The room was so spacious the sofa didn't need to stand back to the wall, there was room to walk around it. It was the first time I'd been in a house as grand as this.

After being offered the job, we were shown around. It seemed like seventh heaven, never had I seen or entered such a magnificent house.

The imposing staircase with it's mahogany banister swept from the grand front door, twisting up to the bedrooms. On the first small landing, a window overlooked the courtyard to the left was the door to my bedroom, slightly smaller than the other bedrooms, but nevertheless I was delighted with it , larger than I'd been used to, it had a single bed, wardrobe, set of drawers, and was light and airy. I was to be allowed to bring any of my own bit's and pieces, being above the pantry it was quite and looked out over the courtyard. Turning right onto the long landing, a left turn found the bathroom, which led on to the guest bedroom, retracing steps again brought us to the front of the house, approached by a long sweeping drive from hall's road, viewed from the window overlooking the magnificent lawn, surrounded by shrubs and bushes, the right hand side bedroom occupied by my employers and to the left the nursery.

A second staircase (never before encountered) led to two large attics, used for storage.

Retracing our steps , at the bottom of the staircase the opposite side to the sitting room was the formal dining room ,continuing down the hallway, it branched right to a study. To the left of the back door was the huge pantry, although as a child, Gran had a well stocked pantry of jam's and preserved foods, this one had shelves stacked with bought preserves and tinned goods of all descriptions with an enormous bow-topped refrigerator. To the right we now entered the kitchen, with its red tiled floor, containing a solid fuel Aga range used for all cooking, also providing never ending supply of hot water. A white, deep porcelain belfast sink with wooden draining board, which still haunts me as I recall how many hours I stood there washing pots, scrubbing difficult to clean pans. To complete the kitchen was an assortment of pine chairs around a large pine table the top needing scrubbing each day. For the most part I enjoyed my time in this job. Finding the hours were much longer than school, on your feet all day I was extremely tired by the end of the first week The biggest shock was the six a.m. start each day. First job, after being banked down for the night was to rattle and rake the Aga into life. Next prepare the full English breakfast then considered necessary, for Mr. Arquile and myself, taken in the kitchen. Porridge had to be made in a pan - no microwave then - fried bacon or sausage, eggs, with beans or tomatoes, all prepared on the Aga hot plate, followed by toast with marmalade. I then took a tray upstairs to Mrs Arquile. After breakfast the day was then taken up with the housework, ironing, washing up, cleaning, scrubbing -the worst being the scrubbing every day of that kitchen floor. The joyful winters of childhood became depressing winters of adulthood when washing still had to be taken and collected from the clothes, line in the adjoining orchard. The eggs newly laid , often dirty when brought in, had to be washed in icy-cold water then placed in corrugated trays, before being stacked in wooden crates ready for market. The Aga ashes still had to be carried out to the cinder path on frosty mornings. Mrs. Arguile did have some concessions to the early emerging electrical appliances, in the form of the toaster a large cumbersome model , a small Hoover for the carpets from hall to the attic excepting the bathroom, a bulky top-loading washing machine. But maintaining standards also made more work, traycloths were used - resulting in more ironing, butter taken from a large slab nicely curled in dishes, marmalades, jams, pickles etc.

were always taken from jars putting them in small dishes, dining tables were always laid for three courses, sometimes more when we had guests - more washing up. Tomatoes I learnt you never take the stalk from when presenting them on the table.

But for the most part the work wasn't as arduous as previous generations had experienced.

I enjoyed gathering the fruit. Raspberries from the canes, strawberries, grapes from the greenhouse. Apart from preparing breakfast I was not expected to cook, but helped on baking day. Lunch was prepared for 12noon. Tea taken at four o clock, trays carried out to the lawn when weather permitted, or the sitting room when inclement, consisted of sandwiches and dainty cakes presented on a tiered platter. I had to butter bread cut so thin it was almost transparent, with no crusts. Dinner at seven was served in the dining room. Sarah seldom joined her parents in the dining room, eating in the kitchen with me.

Sarah proved to be a delightful child, when house-work was done for the day I took her for long walks, usually down to the canal to watch the narrow boats, meandering along the waterway. Another favourite place was the park, these outings were considered 'time off' even though I was still looking after Sarah. After Sarah's bedtime, with one half day a week were the only time I had to myself.

My wages were £1. 10s a week plus my keep. From the beginning Gran saw to it that I saved. My first big purchase I had to save for, was a "good winter coat". When the necessary funds were accumulated Gran took me to Doncaster to make the purchase. For something then so important, that stayed in my mind, I have no recollection of what it looked like, how much it cost, how long it lasted or what happened to it.

I cycled regularly around Grinley on the Hill, then later Owston Ferry - Gainsborough - Scotter or via Epworth - up the Trent-side - crossing Keadby bridge - continuing down east side of the Trent to Susworth then across to Scotter to visit my Dad. It was the only way to get around, no -one ferried you around by car, buses were expensive on low wages, it was also quicker when buses had to be changed at Gainsborough. I once took my bicycle to the local garage in High Street - now gone - for repairs and that set me back £3 3s a lot of money then on my wages.

An amiable old man was employed as the full-time gardener, he was

small, nearly bent double but his neat gardens with never a weed to be seen, a velvet rich lawn with immaculate stripes were a credit to him, fresh vegetables, fruit and flowers were supplied to the kitchen each day, we sat and chatted over many a cup of tea.
Mrs Arquile was kind to me but, she was my employer, however an old lady that lived on our street just opposite the farm-yard entrance became my friend. She was a dear, who reminded me of my Gran. She was kind and lonely and enjoyed my company. I often spent the time with her, staying overnight with her a couple of times when I was allowed a night off. I was allowed the evenings off when Sarah was in bed and all chores were done. Joyce and Janet had been friends from childhood. They became my friends too. Joyce lived in Laycock Avenue on the far side of the village and Janet lived at the end of Finkle Street. We went to St Peter and St Paul's Church together, badminton together, hung around together, cycle rides together. I was sad when I had to leave them. I never saw Joyce again, but I was very surprised one day to meet up again with Janet when our children went to the same school. But then our lives took a different direction again and I know not where she is these days.

I also joined badminton club, held in the village hall and bought my own racquet with press. Badminton was fun, but one obnoxious boy annoyed me so much that on the way home one evening, after yet again being taunted I swung out with the racquet in its press and hit him good and proper. He never bothered me again, nor, did anyone else, it appears I got a reputation for being able to stick up for myself.
Prior to this I had been in other difficult situations, I had not understood the sexual connotations of. A few weeks earlier I had unwisely accepted an invitation to go to the pictures with one of the farm-workers, a man in his late teens who owned his own car. On the way home he pulled into a farm gateway and tried to get over amorous, thankfully after a lot of hostility along with being in a confined space I managed to persuade him otherwise, but it left me very dis-trusting of men.
When I was fourteen years old I was visiting an aunt when another incident had occurred. I have no wish to cause embarrassment to his family, so I shall decline from saying which one. Suffice it to say the perpetrator knows who he was. For some un-remembered reason no adults were present, all but one of my cousins present decided to go for a walk to the shops, not feeling very well, I did not want to go. It

very soon became apparent why one very brutal, irresponsible cousin had decided to remain, trying to prove his masculinity, he satisfied his sexual gratification at my expense in the most abusive way.

Never to dim from my memory is the enjoyable time I spent in the church choir, the words of the morning service and Holy Communion are engraved on my memory. Perhaps it was music which was at the root of my love of Church. Sweet , clear tenors, rich baritones, deep basses, all blending into one triumphant whole to send the spirit soaring. Apart from my absolute love of singing, raising our voices with stirring hymns "He who would valiant be", "There is a green hill far away", "Jerusalem" or the wondrous "All things bright and beautiful" "23r/d Psalm". There was splendour amid the ceremony as we walked reverently behind the vicar Rev. Ivon Baker fitted out in his ceremonial vestments, leading us surpliced figures to the choir stalls, bowing our heads to the alter on the way in solemn procession. Contrast this with the impishness of exchanging glances with the borstal boys - at that time there was a borstal camp in the village- in the front rows. My friend and I safely practised our flirting, as we sang the hymns, psalms and reponses in unison.

On Rogation Sunday the vicar led the choir in a procession, villagers following, around the parish, halting proceedings periodically so that special prayers could be offered, mainly to ask God's blessing on the harvest. Christmas was a favourite time, when the choir, led by the vicar toured the village singing the well known and loved carols seldom heard today, "Away in a Manger"; "Silent night"; "While Shepherds' Watched Their Flocks by Night"; "God King Wenceslas"; "Once in Royal David's City"; "We Three Kings of Orient Night"; with stops at the large residences for mince-pies and sherry. Christmas 1960 members of the choir performed The Nativity of Christ. The Sacred Cantata composed by Caleb Simper. All members of the choir had individual pieces to sing. Mrs Abbott and Mrs. Stevens , sopranos ; Margaret and Fred, baritones; Mr. Yeoman's, tenor ; Sue, mezzo soprano ; I sang a carol called "The Star of Bethlehem" today my family find it hard to believe.

The church choir and Sunday school went on an annual outing by coach. The year I was there we went to Bridlington. My friends went with their parents, adults went off with family's or in groups, I spent the entire day on my own, quite content wandering the shops, in the café or sat around the harbour watching the boats and the world go by.

Mrs Arquiles mother and father lived in Penistone. Occasionally they came to stay with their daughter, but best of all was when we went to stay with them. I wasn't expected to do as much work when there and had more free time. I met my second boyfriend here, although it never stood a chance. It was mainly a postal romance. We used to write the most romantic letters to each other, until one day he wrote me he'd got a new girlfriend that lived locally. I did not blame him, at the most we'd seen each other half a dozen times. It was a sweet innocent romance while it lasted with a few passionate kisses .
Another feature of life in Grinley was the garden party, held in glorious sunshine, in the grounds of the large house on the corner of Finkle Saint. Opened by a local dignity, with lots of side stalls , bowling etc. A variety of games with prizes from chocolates to bottles of whisky or sherry to tempt people to spend
Before the year was out came the day that Mrs. Arquile called me into the sitting room. "She was very sorry, but I would have to leave. She was expecting another baby and she wanted a qualified nursery nurse."
I wasn't hurt or angry, I was sad to be leaving the people I knew, but just accepted it. I left Beacon View farm for next stage of my life.

The edges of the picture become fuzzy at this stage. I drifted aimlessly into the next job at Owston Ferry, with Doctor O' Reilly his wife and family. I know the house on the edge of the village - Ramor house   - was a sizeable rambling old farmhouse, but remember little else except the granary opposite the back door, with the chickens on the top floor , climbing the well worn outside steps to collect eggs. The reason I recall this, is because I'd never come across a granary before.
In the way the mind has of blocking out the things it doesn't want to remember, my recollections are scanty. As I recall I do not remember having to do much housework, I was primarily employed to look after the five children, often taking them on long walks, going as far as the pumping stations either end of the village, which then was sufficiently far into the countryside, to not feel threatened.
It was here I discovered, often going to sleep with the transistor radio tuned to 208 medium wave band, still playing under the bedcovers, Radio Luxemburg the most successful commercial radio

station in history. The only place you could listen to pop, a welcome alternative to the staid BBC. The pioneering young DJs - Emperor Rosko, David Kid Jenson, Dave Christian - bringing Rock 'n' Roll to Britain's airwaves, even if the signal did fade in and out frustratingly. I can evoke memories of sitting on the Trent-side wall outside the crooked billet Pub drinking newly discovered coke a cola with friends, whose names are forgotten. only once did I cycle home to Scotter a round trip of 40 miles mostly On my night off I stayed a friend, who's name may have been Beckett and her family at their house at the end of the long drive, almost opposite in North St.

I have a hazy notion of suffering poor health, nothing significant springs to mind, I never really settled there. It resulted in me leaving after only a few weeks.

I spent Christmas 1960 with Aunt Edna. The new year brought a new job. Mr. And Mrs. Marris who owned the butchers shop at Blyton. From the road the house resembling the shape of child's first drawings , square with four corner windows, door in middle, still stands, virtually untouched on the outside, except the long closed attached shop now sadly neglected. Throughout my time there , the lovely old couple were very good to me, even when I set the kitchen on fire. One evening I put the chip-pan on the cooker to make myself some chips. Hearing Ken, unexpectedly pip his car hooter, I went outside to speak to him completely forgetting the chip-pan. On being alerted, we managed to put out the resulting fire, but not before considerable damage had been done to the kitchen. Mr. Marris was the shop butcher with Ken the rounds man. He was a butcher who took meat out to housebound housewives in outlying villages. I helped with the house-work, with the making of pork-pies, haslets, sausages all made on the kitchen table . Washing was done every day, with all those, 'bloody' whites.

Unfortunately things do not stay the same. Ken left for another job, to be replaced by my employers son. For reasons unknown at that point, he had persuaded his parents to allow me to accompany him on the rounds. At the start I liked the combination, of being out in the fresh air, villages I'd never visited before, Kirton Lindsey, Broughton, Hibaldstowe, the characters of customers, tea breaks with regulars were many, being allowed to serve. Some old dears were unable to walk far, so I would visit the house, establish what they wanted, collect from the van, returning to put the order their meat safe. Before universal availability of refrigerators, a wooden box, with wire mesh door, placed in the coolest available place was used. Weeks later at the end of the day a stop was made in Scawby woods, an ultimatum given, a little wiser now I chose to walk. Thankfully he did the honourable thing, or was afraid I would expose him, he drove back to the shop. Not feeling able to trust him again, finding it difficult to explain to his parents, I made excuses, I was sorry to leave. When I told dad, he insisted I return home to live. But life with Bet did not improve, after yet another quarrel I walked out and went to live in Gainsborough.

New year 1962, lead to a change of direction, a new start. No more living -in, no more being at others beck and call, fixed hours, nine to five-thirty, hour for dinner. Like all shops then, half-day closing Wednesdays and no opening Sunday's or Bank Holiday's. I got a job where Ron worked, Masons a provision shop in town, with a higher class, clientele. This - busy before supermarkets - old fashioned shop had a central entrance door, flanked by large bay windows, displaying tempting goods, led into a spacious area, on entry the delicious, strange exotic smells assailed the nostrils to entice the buyer. Visiting the grocers is no longer the interesting experience it used to be, with almost everything pre-packed. Two long clear highly polished mahogany counters, stretched at right angles. On the right hand side stood glass-topped tin's of assorted biscuits, with sacks of Demerara sugar, dried peas, rice, oatmeal, dried fruits weighed on large white scales with varying sizes of brass weights. Above sloped a glass fronted display, presenting for your selection bacon, sliced in the required thickness, on a huge machine. Whole round cheeses wrapped in cloth-waxed skins which had to be removed before the cheese could be cut with wire, butter and lard came in large blocks , all cut to size as requested, before being weighed, then packaged in greaseproof paper. This counter was considered dangerous, specialist work, manned by trained staff. Eggs as few or many as needed from carefully layered tiers of moulded cardboard in wooden crates. The walls above waist height lined with glass fronted cupboards, shelves of packet and tinned goods with drawers of sweet smelling spices -- cloves, cinnamon and nutmeg. Lower walls were covered with pleasing patterned tiles, all washed down daily. The tang of sawdust covered the tiled floor, routinely swept and scattered afresh. Hygiene was paramount, the day began and ended with scrubbing, cleaning and polishing. In those days people took their jobs seriously, learning about different teas, countries of origin, making good displays, above all look after customers. The customer approaching the counter, met with smiling "Good Mornings/Afternoon" was served, serve being the operative word, no self - service then, by any one of the smart assistants. Nothing was priced in those days, so you had to remember all the prices, requirements were grouped on the counter, until all requests were met, tallied up mentally then ringing the total and placing the money in the till, giving the customer the correct change. Payment complete further pleasantries exchanged, no stood chatting to fellow assistants whilst serving, purchases were carefully packed in the customers shopping bag - no carrier bags - with cheery goodbyes, see you again. A shop with an atmosphere that today's supermarkets do not have, a more relaxed less frenetic era.

The next room was the stock room, stacked floor to ceiling with boxes, not all cardboard, kept in strict rotation. I have a very clear memory of standing on a broken-opened wooden box, putting a nail through my foot. Another thing that stands out in my mind is a craze for eating cheese and chocolate together. *Not until writing this did I realize it would have been early pregnancy cravings.*

Mrs. Bell was working at Foxby Hill an old people's Hospital, painting a glowing picture, I decided that would be a job better suited to me.

This entailed living -in again, this I did not mind as living at number Eleven had not meant to be forever. Neither had marriage been considered, Ron was just my current boyfriend.

Approached through intricate wrought iron gates, the right-side building was the kitchen of considerable size a wall lined with metallic shelves that held the outsize paraphernalia for baking/cooking on a large scale. Off the corridor was a number of smaller rooms. There were two sisters, both spinsters lived on the premises. Sister Dean who had a crippled leg , was very kindly, she had three of these rooms, one for a bedroom, one for a sitting room, plus a bathroom. Offices occupied the others. Sister Scarborough who could be a right tartare had a small independent bungalow at the rear. Myself, employed as a kitchen help with one other lady completed the resident staff. Our accommodation was the building on the left, not then adjoined or covered in. We had our own bathroom , with a bedroom each, plus a sitting / dining room which had to be shared at mealtimes with any staff on duty . Away to the rear stretched the two wards, male and female regularly forgotten or abandoned by relatives, often the old person was there one day gone the next.

Cook, Mrs. Bell, myself plus the other resident composed the kitchen staff. Early 6a.m. starts were compulsory with three course breakfasts - porridge/cereal, bacon and egg, followed by toast - to prepare for patients plus resident staff. Next came mountains of vegetables to prepare. Endless washing up in large belfast sinks, of returned dirty crockery and cutlery, with huge battered aluminium trays and outsized saucepan that needed scrubbing till hands were sore. Dinner over, trays of sandwiches were prepared, with cakes baked by cook cut into neat slices, all covered awaiting collection for tea time. If you were lucky you had finished by three p.m. but everything had to be spick and span before you could leave. We were allowed access to the kitchen to make as many drinks as we liked, a cup of hot chocolate at bedtime was always sleep inducing after a hard day.

Occasionally when kitchen was well staffed, running smoothly; or nurses were extra busy or short staffed I helped on the wards. I cherished these times away from the drudgery, I helped the incapacitated or frail old folk to drink or feed, I arranged flowers in vases, emptied bed pans, lent an arm to walk along with and was taught how to make beds with hospital corners. Not so satisfactory was the morbid curiosity that led me to the morgue, although no body's were there the day I volunteered to collect something, it was a sinister, eerie, spine-chilling experience I was never keen to repeat.

Uniform consisted of overall, cap and woollen cape - like the nurses, different colour- for outdoors. Wearing the cape gave me a buzz, made me feel proud, special like respected.

My working life *with a wage packet* came to a temporary end here as I left to be a mum.

In an effort to ease our money problems I worked at Wolsey's between 8th January - 8th February 1968. I did not have factory mentality and did not fit in sitting at a sewing machine eight hours a day was boring beyond belief I hated it. My first day got off to a bad start unable to do much I became very sick, developing a violent headache whilst being shown the ropes by a girl called Marilyn. By the end of the first week we had managed 40doz. On my 6th day at the machine I had done 4doz in 2 hours on 63 doz. By the second week . The seventh day brought my first repair, the following day I managed 3 dozen in 1 hr, my total for the week 63 doz. But the week ended on a low note when I twice broke the sewing machine needle, twisting cotton round the inside making rather a mess. Not improved by the 12th day when again I broke the machine, managing only 8 dozen all day. By the 16th day I had to unpick and remake a full tin of 4 doz. Because the stitching was too loose. Just not cut out for this, enough was enough only one option leave.

In October 1968, a single mum, still only twenty three years old, as my world fell apart around me, I wanted something more, I wanted a career. With my experiences at Foxby Hill Hospital still fresh in my mind, I felt I would make a good nurse. I made an appointment to see matron at the John Coupland Hospital. She explained I'd probably make a good caring nurse, but in view of the ages of my girls she did not feel able to take me on. Despite having more than adequate care for my daughters whilst I was at work - their grandma, not then working, only to willing to have them, lived around the corner. *Women with young children were not taken seriously then.*

I struggled to regain control of my life. I fought my demons. Variety is the spice of life they tell me, child minding, delivery driver, taxi driver, Console operator to vegetable section at a supermarket. Attempt at self employment, back to college, I never settled in paid employment until I got into catering in 1975 and the greatest experience, working at Butlins.

10. NO HORSE AND CARRIAGE

**The storms that batter
The first get together
To the last goodbyes.
Absorbing each passing incident
As milestones in a way of life.**

I grew into a young women with flawlessly clear complexion along with I'm told, perfectly shaped legs, I had not blossomed the way most girls my age had, I was flat chested, although not bad looking but far from beautiful. I was bright but reserved although at ease with friends, slim and walked tall. My first serious boyfriend Ken, came from the rough area of town, had learnt a trade, and had money to spend. He was seventeen, tall, slim, well-groomed, styled himself on the late James Dean. He was the exact opposite to me, I was just under 16 years old, shy and naïve. He was street wise, a mean, moody, restless teenager, a bit of a rebel, with an intensity in his eyes which drew me to him. We met when I went to work for Mr. and Mrs. Marris.

The months of our love were hectic. He had an old battered Ford car, where during fumbled sexual exploits in the back seat, I lost my virginity. Only the cost of petrol restricted how far we travelled, my first visit to Clumber Park was in that car. Many hours were spent in Laughton Forrest where romantically Ken would spread a blanket, we'd lay blissfully listening to music blaring from Kens other possession a small battery powered record player and a few 45rpm singles. Our songs were Bobby Vee's "Rubber ball" the flip side being "Take good care of my baby", they were to prove prophetic. It was a carefree, happy, unspoiled, innocent time. Drugs, never figured in our youth, alcohol was expensive, so there was no binge drinking.

I tried drinking once, a rare visit would be made to White Swan public house at Scotter, me being underage we'd lean on the cars chatting while Ken and mates supped a couple of pints of beer, I could not stand the stuff, though I did drink, strictly one per visit, my very first Drambuies. You never saw young girls drunk, it just wasn't done, I look at woman now and am appalled. I was seventeen before I tried my first cigarette, Gran used to tell me when friends offered one, it was cleverer to refuse, when I did try a smoke it was menthol one and I thought they were cool, but I never got the hang of inhaling and gave them up , having no more than a dozen and never touched cigarettes since. Frequently we went to a friends house - this was how and where I met my future husband Ron - or in town to meet up with more of our group. I was always on his arm, I was definitely his girl.

One cold but sunny day in winter 1961 after yet another quarrel with Bet, I set off to take dads dog for a walk. I turned left at the top of the lane with the intention of going towards the River Trent, which always drew me like a magnet. I was so upset, so angry, so irritated, so hurt, I just kept going, Susworth, East Ferry, wherever possible staying on the banks. No real destination in mind at this point sheer desperation drove me on and on, Wildsworth, East Stockwith, came and went, now to far to turn back, I continued on to Walkerith, Morton, finally down Ropery Road, knowing that I would be welcomed at Mrs. Bells, one of my friends home in Gainsborough, I'd often visited, a lady always with a welcoming smile the family were warm, open arms thrown to all coming and going. I had no money in my pocket for the call box, when there was no mobile phones, having embarked on a course of action, I'd walked 23 miles to find refuge. I regret the distress I must have caused dad when he returned from work, not knowing where I was, and the subsequent refusal to return home, but I was never going to be able to live under the same roof as Bet . Eventually tracking me down discussions took place, realising if I'd been dragged back- *and it would have meant dragging me* - I would only have left again - neither did I want to live in a village, so far away from my friends - it was agreed I could stay with Ron's parents.

Life in town was a world away from my childhood, such space I'd had as a child, it had come as a great shock to realize people lived in such small houses with postage stamp back-yards and children played in the ten-foots - the ten foot width between rows of back to back terraced houses.

Noel Street is a small cul de sac off Hotspur Road at the north end of town. Fifteen houses on their side and only twelve on the opposite side of the street, I understand a bomb hit three during the war, the site was occupied by garages. The houses were two up, two down with the benefit of an attic. A three foot wide strip of garden, enclosed by low fence led from the path via the ever open gate *no one could be bothered to close it* through the front door, used as often as the back, directly into the compact living room, with only space for a couple of easy chairs, the china cabinet plus television one either side of the fireplace. Passing the bottom of the stairs, rising between the two rooms, you entered the tiny kitchen with a large heart. The hub of that little house, drop leaf table and chairs on the back wall; the gas cooker, one side of the coal fire a grate with 'modern' tiled surround; in front of which was an old all encompassing settee; a small gas water heater, placed above the white porcelain sink with one cold tap, along with the scrubbed wooden draining board set into a cupboard, occupied the alcove on the other side. The walk-in cupboard size pantry under the stairs, contained the ugly grey gas meter, you fed coins into the slot, turning the bar until each one dropped into the metal box. Much pleasure was had when the gas man cometh emptying, counting the shillings required to pay the bill, returning a share. A treadle sewing machine stood under the window. The back door lead out into the postage stamp size rear yard the bottom of which stood the washhouse, outdoor and only toilet with gate directly into the ten-foot. Upstairs the front bedroom was occupied by Mr. And Mrs. Bell, sister Linda had the back bedroom, now shared with me, Ron and brother Derek slept in the attic. Each room had a tall, narrow sash window , a contraption of pulleys, cords, and weights, four large panes of glass divided by wood, the whole surrounded by wooden frame, the front room window being a bay had a further two panes either side. You quickly learnt to keep your fingers out of the way when opening these windows, as I learnt to my cost, there being nothing to hold them when the cord snapped. To hold an already broken one open it was wedged with a piece of wood. The attic did not receive a lot of daylight, having only a tiny window in the roof with a very stiff old catch.

Those houses although small and cramped were cared for with a passion. They were the people's homes and much loved, pride was taken in appearance, scrubbed and polished inside, the windows sparkled with clean pressed curtains hanging neatly, yards and frontage - even your stretch of the front pavement, likewise the ten-foot - was swept daily, often women leaning on sweeping brushes catching up on the gossip.

Recently on a visit, I was extremely saddened to see what that little street had become. Even though everything was the same, everything had changed. Gates were hanging from broken hinges or missing altogether; paint on doors and window frames peeling, some even boarded up; torn, raggedly curtains hanging, in most instances barely open at grubby windows; guttering hanging precariously from eaves; garden walls dangerously unstable; dogshit, broken glass, littering the lane; weeds sprouting from every orifice; rubbish including an old mattress haphazardly discarded; busted dustbin bags the contents strewn along with pages from newspapers blowing in the wind, circling like demented spirits. Terribly neglected, scruffy, the street that used to be filled with women chattering, children playing, was now deserted, the twitching of curtains, blaring music heard from the end of the street the only clue that people actually inhabited this dump. Nowadays not a problem exclusively of Gainsborough. Two new houses or flats, wretchedly out of place have been built were the garages stood. But why wasn't the whole street modernised, making much needed homes for single people. Gainsborough has a lot of new development taking place, but ignore these once cherished homes.

A totally different lifestyle became the norm, all so different. We still sat to table for meals but with everyone coming and going at different times, although until then I'd never seen a loaf of bread, ready sliced, packed in its own wrapper. She never knew how many friends her children Ron, Derek or Linda would bring home, but whenever and whoever, they were always made welcome she embraced people the same way she embraced cats, if it was meal times even with meagre resources the meal was stretched further. Likewise, happily going to bed without the door ever being locked she was never surprised to find lodgers in the morning.

There was a genuine feeling of care for one another, neighbours really looked out for each other, driven by generosity and humanity. Though all were poor there was a powerful sense of community, neighbours were genuine, honest, working class folks second to none, not simply anonymous figures seen only entering or leaving houses. Gadsby number 13, Parker number 15, indeed the whole neighbourhood, Dixon, Doyles, Warriner, Clayton, Sampson, Golland, of Noel St., Edwardson, Addison, Taylor, Hardy, Atkinson, Wiltshire, Tye, Alcock, Howard, Wood, Crossland, Hines, Stothard of Melrose Rd. just some of the names I recall. Nor were those homes the secured houses of today, doors were never locked day or night, nobody had any money, nobody had anything to steal, in summer doors and windows were left open.

Chatting over garden walls, smiling faces, problems aired and shared, people were seldom judgemental, chatting in the street, at the shops, would wile away the time. If someone in the street died everyone drew their curtains as a mark of respect, if a funeral cortege passed men removed caps, everyone stood quite and motionless with bowed heads.

Within a hundred yard radius, was the pattern of corner shops that once littered England. Shopkeepers knew their customers and welcomed them by name. The co-op branch butchers and groceries in Hotspur road, - currently private houses; Noel street's thriving corner shop, - at present stood empty, forlorn, now enclosed by fencing, if run out of milk for breakfast no problem, pop in in your dressing gown; Collinson bakery, currently undergoing renovation; the candlestick maker, *only joking, no candlestick maker.* Underwoods, - then solely, not even pies - fish and chip shop, now a Chinese takeaway, both in Melrose road; shops you could pop to wearing your apron, children running errands with scribbled shopping lists were welcome. On Ropery road, Tinkers post-office, where you collected your pension or family allowance in cash weekly over the counter - seldom dole money - a well stocked wool shop and the newsagents at 294, men in work clothes called on their way to or from work, the newsagents the only one still going strong.

I found town life to my liking, friends nearby, no waiting for buses, no last bus in early evening, when at Blyton the last bus left Gainsborough at 7.05pm. How well I remember the open air swimming baths at North Warren Rd. Only on scorching hot days did you need to queue at opening time, to enter the cold, cold water - 75 feet by 24 feet, varying in depth from 3 feet to 6 feet - where you could swim all day for 6d. Plunging in after leaving your bits and pieces safely in the sparse changing rooms, - little boxes with short doors, gaps top and bottom - thundering with noise, choked with bodies, we jumped, dived, and bombed, crashing into the water that stung the eyes from chemicals, whilst everyone swam in all directions at once, twisting to avoid collisions.

The State Cinema as well as the Theatre. A free town library where I could lose myself in the reference section, a reading room for daily newspapers, magazines or take home reading, from fiction to biography, along with books embracing the widest variety of subjects. I was in seventh heaven.

Ron's mum became the mum I'd never had, she readily embraced me into the family, a small, roly - poly bundle of laughter, always wore a pinny and headscarf, the triangular fold starting in the nape of the neck, being tied at the top of the head.

In Nottingham she had been a member of a spiritualist church. She owned a crystal ball, all things mystic appealed to her, a love of, she passed to me. She correctly predicted I would have three children even as Ron and I parted. I think there was many things she knew, but would never divulge bad news. She often entertained us by reading tea-leaves or reading the palm of our hands.

Together we whiled away winter evenings playing cards she taught me to play Solo Patience, which I still enjoy, but now the lap-top deals the cards for me.

A saying she oft repeated in a morning "I'll have a lick and promise" translated meant *a lick,* wet flannel round face, with a *promise,* to wash the neck and behind the ears at bedtime.

She adored cats, keeping three or four at a time, it would have been more if her husband had allowed it. She was a sucker for strays or any she thought were strays. The neighbourhood cats never went hungry. They made no demands, they never let her down, she admired the cat's free spirit. She wanted to grow very old and eccentric, surrounded only by her cats - but would still have wanted her children, grandchildren to visit regularly. Sadly it was not to be. I like to think she's now found her idylls. We remained close till the day she died in 1994. I went with my daughters to the funeral, I had lost my adopted mum.

Being a teenager then, to me was a perpetual quest to make reality fit. I still feel that actually to be a member of that first brave new world of teenagers wasn't quite what I kept reading about. The word 'teenager' was coined by Bill Haley and the Comets first of the Rock 'n' Roll stars during a UK tour in February 1957. He revolutionised the music scene with 'Rock around the clock' the film became a smash hit. Before, there had just been girls and boys waiting to be adults, suddenly we were the newest group in the world, once called the war babies, raised on rationing and the welfare state, overnight we were reclassified as that bouncing new modern generation. We were they said, uncouth, rebellious and sex mad, the clothes we wore were loud, and the wild music we listened to on Radio Luxembourg would lead us into 'moral decline'.

The reality of my teenage years was we had the innocent luxury of being far removed from issues of race, thanks to our parents generation we took racial equality for granted. Looking back now I realize how extraordinary lucky we were, there was a better spirit to mankind. No aids to worry about, money was just money, not the all consuming god it has now become, drowning in a materialistic flood. Gun crime, drugs and knife culture was non-existent. We had no interest in what was going on outside our direct line of vision. I would not want to be a teenager today, the constant pressure to pass Sats, we'd never heard of Al Qaeda or New Labour. I'd also hate to have been exposed to today's harsh, judgemental body culture while my own body was still developing, we did not know what size zero was. We were free to experiment with love and ideas and that is I believe, every teenagers right, compared with today there was an extraordinary innocence.

Now there were 'teenagers' with fashions and way of life to match. I along with my friends were to discover and love Rock 'n' Roll the first type of music all our own, entirely for and by young people with our own dances such as jiving and the twist. Then a twenty-one year old Elvis Presley burst into fame with "Heartbreak Hotel". He was hard, fast and sexy with wriggling hips which outraged adults and excited us teenagers all over the world. We had our own cult, own fashions, *never wore jeans or trousers,* language and style. The boys dressed as "Teddy Boys", with their long drape jackets, bootlace ties, thick-soled shoes, along with slicked-back hair, constantly combed in quiffs and DA's whenever they passed a mirror or shop window. We girls wore our hair long in pony-tails, wore short sleeved cotton blouses with very full polka dot, dirndl skirts or flowery paisley over net petticoats dipped in sugared water to make them stiff when dry, which swirled out as you turned, wide belts tight at the waist, complete with flat black pumps with bobby socks, pop-it bead necklaces with clip-on ear-rings. In the fashion stakes along came black and white dog tooth check dresses, fluffy cardigans buttoned up the back, often with stuffed tissue in bra's because of slow developing busts. Suspender belts - a small coin replacing a lost button - with nylon stockings, seams up the back of the leg checked to see if dead in line, a cry of "are my seams straight", expensive to keep replacing often had a dap of nail varnish to stop the runs. Feet squeezed into five or six inch high steel-capped stiletto heels, would not be seen dead in anything else to totter around in. beehive hairdo's, green eye shadow, experimenting with make-up, we looked years older than we were.

We roared in on our motorcycles to the then 'new, all night' transport café at Blyth roundabout - situated opposite today's. Much smaller than the current one, where before the advent of Radio 1 we met to listen to the latest hits on jukeboxes. Another rendezvous was a café - long gone at West Stockwith, opposite the basin, now a cottage, to linger long contented hours, at week-ends often all-night, hanging out, chewing gum, supping - nothing more than coca cola's, playing the pin-ball machines, analysing life, love and the relative merits of various motorbikes whilst listening to the juke box.

First love has a special significance, I was totally besotted, I adored him, worshipped the ground he walked on, I thought Ken felt the same way. Things started to cool, - he had other things on his mind, he felt he could not share with me - days went by when I did not see him, he'd let me down when he'd promised to take me out, but like the words of the song "Rubber Ball", he'd come bouncing back to me. Till the day he could not bounce back so easily he'd been sent to prison. Years later in a certain woman's handbag I was to find six beautifully written love letters to me, that had been withheld. Not receiving the letters I could not write back so Ken had thought I no longer loved him. Likewise I not knowing, eventually believed Ken no longer loved me. Eighteen months later upon release Ken was devastated to find I was married, and told my husband "To Take Good Care Of My Baby".
They say first love seldom lasts but would it have worked if there had been no intervention? no-one knows, but later, the two years he was around we fought with our emotions, and ten years later when we met again we still felt passion. Today I have no knowledge of where he is or what sort of life he has. I know I would not trade places but I will never forget my first true adult love.

To take me out of my despair Linda took me to a Saturday hop - dance - at the Drill Hall, it was a far from pleasurable experience for me, I only went the once. I suffered from extreme apprehension as we were propelled into an already thronging noisy room to join the multitude of girls in their finery, gangs of boys strutting around in their Vaseline sculpted hair. Having grown up in town gone to school with these people, although younger, Linda was far more confident than me. Locating friends she knew, attaching herself to the group, joining conversations came naturally. I sat like a wallflower watching, all evening they criss-crossed the room, exchanging glances and giggles, nothing aroused a young man's interest more than the challenge of a confident girl who for some inexplicable reason did not want to find him the sex symbol of the dance floor. But I, due to intense anxiety was giving off an air of unapproachability. The few times I was asked to dance, I refused, a coy wallflower so nerve racked, so afraid of looking a fool, so out of my depth.

Ron offered me sympathy, became my shoulder to cry on, comforted me, courted me.
Sex education had not been on the syllabus at school or home, no books to glean information from, deep sexual ignorance resulted. No advice had been given about remaining a virgin till marriage, or that sex should only be an important part of marriage. As I grew up I had to learn about dirty old men, wanna' be men, take advantage men, the hard way from experience. As a child at the cinema I had quickly pulled away from the repulsive man, simply because I did not want anyone, let alone a strange man attempting to stroke my hand, or place his arms around me trying to pull me closer. When a cousin had raped me at fourteen, I had resisted his advances because I had not found his presence favourable. He saw me as an easy target when the chance had arisen, without warning he abruptly grabbed me from behind, pining my arms behind my back as he forced me to the floor. I was no match for his size and massive force. He violated the trust his parents and siblings would have expected of him and took advantage of my naiveté. A year later, a very unsophisticated fifteen year old, I had foolishly accepted an offer to go to the cinema. When the farm worker stopped in a lonely place, he "claimed a ride for a ride", a vulgar description I did not understand. I constantly fought off his advances as he tried to put his hands first down my blouse, then up my skirt, all the time muttering "come on you know you want it". At school we had immaturely sniggered but had no real understanding of sexual behaviour.
Ken had taught me emotions, loving reactions to passion lead to arousal, affectionate persuasion to sex. I was so naive I thought or can only assume I thought, pregnancy only resulted from marriage. I knew little or nothing about contraception, believing it was a man's responsibility. So I threw away my youth by finding myself pregnant. Having missed my period I confided in Mum (Bell).
First important step, was to confirm and establish the expected date of arrival. Whenever I had been ill as a child the doctor had visited the house, so having no knowledge of visiting a surgery Mum accompanied me. What a shock to the system, no appointment

system existed, you just went along to the surgery. Upon entering this tiny crowded waiting area you found a hard chair if lucky, taking notice who was already there and who followed you. This memory game had to be played due to no assistance, no device to monitor rotation you just went in to see the doctor as your turn came around. With trepidation I enter the lair trembling with fear of the unknown. Sat behind his desk, he coldly without an ounce of understanding, looked me up and down - nothing like the old family doctor, scribbled his notes, gave me orders to book into the maternity home and condescendingly dismissed me. More afraid than ever I visited the maternity home, conveniently for me in North Marsh Rd. A vaginal examination was given to see how far on you were, not a pleasant experience, unlike nowadays no tour took place, odd visits to the doctors for check-ups and that was the sole anti-natal care received.

There were few options, unmarried mum's were seldom heard of, either an abortion followed, the child was adopted, or raised by another member of the family, so we became engaged, as proposals go it was no 'down on one knee' romantic affair, but I thought I could grow to love him in due course. I started my bottom drawer. Not always a drawer, but in those days, so called as you saved and bought a few things while you were working , ready for your future home. One such item was my first set of sheets, advised to buy unbleached calico for strength and wear, a grotty yellow colour, they were so thick with 'dress' as to be like thin cardboard, in the first frosty weather I washed them, I left them on the line for a couple of days in hope, as it was said, that this would whiten' them. By the time they were wore out they were both soft and white.

At the local register office at Ship Court Gainsborough. on June 16th 1962 I became Mrs. Bell. A married women took the name of her husband, even her Christian name disappeared. Only a handful of close family was present with dad providing sandwiches and cake we enjoyed on the lawn at Scotter on a beautiful sunny afternoon. I made my white dress myself, just below the knees, boat neck, long sleeves with belt over the full skirt gathered at the waist. White court shoes with small heels completed my outfit. My naturally short hair was shoulder length, permed which was usual then. It seemed a sensible step to take, it wasn't the done thing then to live together, you 'made your bed and lay on it'. Not being able to afford our own house, few available to rent, council houses like gold to get, we first lived with Ron's parents. A few weeks later a walk up to see my aunt Edna was about to reveal the long concealed secret. Curiosity got the better of me. I wanted to know what she was like, was I anything like her. Aunt Edna arranged for mother to write to me.

Like most girls then, I gave up work on marriage, making good use of awaiting my confinement by preparing for my coming baby. Knitting matinee jackets, mittens, bonnets, bootees all sets to match. Different patterns but all in white or lemon until after the birth, no pre knowledge of which sex your baby would be, no ultrasound scans. I claimed my maternity allowance, a layette was purchased, consisting of vests, bibs, nightgowns, three of each, one to wear, one to wash and one airing . Only these were worn until baby was a few months old. A pram set, two dozen terry nappies, with three pairs rubber pants. Closer my bag was packed ready, just nightgowns and toiletries. Everything for baby was provided until day of discharge.

I awoke On 2nd December 1962, to find my waters had broken, so Ron being at work, and couldn't leave, customers still needed their bread, my sister in law walked with me around the corner, but was not allowed to stay. Ron would not have been allowed in the delivery room even if he had come home to go with me, they were expected to wait in the corridor. It was a strange day, with strange feelings, not at all how a birth should be. Alone, no-one explained anything and I had seen no books to prepare me. I was put to bed in a side room, suffered the indignity of the perineum being shaved, (it was thought to make the skin cleaner for delivery). Given the far worse enema, a preparation used to empty the lower bowel, given to all women at the start of labour, administered in the belief that it would stimulate contractions, making space for the baby to descend. A nurse checking periodically as my contractions raged, the strength of the pains terrified me. Eventually about 11pm I was wheeled into the delivery ward. I took one look around the room, the walls adorned with glass fronted cabinets, full of strange and weird surgical instruments, and wondered what the hell they were going to do to me. I was petrified, thankfully none were used on me. After being given gas and air which stopped the screams a daughter the image of her father, was born at 3mins. past midnight, weighing 6lbs 3ozs. Sunday' child is "bonny and blithe and good and gay". Next day I was to learn the clocks were all ten minutes fast so really she was actually born on 2nd Dec. Saturdays child "works hard for a living". Minutes after she was born when its all over, its beyond doubt the most amazing sensation as she was placed in my arms to hold, my tiny exquisite daughter, perfect in every way, this little thing I felt a great surge of love for, who stared at me with such trust, a short while later, they whisked her off to the nursery. No father was present. I was transferred to the ward and fell into an exhausted sleep, till woken with a cup of tea at 5.30 a.m. The babies were carried in to mums for feeding, as I attempted to breast feed, I looked around the ward. The whole of maternity was upstairs, a long oblong room, with one large window on the end wall, looking down to the road. Very sparse, between 10 - 14 beds, each with curtains which were seldom closed, a bedside cupboard each but no easy chairs, a stack of hard chairs for visitors, to be stacked again neatly at the end of the allotted hour. There was no-one I knew and all were quite a bit older than me. After feeds babies were always returned to the nursery which was never entered by a mum, dad being allowed a peep at visiting time, strictly adhered to. No-one was allowed out of bed except for going to bathroom, meals were served on a table that straddled the bed, pulled close or pushed to the foot as needed. Mornings were incessant clatter, toiletries, bed-making, cleaning all essential to make the ward look 'right' in time for the duty doctor to make his round. With each mum's own doctor visiting once a week. Afternoons you had to lie down on your stomach in complete silence, window curtains were closed to encourage a nap. Whilst pregnant I developed a craving for picnic bars, munching through a mountain. When I was in the maternity home, the corner shop sent me half a dozen, sadly I was never to eat them, I'd lost the desire for them and never ate another.

Cards were not received and displayed, they were brought to you after returning home, by well wishers come to admire the new baby, always silver being placed in tiny hands. In those days you were confined 10days. How grateful I am things have improved, as I'm sure my Gran would have thought the same, when comparing mine to her confinements.

When you got home reality set in, a routine of night feeds, endless terry towelling nappies to wash then boil, and never ending housework, followed, despite this I enjoyed being at home with my daughter. Women did not even consider going back to work. Everyone knew their role, the housework and children were the women's domain, men never gave a hand, men earned the bread. It must be terribly difficult for today's mothers leaving their children in order to return to work, so much more opportunity, so much more wealthier materially but, are they any happier than we were

Ron now working at Collinson's the bakery at the rear of the shop , had managed to save enough to buy Jacky a new pram as a surprise, I was secretly disappointed, I'd always dreamt of having a large silver cross, besides being terribly expensive this would have been totally unsuitable with space at a premium. The body of the new pram lifted off the wheels to form a carry-cot which was also used as her bed, proving to be much more practical.

Providence saw fit to favour me with a wonderful mother in law, who had a raw deal in life but took it all with cheerfulness. Born in Nottingham, she had two sisters, the older one Annie was a cook at Nottingham and Ada put in a home when they'd lost their mum, while Winnie was still very young, she looked after her dad for many years, then came to live at Gainsborough on marriage. In addition to a difficult husband, she raised three children, nursed Ron's Nana (on his fathers side) who was bedridden. She did the cooking, cleaning, washing for both households which included great uncle Jack, Nana's unmarried brother who lived with her in Melrose Road, The two streets were back to back with the 'ten-foot' between, the two back gates fell directly opposite. As if that wasn't enough no matter how many friends her children brought home, all meals were stretched to include everyone, without a word of complaint, she took it all in her stride. Winnie was a very charitable woman, with patience, love aplenty, that gave all her help, advise, to her new daughter -in - law with a new baby. Later, she was to bring her younger sister out of the home, to live with her, her husband had a stroke, which entailed extra work, along with the eldest sister who was nursed there in her final years.

Jacqueline Ann was christened on 24th February 1963 the 4th generation of living Bell's. In appearance physically like her dad, perhaps a personality trait or two also. I could not help but wonder what the future held for my tiny daughter, our behaviour and actions would certainly affect her for life.

By the end of the year a solution had been found to our overcrowding. Nana used only the front room of her house, with Jack only using the front bedroom. The kitchen and back bedroom were not used. With our new baby daughter these rooms became our new residence, I set about making a home, doing the best I could given the circumstances. Entering the back door, the stairs rose immediately in front of you. Opposite was the door to enter the front room, with a small stretch of blank wall, we purchased from Sills Furnishers on weekly payments, our first piece of furniture. The newest space saving design kitchen cabinet, 6ft. High , 4ft wide. Two door cupboard at the bottom , two glass doors at the top, in the middle being a drop down enamel door that made a table. No refrigerator, it was 1969 before I had one of those. Next wall came the grate the sole form of heating, but the oven made a great place to air clothes and keep baby things warm, turning back under the window was a gas cooker in the corner, a white belfast sink, cold water tap, with a wooden draining board. Over at mum's I used the sewing machine, I made a curtain which I threaded a wire through and hung under the sink to hide the dated old plumbing. Two (not easy) chairs completed our kitchen / sitting room. The bedroom already possessed a double bed, old heavy wardrobe and large deep set of mahogany drawers. We had our few basic bits from my 'bottom drawer' including new cellular blankets, the open-weave said to trap in air to keep you cosy on cooler summer nights and good insulation in winter without adding extra weight. The yards had a narrow path from gate to door, on one side a shed with copper, a coalhouse and outside toilet No bathroom, meant strip washes in front of the fire, hair nights was endless boiled kettles to wash and rinse with jugs of water over the sink.

Washing was done over the road. Mum had the newest, all be it second / third, hand , washer in the shed, carried into the yard for use. A heavy contraption, square body on four legs, no heater, to be filled from the copper. A handle swished the paddles, also hand turning of the rollers on the attached wringer. A tap emptied it, to be filled again with clean water, using a length of hose attached to the cold water tap. Woollens had to be hand washed in the sink, after squeezing as much of the rinsing water out as possible the garment was rolled in a towel, twisted to extract as much moisture as achievable, then dried flat to preserve the shape. Each house was reversed so the two out buildings, backed to each other, likewise your neighbours path adjoined yours separated by a four foot high wall. Above the wall was your drying area. That winter it became impossible to dry clothes outdoors, drying around the fire become a nightmare of steamy rooms as you struggled to get to the bottom of endless nappies, as well as the normal washing. Meagre finances were stretched to buy an electric dryer, this was a 3' by 2' cabinet 4' high with an element in the bottom, clothes were draped over rods hooked in grooves at the top, the lid placed on the top. Running the thing proved so expensive, it was back to the clothes horse round the fire.

Wages were paid in cash, the boss handing over a little brown envelope pay packet on Friday nights. Bank accounts, cheque books, credit cards did not exist for working class people, hire purchase was difficult to obtain and undertaken with great caution so this was bought from Wildbores, arranged entirely between the shop and you, (well the man that was, married women had little rights), were deferred terms was discussed in complete privacy, no hire purchase agreement, just a payment card, pay early the bit of interest added was waived, default a payment the shop reclaimed the item.

A visit was made weekly to the clinic, in my case just around the corner in Woods Terrace. It did not matter to those at the other end of town, walking was the norm. The corrugated roof lean-to just inside the gate, being safely used as a pram park. Inside the prefabricated building, a hot-house in summer, warmed by a huge coke pot-belly stove in winter, was the large room, where most mum's knowing each other, waited their turn with baby talk and gossip while baby was undressed ready for the weigh in, and general development checks. Everyone was made to feel welcome, the health visitors knew everyone by name, trust was built, mums could talk about things they found difficult to express to family or even doctors. One of the small rooms off the main area was used by those who wished to see the doctor, immunisation, hearing and vision checks. On the way out you handed in the coupons you were issued in exchange for free tinned National Dried milk for baby to those unable to breast feed.

I had not made a success of breast feeding so Jackie was fed every four hours, wake them if they were asleep, 'don't - you - dare - touch - them - in - between - times' rule imposed. With only one, straight-sided, octagonal shaped, glass bottle, one feed at a time was mixed carefully with measured level spoonfuls, measured amount of boiling water added, thick rubber teat had to be stretched across neck of bottle then shook to mix. After feeding sterilized ready for next feed. Amounts increased with babies weight. Cooling the contents followed, shook on back of hand to test.

In that extremely desperately cold winter that started on Boxing day

1962 when temperatures plummeted we sat close to the fire, were legs became mottled, shivering every time you had to leave. Recorded as the coldest for 300 years, a two day blizzard swept across southern England and Wales, with the worst snowstorms in England recorded since 1881, the storm left snowdrifts more than 18feet deep. In February 1963 winds reached 119mph, force 8, the snow, freezing fog lay over much of the country for sixty seven days till March 2nd. The night feeds became a nightmare, sod the expense we had to have an electric fire on all night. Cheating with a pre - made bottle, heated resting on the protective wire, turned frequently while changing her nappy, it was a blessing when Jacky slept through the night.

Money was always tight, no garden to grow your own vegetables, no large pantry to store preserves. A walk to the town centre, returning with the pram loaded with fresh produce became a weekly chore. Tuesdays and Saturdays to market for meat, vegetables, cheese, eggs, fruit like gooseberries, apples and rhubarb for pies. Friday night, pay night, round the co-op for basics, tea, sugar, flour, margarine, jam, custard powder, gravy salt, soap, wash powder. Occasional tins, luncheon meat, fruit like peaches, pears or pineapple, cheaper than fresh.

Bread was fetched daily from the bakery, yes I still had to buy it even married to the baker. For emergencies the local shops ran 'tick' - get now pay later . Milk - which froze in the bottle in 1962/63 -was delivered to the doorstep daily, milk checks bought immediately when paid, from the Co-op, left on step for exchange. Coal money for two bags weekly put in tin, touched under no circumstance, till coalman came, along with a bit put by for electric and gas, taken and paid by cash at their respective showrooms in the town when the bill arrived.

Breakfast was now skipped, no time. Dinner was at twelve, faggotts; or thick slices of spam dipped in batter then fried; sometimes a pan of stew, vegetables from the market cheap and plentiful - no pre-washed/packed - with cheap cuts of meat, one pot cooking cheaper on gas too. Sunday dinner was chicken, seldom could afford a joint, vegetables, roast potatoes with Yorkshire pudding. Friday dinner a real luxury with last few pennies, chip shop was comparatively cheap, fish and chips smothered in vinegar, no cooking, straight from wrapping (grease-proof paper , then wrapped in newspaper) no washing up. Bag of chips if things were really tight before wages came home.

Basic staples provided tea-time meals, often bread and jam; eggs, hard-boiled, poached or scrambled on toast, fried in a sandwich; cheese omelette, sandwich, or welsh rarebit - melted on toast. Sunday's a treat, tinned luncheon meat or corned beef , cheap store cupboard standby's, with lettuce and tomatoes, followed by tinned fruit, evaporated milk if the budget had stretched to it, or pie and custard.

No money for nights out now, we had a Philips radio/tape recorder, I was a huge Elvis fan, not having money for the latest records we spent hours making tapes of favourite's from the radio. A bulky thing by today's standards, about the size of the box a new pair of boots come in, weighing a couple of pounds, great excitement could be had, great disappointments too when even the slightest noise was picked up, even when you tried to remain silent the dog barked or some-one knocked at the door. Our still single friends came round in the evenings, sporadically we exchanged visits with married friends who had small children. Drinking strong tea, eating artery clogging fish and chips, chatting about life and the meaning of it, topics of conversation ranged from the latest releases in music and films, or photography, Ron's one luxury, he did not smoke, he'd had his own darkroom in the attic, since bachelor days.

In February 1963 we decided we'd like a place of our own, a bit more privacy. Our one room could be a bit like Paddington station. Visits to chat to nana, sometimes to give her a bit of company, sometimes to escape 'the old man' (father in law), coming and goings of Jack, cries of "turn that music down", "stop that crying baby" (teething).
A furnished rented house was found in Saville street. similar terraced house, but all ours at a price. With rent of £5.5s weekly, this was the most financially difficult period of my life so far. The whole electric, gas and rates was our responsibility. Jacky was growing, needing new clothes, I made her dungarees, cotton dresses, nighties, knitted cardigans, but that still entailed buying wool and material. Ron no longer on the doorstep to come home for dinner wanted pack-up and not just jam sandwiches, petrol had to be found for the motorcycle now used daily. Mum the other end of town. Not owning a washing machine, I had two choices; wash by hand which I did as much as possible, but no good for whites or dirty nappies; or use the new launderette on Trinity street. A shop that had porthole-fronted

washing machines with the addition of coin slots on top. After loading your washing, adding detergent (if not bringing your own, it could be purchased from another machine, dispensed into paper cup for 9d) insert two separate shillings. Twenty minutes later the machine stopped itself, having lathered, rinsed, and swirled around totally mesmerising (this was better than the old washing machine at mum's). The wet items could be transferred to the huge drums that tumbled it for six minutes of drying for 6d. in the slot. Only affordable in times of dire need with long queues on rainy days.

After receiving a letter saying how jobs were easy to come by in Bristol, the wages being far better, Ron decided to take the chance, we scrapped the money together for petrol leaving for the unknown. He resided with mother, quickly finding better paid employment. Painting a rosy picture, before the end of April I had my bag packed with my mine and Jacky's few clothes and was on the way to a different life.
I was to discover a very different environment from where I'd been born and raised. Miles from home, but one I never the less came to love, returning regularly to visit those scenes that became so familiar to me, *all be it now more touristy.*
Mother never drove a car but John and I got on really well he was after all my uncle, when not at work we'd all pile into his car, introducing me to his adopted county. A vast opulent city; magnificent buildings, like the Council House, a long graceful curved building terminating either end in pavilion entrances; the Victoria Rooms, having the appearance of a Greek Temple; compared to the austere high-rise blocks of tower flats; immense luxurious hotels; lavish restaurants; huge department stores with these things called lifts, with attendants in smart uniform that monotonously droned the goods sold as the doors opened at each floor. Unfamiliar citizens of many different nationalities; beggars and meths drinkers on street corners contrasting with the sleek, fashionable, wealthy community; the unbelievable amount of traffic all rushing around, compared to the sedate pace back home. The incredible assault on the ears from street traders, car radios blaring, brakes screeching, police and ambulance sirens.
The thing that was to make the greatest impact was Clifton Suspension Bridge. My first sight of the bridge was breathtaking, this impressive masterpiece, once seen never forgotten, 702 feet span, a spiders web of steel spanning the River Avon, seemed to

float in the sky - 245 feet above high water.

With Blaise Castle Estate within walking distance we spent many happy hours exploring its immense acreage. Walking along the winding carriage drive you approach the house built in 1795-7. A branch of the City Museum with collections illustrating the history of everyday life in the West Country, (a little known fact - seldom available to see, the vaulted wine cellar contained a real horse that had been preserved). Outside in the grounds is the charming thatched Dairy. The castle is a Gothic style folly, situated on the summit of a high plateau on the ramparts of an Iron Age hill fort. In the valley of the 400 acres of woodland by the tiny Hazel Brook is an 18thc. Stratford water Mill, unfortunately the volume of water was rarely sufficient to turn the massive wheel. We scrambled up and descended *often on our back-sides* the steep wooded areas, discovering the Butchers Cave, a grotto where the massive stones of the roof appear like joints of meat; the Robbers Cave; the footprints in an exposed rock of Giant Goram, who reputedly lived here about and whose chair, a crag of rock, may be seen across the valley from Lovers Leap.

Sitting in the splendour of the surrounding landscaped gardens, twelve acres in extent, the fifth oldest zoo in the world, was only a short bus ride away. At the circus, I'd considered the animals as tame, not exactly pets, but not really wild - I remember exactly my first vision of wild animals - the famous family of white tigers, gorillas, polar bears, hippos, long-legged haughty flamingos.

John liked nothing more than the novelty of taking us across the 3,240 feet long Severn Bridge in the evenings after work just to have a pint of beer in Wales.

Living with mother was fraught with problems, we stayed with my newly acquired family until June. when we rented a holiday chalet at Severn Beach. Just a hut really, not big enough to swing the proverbial cat. Entry at the front, by a central door straight into a room, which contained a sofa to make into a bed, the only other furniture a couple of chairs with enamel topped kitchen table. Through a curtain, a narrow kitchen, if that's the right word. Barely a cooker, a tiny calor gas oven below two rings. The sink unit the only cupboard . Some of our happiest times were spent here. We were on our own, with our gorgeous baby daughter, we were a family enjoying life.

Whilst at Severn Beach we went to the picture house, a tin hut,

where for a few pennies you could leave reality behind, dream, plunge into a fantasy world. I watched Cliff Richards "Summer Holiday", thereafter my fantasy was to live on a bus. I had to wait thirty eight years to achieve the next best thing, a campervan.
We did not need to dream. That summer Ron did not work in the conventional sense. We worked the waltzes, and the boating lake for the owners. The beach on our doorstep, lazy days and heady nights, what could be better at that age than being paid, all be it poorly, *our needs were little,* to enjoy ourselves.

Here I regained some of my teenage years, in the name of one of Cliff Richards songs we were the "Young Ones".
Sadly it could not last November came, losing the holidaymakers, bringing danger. The camp-site flooded in winter gales. We left how we arrived, a pram and our clothes.

Ron went back to what he knew, got a job at Langston's bakery, High Wycombe, Bucks, living accommodation provided. Our new home West Wycombe Rd. a very large Victorian house. Using the front door no room for pram (carried up and down stairs every time, thankful to Ron for buying the one with lift off body), the stairs rose straight to the upstairs flat fully furnished. Off the wide landing, large rooms each bigger than the total area we'd so far had to call our own, fitted carpets, large windows, what a size the whole house must have been. Nice bathroom at top of stairs , no shower, but running hot water. Long, covering one wall , tall mahogany wardrobe with enclosed drawers , stood in our bedroom along with matching carved bed. Kitchen with electric cooker, run of cupboards filled with pots and pans, overlooking the side drive. Sitting room with large shabbily comfortable three piece suite placed around the fire, coal to be carried up and ashes down; four dining chairs, drop leaf table I placed in the huge bay window, overlooking the street. The only smaller room Jacky's bedroom, thoughtfully provided us with her first cot and small set of drawers. Such luxury's what more could a girl want. The drawback, Ron had to work nights.
Just a path to the front gate, but at the rear a large lawn, shared with but not used much by those downstairs, the man's name was Don but I have no recollection of his wife's name. Next door lived an Italian family with a boy around Jackie's age, neither spoke the others language, but when we were out in the garden the two of them played happily for hours.

By Christmas I knew I was pregnant again, we came home to Gainsborough to spend a few days of Christmas, and share the good news. Mum had bought Jacky a brown doll that stood as tall as her, Great aunt Annie had sent her a red jacket with matching trousers and hat, knitted in her spare hours.

On new years eve, although afraid of the dark, *alone, I still am*, desperation drove me to put Jackie in her pram, wrapped us both warmly, I walked to the bakery to wish my husband "Happy New Year"
We bought a sewing machine, many hours spent making the growing Jackie new clothes, I even made myself frilly nightdresses. We could also afford the luxury of a playpen to keep Jackie safe from falling down stairs, plus a high chair. This like the playpen was wooden, a remarkable piece of engineering. A tray was brought over the baby's head from the back for meals, firmly enclosing the hungry child. To become a delightful cart the whole chair hinged from the middle, the underside of the base provided coloured wooden balls strung on wire across a tray. Fiercely independent early self-serve meals were quite messy, hit and miss the mouth, seldom liking the food, spills were many, the chair, floor, dish on head, completion meant a strip wash or bath, scrubbing of chair and floor. None of your jars of baby food then, mostly same as us put through a mincer, home-made milk puddings, sandwiches made with cheese triangles or tinned spaghetti in tomato sauce were favourites.
Ron bought our first motorbike and sidecar (He had previously had solo motorbikes). We now had many outings on his days off, often to motorcycle scrambles . My dad visited often, the most miles he had, or was ever going to drive. I shall always remember 3rd May 1964, a marvellous day we all went to Henley, taking a rowing boat on to what to me then , was the vast Thames.
I met Isobel about the same age with baby Paula, at the baby clinic, her husbands name was Michael. We became good friends, some afternoons we met at each others houses, "I'll put the kettle on ", have a natter. We discussed our girls progress, we gossiped, we giggled, we talked nineteen- to- the- dozen. Living about a mile from town centre we walked everywhere we wanted to go , it never occurred to us to get on local buses with prams, even less to use taxi's.
I tried to adjust to living so far away from family. I threw myself into the W.R.V.S (Women's Royal Voluntary Service), at the clinic,

two afternoons a week, serving teas, along with distributing the baby food.

I wanted to have the new baby at home, I did not want to go into a strange hospital. The arrangements were made, the midwife booked I figured it would be nice to have the dad present, Jacky quickly seeing her new-born sister or brother, no scans available to determine the expected sex of your unborn child.

As the day of expected arrival got nearer, I had second thoughts, what if Ron wasn't at home, what if it was in the night, tales of midwifes not being able to reach you in time, how would I manage.

The decision was taken to return to Gainsborough in time for the delivery in the maternity home. On Thursday (child has far to go) 4th June 1964 at 7.30 a.m. I safely delivered our second angelic daughter. Slightly heavier at 7lbs. 4ozs. Waves of adoration washed over me for our adorable, chubby, perfect, contented baby, looking just like her mum. A slight touch of Jaundice, plus an exceptional busy time for births, led to our daughter being baptised, before the following day a number of us being transferred by ambulance to Willingham nursing home. Ron returned to our home and work, we stayed there until the 13th when we were collected by my dad, who drove us home to High Wycombe. I decided there and then no more for me, so I made sure I found out about reliable birth control. I went to the doctor and pleaded with him to prescribe the pill, which served me well until I decided to have one more 15years later, how things had changed, pre-viewings of maternity wards, information and explanations, scans, fathers present , relaxed visiting.

Both my girls were deliberately given what I considered to be ladies names, because that's what I wanted them to become. Caroline *who looked so much like me, was given one of my names,* Lynda *I wanted a girl called Linda since I was a child but having a sister-in-law with the name, I chose it for a second one and changed the spelling*. Boys would have been named Michael and Phillip.

Caroline was a more placid baby, probably due to my greater understanding of a baby's needs. When Jacky had been born it came as a great shock, I'd never had experience of a tiny baby, but I learnt with the aid of her grandma. From her I learnt the practical side, how to recognise and cope with childhood illnesses, along with all the nursery rhymes. One that had both in fits of laughter went

| Knock at the door | (tapped on forehead) |
| Ring the bell | (pulled ears) |

Peep through the keyhole   (ringed eyes with thumb and finger)
Lift up the latch   (lifted noses)
And walk right in   (put a finger in mouth)

From the beginning Jacky adored Caroline, always bending over her to kiss her, always wanting to hold her. Jacky whilst not a noisy baby, just had an inexperienced mum, became the quite, studious, toddler, Caroline grew to be more curious, more mischievous of the two.

Dad visited in early August, after much pleading on his part, I allowed him to take Jackie home with him until the following weekend when we were due to pay a visit to Lincolnshire, but two days later the oil pump on our motorbike ceased it was five weeks, *seemed a lifetime* before we could collect my treasured daughter.
I could not take anymore. The better standard of living could not compensate for being so far from family, or the lonely nights. Always afraid, in the evening I sat in the window, sad and forlorn watching the world go by as I took pleasure in knitting and sewing for my girls. That way I would know if anyone approached the door. I'd brought the cot into our room, when I finally went to bed I took Jackie into our bed with me , thankfully the bedroom door locked. I reasoned no-one could climb in the bedroom window, due to the driveway sloping, the bedroom was three stories high. Fitfully I slept. When dad was staying, the spare bedroom now containing a double bed, he thought the sleeping arrangements were for his benefit. I never let on. Ron thought I would get used to it, he could not understand why I was so depressed, I felt lonelier and more isolated than I'd ever been in my life, living in unfamiliar surroundings, miles from everything I called home.
We returned two months short of a year , September 1964, I was disheartened, older and wiser, my life lay in Lincolnshire. How ironic that seems now.

Chances of a council houses being nil, although we 'put our name down' joining the waiting list, chances of finding a private rented house as likely as flying to the moon. So desperate were we, I even rang James Forrest, who had a cottage stood empty, this man who had played such a large part in my family's life could not find it in his heart to help me. We managed to find a small touring caravan to rent, not far from dad's. Like a yo-yo I lived in big places and little places, this was the worst. Twenty one months I lived a wretched

life first stood in someone's back garden in Sands Lane, Scotter, till May 1965. Then we managed to buy it at an inflated price, to enable us to take it to dad's garden, where things were slightly better. Two adults and two children living, eating, sleeping in five foot wide by 15foot long. The girls never went to bed until we did, no point, they would not have gone to sleep. Nightly the girls bed had to be made from the two seats, now no table. Our bed pulled down from a partition , behind which was The tiniest area, containing a two ring and minute oven. Tiny sink, with one cupboard under for pans. All had to be reversed in the mornings. Everything was repetitive, walks to the shop, were regular, no storage, but not as if I had much else to do. What few clothes we processed had to be crammed into the narrow wall cupboards. No inside toilet, Ron and I had to have strip washes when the girls were asleep, a miniature tin bath for the girls. Seven months all washing , had be done by hand, in buckets of water heated on the calor gas ring, rinsing in cold water, even though winter , wrung out by hand, hung out, left until it dried. At least when we got to dads, bet had a copper and a hand turned wash tub.
A never ending treadmill, with seemingly nothing else in sight , came to an unexpected end quite suddenly. Nearly two years of purgatory ended with, not what you know but who you know, in our case who my dad knew. Not a moment to soon.

Dad had been a gang master since 1958. Farmers could not afford to keep employed the amount of workers needed for some seasonal jobs. Not all farmers had new machinery capable of doing the work of farm labours either. Dad was doing okay, not enough people willing to do land work, meant he was always in demand, at this point he had plenty of work, One evening he was visited by a farmer who wanted his potatoes picking, and he wanted them doing now. Dad was currently engaged by another farmer. More money was offered but dad would not budge. During the conversation the farmer who happened to be a local councillor, ask who was living in the caravan. Dad gave him his answer, stating we were on the list awaiting a council house. The farmer says "you start at my place on Monday morning, and your daughter will have her house in this village within a week". Hands were shook, a gentleman's agreement. Both kept their side of the bargain.

We got the keys to Franklin Rd. within two days, May 1966. Not that it was going to save our marriage. On looking back the damage was done, poverty had come in the window, and love was flying out the door. The women's role was almost totally subservient, women very rarely had control of finances and seldom knew how much husbands earned. I was supposed to have housekeeping money and Ron pay the bills, but often it wasn't forthcoming and we often lived on chips, bags of potatoes provided by Dad. We quarrelled frequently, we were always short of money, two growing children, large rent - wasn't used to this - electric and coal bills to pay, a motorbike that ate money in petrol and spares, always seemed to be broken down, many times stopping Ron from going to work. Two years we struggled to keep a place of our own. Owing rent and hire purchase, we had to get out before it got worse so by July 1967 we headed back to his parents in Noel street .

We had previously been members of the local Hubspinners motorcycle club, so we re-joined, attending other clubs events; dinner dances, 1966 at Corringham village hall, 1968 at Embassy restaurant Gains borough; along with runs out Sundays and summer evenings. We went to weekend Camping Rallies, once we had been to one in Wales whilst Jackie was only a few weeks old. It was bitter, with snow on the ground, she was the only one warm snug in the body of her pram, - which went everywhere in the sidecar - it was so cold when I attempted to crack the eggs for breakfast they were frozen solid in the shells.

For the next thirteen months I did what I'd always done when unhappy I flung myself into something that temporarily takes your mind off the problems. I joined the committee with Ron, attending weekly meetings, represented our club at the A.G.M. of the E.M.C. (governing body of motorcycle sport) at Pier Pavilion Nottingham, attended meetings of L.S.R.A. at Market Rasen. 12th-14th July 1968 we helped to organise the 1st Aegir rally at Beckingham which was a huge success. We'd had a smaller rally in August 1966 at Station road, Knaith, whilst Ron was at work I'd loaded the sidecar with the things needed, i.e. camping equipment, when he unloaded to set up camp, he was in for a surprise, I'd included the mattress, well I intended being comfortable. We chopped trees and bushes down when the club built a trials course at Newton Cliffs, the first trial took place in March 1968. We marshalled road racing at Cadwell Park, In May I helped our club win the ladies darts match 11 - 4 against a team from West Burton Power Station. I wrote letters to company's asking for raffle prizes, addressed hundreds of envelopes to send application forms out to trials competitors, did a weekly press report of events for the Gainsborough News.

Although I enjoyed all of this, I was still trapped in a desperately unhappy marriage, however hard I tried, there are always things that gave cause for a troubled mind, its all to easy to find the imperfections which over time become intolerable. I could not hack it, in the evenings after quarrels I walked miles along the River Trent it drew me like a magnet, the flowing water soothed my troubled soul. In early February I had visited marriage guidance councillor's in Doncaster in an attempt to mend our relationship. I couldn't see a way forward , the damage was done, but still I tried. Then in August, Dad brought me the news that my beloved Gran had died, I was very low in spirit for weeks then the whole thing came to a head. 1st October 1968 it was all over.

I have no bad feelings towards Ron. We had the good times, we had the bad, the ups and downs. He gave me two cherished, treasured daughters.

At that age you think it's the best thing ever but marriage can be very random, involving many variables, throw into this haphazard mix two young people, one vulnerable, emotional insecure, it is hardly surprising when it goes wrong. It's easy to say "If only ---------, then we'd be blissfully happy," but of course life's not like that.

I made my choice in a rush, not stopping to consider whether it's a good long term bet, then had to discover the reality. We lived and struggled through six years two months of hard times, some of it of our own making. We had good times too, life was what you made it. No blame. We grew apart I had to move on, a chapter of my life closed.

11. LOST

No-one chooses who they fall in love with, I never thought when I woke up that morning, that I was going to fall in love at first sight. Much less the consequences it would wrought, and the price I would pay for loving him. 20th September 1968 my whole world tumbled out of control.
Two drivers drove the town buses from Morton - Lea, Lea - Morton every half hour, passing in the town centre. This morning I waited outside the shop like I had done many times, I stepped on the 10.10am , paying my fare, our eyes locked, his smile spoke a thousand words, my heart pounded , spell -bound, unable to speak , we held the gaze for what seemed an eternity. My head spinning, feeling quite faint, I collapsed into a seat. Every time I looked up he was watching me in his mirror, lowering the eyelids, trying to catch my eye again, winking as he did so. For a few moments I stared, mesmerised, anxiously trying to contain any outward hint of excitement. Alighting at the town centre, he ask my name. Saucily I replied "when you tell me yours, I'll tell you mine" before disappearing into the crowds. Without a thought, or was it subconsciously, on completing my shopping, who's bus should I catch home but his. Holding my hand that fraction longer as he gave me my change, with a coy note in the voice he said "Will". Legs like jelly I took a seat, desperately trying to keep my emotions in check. The next time I caught the bus he ask me to stay on the bus to Lea, foolishly I did, there the drivers had a few minutes waiting , to keep to the timetable. Just the two of us alone in the world, we chatted none stop, he was charming, funny, alluring, considerate, his magnetic attraction overwhelmed me. Before the week was out, all hell broke loose, there was vast upheavals. Returning from my friends Val and Keith, Ron having heard rumours, forcibly refused me entry, it tore me apart that he would not let me see my beloved daughters, I had no choice but to return for the night with those friends. The next morning early, I was at the solicitors. Ron could not keep the girls away from me, so that night he had to hand them over and we went to live with Val and Keith . At that point I did not see my marriage as over, I had a husband and two children. If there had been romance in my marriage, if it had been a strong marriage, I am confident it would not have gone any further. Having forced the issue I now just wanted some space, I was angry at the

accusations made. Since teens I'd been happier in the company of men. I had just been playing a game, someone was paying attention to me, making me feel good about myself - for the first time in my life - making me laugh. Some-one was flirting with me, made a fuss of me, made me feel like a woman again, variety along with magic entered my life.

Thereafter I made excuses to myself, reasons to go to town, every day I looked forward to seeing him. Hemlines rocketed and so did the passion. When Will wrapped his arms around me, kissing me, I found myself responding, I could barely think, the seduction continued, the smile, the passionate glance, the affectionate laugh, the tender touch that stirred a sexual passion, we became ever closer, my feelings were changing from friendship to something deeper, I did not want them too, I hadn't planned on falling in love, sense, logic, wisdom, judgement went out the window. I felt sexy. It was exciting, dangerous, I was not a bored housewife anymore, the light remained on twenty four hours a day.

Life became hectic, what a tremendous time we had, as our favourite singers, Leepy Lee and Mary Hopkin sang 'Little Arrows' and 'Those were the days my friend' it seemed as if it would never end.
For two months I accompanied him whilst he was working erratic hours. Apart from driving the town service route, another aspect of his job on a shift pattern, was collecting and returning women from outlying villages, who worked at the chicken factory. Some mornings we had a 5a.m. start, Some days he drove a tanker delivering oil to colliery's, everything was a new experience. Week-ends would be coach day trips. Matlock illuminations was (up to that point) the most marvellous day of my life, we climbed to the top of Abraham heights and made wishes in the wishing well, buying me a commemorative spoon as a keepsake. An evening tour took us to the Lumly arms, I was happier than I'd ever been. At Hull fair, we had a fantastic time, but then the bombshell dropped, he was married, just when I was happier than I'd ever been my world crumbled. The night was so long, I watched the hours go by one after another. My mind was in agony, so tired, I couldn't stand it, I was so scared of myself, I'd never felt like that before. The next day I refused to go with him in the tanker, but in the evening , I relented when he came to take the girls and I to Morton fair. I would no longer accompany him in the tanker although he came down for the

evenings I would suffered terrible mood swings from happiness to sadness within a day. I was frustrated, angry. It ends by being destructive.

On 26th October we went to see Tom Jones in Bradford, come the end of the night I did not want to part, seeking to hold on forever, but knowing he wasn't mine. Every hour without him was unbearable I wanted to be with him 24 hours a day, an impossibility, but it didn't stop me wanting.

He wanted to be with me but could not bear the thought of living without his children. I knew we were close to parting, but I could not just give up. *I have got to be patient , help him, fight it, I can-not give in, I love him too much.* The problem with fire's of passion is, once lit they may burn out of control. It was so intense, so selfish, jealousy wrecked havoc, I could not love him unconditionally.

The girls and I went to Bristol for a few days, my brother was getting married. I missed Will terribly, I wrote to him daily, I felt strange and out of place, very lonely. Will hired a car for the weekend and came down, we returned to Gainsborough early hours of Monday morning, having thoroughly enjoyed the break. The next few days were torture, sometimes he would not take me with him, then he'd collect me expecting me to drop everything, when on town service run, as always he piped his hooter each and every time he passed the house , he'd drop in to see me, but would not discuss things with me. I wanted to hold him close, make all the problems go away. He refused to stay for a meal, I begged him to spent a night with me, all to no avail. loving Will was like a volcano, I felt as if the sun had stopped shining, he said he loved me yet he remained so stubborn. For six weeks I lived in heaven and hell, we had a marvellous time filled with a million good things and a thousand emotions. On November 11th still loving each other, it seemed we had to part, we did not want it to end but I could not share him with some-one else. We said our goodbyes, it was fun while it lasted, now I had to re-build my life again, I had to deal with the pain without anything to anesthetize the grief, a little bit of me died. Why, why did I love him? The heartache was torture, this was the first time I had experienced a broken heart. I didn't ask for this, I didn't go looking for love. The next day when I saw Will in The Coffee Pot, he bought me a coffee, with that self-same heart stopping smile, which always made me melt, he told me how much he was missing me, how he thought of me all the time. Later that night I saw Ron, he asked me to go back. The following night we went to motorcycle club together. I was bored to death, I did not belong any longer. All I could do was think of Will, I loved him and thought of him constantly, every minute of every day. Whatever the future held I knew Ron and I could never make a go of it.

He promised he'd ring. "I love you he'd called" as he reluctantly went back to his bus.

I feel so utterly miserable , I'm bored, unhappy, trapped, helpless, lonely, aching. I have tried everything I can think of, but I want to love all of you, not part of you leading a secret life.

It's stupid being like this, nothing can come of it. Yet I can't help myself. I want to see him again. I need to know. I imagine life with him, life without him. Can you love some-one you hardly know.

Please ring.

If only wishing and wanting would make things happen. I can't get him out of my mind - day or night, remembering the familiarity of our bodies, the ecstasy of our love-making. What am I going to do? I'll end up destroying everything and gaining nothing. I hurt, I can't eat, can't sleep, I can't stop wanting.

Why! Why! Why!

I feel cross, hurt. Trapped in emotions I can't control. I can't get you out of my mind. I wonder what you're doing, if you're thinking of me.

A week later I again ran into Will in the 'Coffee Pot'. I'd missed him more than anyone would ever know furthermore I knew he still loved me or he wouldn't have wanted to go on seeing me. We could not live together and we couldn't live apart , I loved him so very, very much. My emotions played havoc, torturing me, suffering anguish from guilt to euphoria, feeling joy to sorrow, love to hate, uncomprehending the power of love.

Despite everything we clung to the belief that we were meant for each other. So I accepted the situation for what it was, we picked up were we left off, not putting to much pressure on him. Seeing him a little was better than not at all.

We regularly went to the new Chinese restaurant for a meal and he started coming down again for the evenings, but the pressure was to much on 24th November without any tantrums, quarrels or recriminations I walked away, I'd made up my mind to keep out of his way, but invited to the Chinese restaurant five days later we had one last meal together, still professing his love for me, he rationalized he could not walk away from his children. We'd been so happy, I had thought it would last forever. We'd had a deep intense, passionate, amazing love that was too strong, when you love someone that much it was never going to be that easy. The heartbreak continued as I saw Will about town, I knew he still loved me, the way he smiled, that misty look in his eyes, the persuasive voice, the one person I wanted I couldn't have, and I didn't seem able to function without him. Whilst out with friends on Christmas eve seeing him out with his wife, I knew it really was the end. I returned home and completely broke down. I was moody, felt angry, betrayed, he'd abandoned me. His marriage was obviously not one of the best, but he was abiding by it. I wished with all my heart it could be myself who was his wife.

How can I break the hurt that I feel. I know where the heart is concerned every love has a meaning.
But, what can I do? How can I control the love that I feel.
In it's miraculous way, fate brought us together, together we become as one person.
Is nothing going to ease the heartbreak, I'll never love anyone again like I love him.

I felt terrible, sank into depression that destroys everything in its path, I lost interest, I couldn't cope. I suffered mood swings, cried for no apparent reason, lost my appetite, found sleeping difficult, but was always tired. Drained , exhausted......postponing things, washing up got left in the sink, ironing piled high, cleaning undone, dust three inches thick, I only existed to look after my girls.
I missed the joy and passion and richness in my life, there was only pain now, I was being punished for loving him. I loved him more than words can ever say, and in some small way I always would.
I was two completely different people, I had retreated into thinking nothing, feeling nothing. I had an intelligent, rational mind why did I feel this way, my girls my family, my life , was completely at odds with my love for him
My problems began due to a overwhelming intensity of not being able to cope. Sometimes I felt I was going completely mad, I could not understand what was happening to me, why I was behaving this way a feeling of fear gripped me.
As my depression grew my doctor sent me to see a psychiatrist , he wanted me to talk but I did not know how to put what I was feeling into words. He gave me anti-depressant pills, which had no effect at

all on the state of my mind, Disinclined to get up, all they did was substitute my troubles for sleep, only sleep gave me withdrawal from this unendurable world I'd found myself in. I didn't want to be awake, awake meant thinking, only sleep took the pain away, sleep meant delaying a decision.

Depression has no word to describe its full horror, its devastating, evil, mindless, volatile, unforgiving, relentless, despairing, powerful, dominating, suffocating, manipulative thoughts, choking, murderous, horrific, hateful, degrading,

I lost my way, I saw no way out so I withdrew into my own world, became dead and emotionless. I wanted to shut off, forget life and hoped my insurmountable problems would go away - but of course they didn't , they just lay simmering below the surface until I could cope again,

Great wall of concrete crushing me I floundered in the disaster that had become my life. I wanted to be relieved of the responsibility of making decisions, or taking action to help myself.

Lost track of days, sense of time and sense of purpose I did not want to eat, I wanted no complication of thought, It was sunny but I could only feel cold.

I didn't want to see anyone, or anyone to see me, I was completely miserable, My emotions kept overwhelming me, I despised myself, life was like a fog, a surreal nightmare world , a struggle to wake, a struggle to eat.

All the time There was an argument going on inside my head. Inner turmoil gave me no peace, an internal battle to live.

> *I can't go on living like this, unhappiness is like a disease, for weeks on end I haven't lived, I have been existing , no-one understands, I do not expect anyone who hasn't felt like this ever will. People try to sympathise , they say, "Oh things will get better" but they never do. I have been waiting and waiting what seems to be a lifetime, but you can't cure your mind and it is all in the mind, I know this, because I have everything I could wish for to make me happy. We had a nice rented house, nice clothes, I had money in my purse, on the surface, after all the lean years life was seemingly good. But somehow its not what I want, I'd rather be poor and have him, but this can never be. He says he loves me, but he no longer calls. I love him, I love him, I love him. I can't go on like this, there's no future, nothing to look forward to, slowly I am destroying the*

> *love and trust between the girls and I, they are so young they can't understand my moods, why I am so unhappy. Life's so unbearable, so empty. Why can't I be thankful for what I have got, many people have less and find happiness. I think what people will say, they'll think I'm mad, perhaps I am. They'll say she had so much to live for. They would say pull yourself together, but I can't. I have tried to tell them all, but without success, it's not easy to put what you think into words. While I live my heart is broken. Doctors can replace hearts but they can't mend broken ones. All I'd asked of life was for our future to be together.*

I could not find the will to live, but suicide was not an option, throughout all the pain and heartache the one thing that kept me going was my wonderful girls.

I was a nightmare to be around I drifted aimlessly, I inflicted a strain on those around me, I felt a real nuisance, it became impossible to stay at home, I knew I needed to be looked after at that point in my life.

Desperately unhappy, reluctant to face life, to remove myself from a stressful situation, after a two and half hour session with the psychiatrist I was offered a stay in hospital, so I 'voluntarily' entered St. Johns in Lincoln on 18th June 1969. I thought the hospital would be my sanctuary, my protection from reality.

I had never heard of this hospital, I had no way of knowing the imposing , enormous sized building, I was admitted to was a hospital for mental patients, built sometime between the 19th and early 20th centuries set in rambling grounds with locked doors everywhere, this frightened me.

I was escorted to a single, large, long, all female ward. Gloomy - a coat of paint would not have gone amiss - cheerless, with little privacy, beds ranging down each side, only to be occupied if seriously sick or for night-time sleeping, strictly out of bounds during the daytime. Suddenly I was a non person, with no rights. Nurses put on a show of being nice, but underneath the veneer no-one really cared. Patronising, saying little but implying much.

> *I hate it. I hate it. I feel terrible. I want to go home. I hate this place, it's so depressing.*

I hadn't really wanted to go in the first place, but I thought it for the

best if some-one was able to make me feel better able to cope.
I hate it. I hate it. I can't sleep although I'm tired.
Every day was the same, woken at 6.30a.m. to take your temperature, even though you may have had little sleep. An endless routine made to take foul-tasting drugs, eating, sleeping and sitting about. Forced to take mind numbing pills , but didn't explain why, if you refused you were forcibly held down and injected, you felt woozy, frightened unable to think straight. Handed out four times a day, to create a perfect stupor, with no explanation given as to what they were or what they were supposed to do for you, then left sitting dazed, in a chair till the next dose. The constant drone of the television drove me to distraction, meals were awful, cold and tasteless, I did nothing much but cry silently.

You did not know where you were or why, being medicated four times a day, I did not know what I was being given, I guess strong tranquillisers I was dull and listless, a pallor in the spirit, a loss of control, a passive acceptance of fate, a zombie. Wiped away everything, joy as well as pain.

Petty rules abounded, anyone questioning them, let alone disobeying them was in for further 'punishment'. Taking a bath two at a time a nurse must stay in the bathroom. When not confined to bed you were expected to go into the sitting room, joining the deranged patients, sat too institutionalised to be cosy on upright chairs, a few even on the floor, with vacant looks glazing their eyes, rocking, moaning, nobody smiled or spoke. Cups of tea were scarce, only allowed at meal-times. No attention was paid to the neglected, abused, individuals , except to place meals in front of you, dish out the drugs , so you sat still, shut up, didn't give any bother ,obey the rules and you'd get on fine. I cried myself to sleep each night, spending most of the time trying to create an invisible barrier around me to keep other patients at bay , I was not mad, shock and stress had tipped me over the edge, I did not want to be tainted by their insanity. Few of the patients were capable of having a conversation , another girl called Christine arrived a few hours before me, at first she slept a lot, she was very despondent. Shirley was brought in later, she'd taken an overdose - you've got to be desperate to do that. The next day a grandma from Kirton Lindsey arrived, I liked her and we talked a lot, of family's and the old days, but I never ask her what she was doing there, I never pried. Pat arrived later in the week, she was in a bad way, she'd cried for help previously trying to gas herself, then slashed her wrists with a razor blade.

Not wanting to be in the hospital but not at home, nor with friends only with him. We'd been so happy, had so much fun, I thought it would last forever, I was to painfully learn that we all get one love of our life who hurts us.

Real love, like a tender seedling, flourishes in the right soil and right climate. Tender care keeps it healthy, then it can live for as long as life itself. I did not know this then. I could not get him out of my mind. I wondered what he was doing. If he ever thought of me, if he missed me.

Sometimes in my dreams I could even feel his presence, he'd come back, everything would be alright, but when I opened my eyes he wasn't there and never would be again.

On our section were housed patients with a temporary inability to cope with the stress of life, those like me with depression, those who had felt unable to cope and had attempted to take their own life. People in early stages of dementia - not widely talked about then - referred to as senile. Old, confused failing to grasp what was going on in the world around them, put away by family no longer able to cope. Emaciated anorexic's , not wanting to grow up, controlling their lives by trying to keep childhood shapes. Bulimia girls, seeing themselves fatter than they really were, alternately binging and vomiting. Both eating disorders, dieting to excess with a morbid fear of getting fat. There were also the schizophrenic, split personality's, with disturbances in thinking, emotional reactions and odd behaviour like seeing things not really there, some had delusions of a belief in being some-one else. Some hallucinating, with voices in the head, leading to odd behaviour or thoughts. Disordered, muddled thinking led some to engage in outbursts of repeated movement like kleptomania, not pre-planned, not wanting the things collected, no thought given to the consequences. One such person nearly sent us crackers, she kept touching other peoples things, collecting them up onto her locker. She did not see it as stealing, she did not want them and did not know why she did it.

Some were given ECT,- electro convulsive therapy- , taken away, forced to lie on a table, with hands and legs tied down.

A general anaesthetic and a muscle- relaxant drug were given before two padded electrodes were applied to the temple, delivering a controlled electric shock, until a brain seizure occurred. Twitching of the limbs and eyelids followed, making them even more frightened and disorientated , often coming back from 6-12 sessions weeping.

I did not understand depression how could I, I had no experience of this feeling how could I feel so low, floundering in a deep hole with suffocating black clouds overhead, a heavy feeling in my chest weighed me down. I wanted to float like the fluffy white clouds hovering in the blue sky's, as a child, in my own private world, for all eternity, until I could smile again without drowning.
Instead of the period of rest I had been promised , I had to fight the psychiatric system, a loveless environment, that deadens the soul, try's to make you conform, with no encouragement to reclaim your identity.

I try to keep my patience, but if they keep treating me like this I will go insane. My nerves and depression are worse now than when I came in.

At the best of times always treated like prisoners, but one sister was very unpleasant, she treated everyone as though they were insane, she thought no-one knew their own mind. One morning I'd had to ask twice before being allowed to get dressed - that's how petty she could be- another time she refused to let me use the phone. We were ordered around, the place was riddled with unwritten rules and regulations, how you were meant to understand or obey them when you'd never been told was beyond me. For one supposed misdemeanour, speaking up for myself, the psychiatrist was sent for he said "I was being childish, do as I was told". I was locked in a bare room alone until I conformed. Without clothes, a radio or any personal possessions, like I was being punished. It was like a prison cell -- just a steel bed with bars on the window.

I came in with depression, I'll go out a nut-case and not the fruit and nut kind, that's if ever they let me out. Everything is building up and gets on top of me, making me even worse.

When I'd served my sentence, I was allowed to see a different doctor, who returned me to the big ward, given a rare privilege, sanctioned to walk around the grounds.

I want to discharge myself, but if I do I may never recover and if I stay here, well who knows.

How can I break the hurt I feel so often. What can I do, I don't know how to get through my sadness, my pain, my unplaced love, how can I control the love that I feel. I see-saw between emotions, ranging from being the player to being simultaneously in the audience as well .

Eight days later I could not understand the purpose of being in a psychiatric hospital, my mood felt exactly the same. Life was for living not 'getting through' popping 'little miracle pills' wasn't an option. I was not receiving any other treatment, indeed my depression became more intense because I was incarcerated.

I feel so utterly miserable, bored, unhappy, trapped, helpless, lonely, aching. It's stupid being like this, nothing can come of it, yet I can't help myself. I imagine life with him and life without him. If only wishing and wanting would make things happen. I can't get him out of my mind - day or night, what am I going to do. I'll end up destroying everything and gaining nothing. I hurt - I can't stop wanting. Why, why, why. Trapped in emotions I can't control. Six months and I still can't get you out of my mind. I wonder where you are, what you're doing, if you're thinking of me. I thought it would get easier.

Rather than healing tangled thoughts, the lack of compassion for those with troubled minds, led to me discharging myself on 26th June feeling much worse than when I entered the institution. I had realized it was only I who could pull myself from the depth to which I'd sunk. I was not going to let it destroy me.

A part of me had wanted to return home, but a part didn't want to face up to what the future held , I felt weak, I was fragile, vulnerable but life had to go on. I had to help myself.

In the months that followed I discovered my strengths, as well a my weaknesses, a large element of hope and faith remained throughout everything during that difficult time.

I reclaimed my life. The person I had been, got lost, but I couldn't to it for doctors, or anyone I had to do it for me.

The day I walked out of that hospital, I vowed to myself it was the first day of the rest of my life, moreover I wasn't going to waste one minute of it. On the road to recovery I gave it everything I'd got, I threw myself not only into rebuilding my life but making myself a better person. I also vowed to myself one day I'd write a book about my life.

I hated then and still do, housework, shopping, so I did it quickly so I had the rest of my day to myself.

Poor I may be but common I was not, I studied etiquette. I learnt to swim, had driving lessons and passed my driving test. I renewed my interest in all motor sports, show jumping, ice skating,

When you leave school you go on learning, I discovered there is still plenty to be learnt when teachers days are done. I set about educating myself, I made good use of the library, devouring books. I improved my grammar and maths. History came alive when I started with my family , during research I became curious about other events in the time scale. I wanted to know 'What makes us tick', so I studied psychology plus the psychic sensitivity to phenomena outside the range of normal experience, also sociology, studying how people live and organize themselves in society and how that society is changing.

I discovered a talent for house design and would have liked to have taken technical drawing.

A weakness for crosswords began. I became an avid reader of the newspaper daily. Realising it always gives you something to start a conversation with. I began to take an interest in World affairs. On 20th July 1969 I along with half of Britain sat up all night to watch Neil Armstrong an American, first man to step out on the moon, 'taking one small step for man and a giant leap for mankind'.

Always good at figures I was to take my book-keeping exams and would loved to have been an accountant Even with qualifications I was still first and foremost a mum and housewife, women like me did not have careers.

Writing this book has been a difficult emotional journey into what constituents a nervous breakdown a destruction of your rational thinking process, a passing disturbance, a reaction to circumstances, a crisis, poverty, sexual abuse, severe anxiety, tension. There's a million reasons why some-one can't cope with conditions in life at that moment in time, and you feel unable to survive, leading to a distinct social withdrawal.

Few now know I was once chained inside those walls of a broken inner self. There's always a good reason, people break down, it could happen to anyone. Some inmates I was to learn years later had been locked up for a lifetime, institutionalised for no greater sin than having a baby whilst unmarried, banished to the lunatic asylum.

I still faced a long hard battle but gradually the day came when I made friends with myself and my insecurities and took the decision to fight back, regain a hold on my true self, I'd faced my demons, decisions had been made, my emotions had been conquered, My inner strength pulled me through in the end. I always believed he

never really meant to hurt me, he genuinely loved me , yet he was the one person in my life who hurt me the most. I swore no-one would ever break my heart again.
I could live without him at last……..part of me died ….I will never forget the bitter sweetness of loving him.

12. LIFE TOOK ON A WHOLE NEW MEANING.

I vow to thee, my darling
All earthly things above,
Entire and whole and perfect,
The service of my Love.

The Love that asks no question,
The Love that stands the test,
That lays upon the alter
The dearest and the best.

The Love that never falters,
The Love that pays the price.
The Love that makes undaunted,
The final sacrifice.

Afraid of being hurt, emotionally and mentally, in 1977 at my lowest ebb, I met Derek. My whole life was to take on a whole new meaning, I didn't know it then but I found what I'd looked for all my adult life. Convinced that this would bring the happy ending, I went for third time lucky. I came to love the guy.
Why did I love him so much, because he was "my best friend" (Don Williams). We were Soul mates, before him , no other fella had been able to sustain my interest. A love that's wholly and exclusively, a love that knows no bounds, a faithful love, built on trust. Love grows between two people the way a delicate seedling grows under glass, it takes root slowly and develops gradually until it is strong, powerful and firmly established in the soil that suits it best. Real love like the tender seedling, flourishes in the right soil and the right climate. Tender care keeps it healthy, and it can live for as long as life itself . But not every person has the ability to cultivate that love. Love if its to last, needs stimulation. It needs excitement and surprise, constant revitalisation or it can become sterile and die. Additionally a happy stable life, not rich but comfortable. Not all work and no play. He gave me freedom, freedom to choose what I wanted to do and when I wanted to do it. I had time to pursue my interests, my own car to go were I liked, when I liked and enough money to do it with. Happiness at last, until 2013 when my world shattered.

Back in 1977 it was difficult living in a world of couples, so in order to get out and meet people and make friends, I had joined the local group of single parents. We were enjoying an arranged evening of country & western music in the Peacock pub, when in walks this good looking young guy, with an easy outgoing personality. As he passes he says "Hi I'm Derek " "if there was anywhere to sit I'd stop and chat" "sit on my knee" I say . "Better still you sit on my knee " he says. We got on like the proverbial house on fire. He arranged another date and as the saying goes the rest is history, there was a sense of ease between us an instant rapport as though we'd known each other for years.

Although charming on meeting, in the beginning Derek's manner could be off putting to this fragile woman, he had his own views and opinions and wasn't scared to voice them. But as I got to know him, I realised his lack of elegance covered a sensitive heart. On a subsequent visit to the Peacock, he wowed me and the crowd when he took me in his arms and sang Peter Starsted's "Where Did You Go To My Lovely".

We didn't appear to have much in common. Like a true Pisces I had been enjoying boating with new friends when we met, my greatest wish was to own my own narrow boat, spending my life on a slow boat to China, well maybe not China, the canals would be nice. A watery journey the length and breadth of England, but it dropped by the wayside when Derek informed me he didn't like water. Derek's idea of a night out was a game of darts or dominoes down the pub, weekend's entailed a spot of fishing, occasional matches entered.

On the surface we had little in common, we had very different tastes, our interests and hobbies being vastly different, but Derek accepted me for who I am.

Derek enjoyed a joke, loved comedy in all forms, laughed heartily at comedians and comedy shows. I'm told I have no sense of humour, jokes nor comedy shows do nothing for me. I seldom see anything funny in comedians and jokes, but see the funny side of things naturally, in everyday life. Once when seeing Mike Harding live on stage , Derek was creased double with hilarity, I found Derek's antics more amusing than the jokes. I loathe all forms of humour derived from making people look stupid or foolish. (skirt caught in knickers after toilet, no-one tells, just keeps sniggering,) people who play practical jokes on others and make them look idiots.

For one so sporty at school, Diving, athletics and javelin throwing, I found it hard to believe he no longer participated in sport. Derek's mantra was "why run when you can walk, why walk when you can go in the car." Fishing long since abandoned. Derek loved watching most sport, on television, Olympics keep him glued to his seat, thankfully not football. I like watching, show jumping, and all motor sports, we both watched the Grand Prix's. Although never a strong swimmer I have always enjoyed it, Derek only went swimming under protest.

Television has never played a large part in my life, as a child Aunt Vi did not have a television; Aunts Alice, Joan, Edna, Maureen, had television I watched when visiting, mainly evenings, life was to interesting to sit in front of a television. Mum Bell had a television, but I only re-call watching Coronation Street. I did not own a television until 1975. Today we have television in every room but my viewing consists of only about six hours a week, mainly escapism, its never 'on in the background', I prefer peace and quite. Derek was an evening couch potato, he loved the television and videos particularly films, and wildlife programmes.

We both loved Country music, that brought us together, we were not to know then that we'd end up running a successful Country and Western business, but there are music tastes parted company. Derek liked Elton John, the Beatles, Genesis, none of which I can stand, but then he didn't think much of my taste either. Elvis,

I often experience spooky feelings. I have this feeling of affinity with certain places, as if I've been there before.
Sometimes I can be quite logical, sometimes I just can't 'see' it, I just do not get it.
My spelling is good if I'm writing a word, but if someone asks me to spell something, I sometimes can't see it - I have to write it down, likewise when I'm typing and not watching the screen, I can spell even simple words wrong. Presented with a choice of two written words I usually pick the correct spelling. Derek was poor at words, but I could not beat Derek at mental arithmetic, which I have always been poor at, I can not 'see' hold one set of figures in my mind whilst I complete the next stage of the equation. 1 simple 'trick' Derek taught me was (a simple example,) adding say 10 x £39 in your head , 10 x 40 = 400, less 10 x 1 = 10 answer £390, as silly as

234

this sounds , this method had never occurred to me. But give me a pen and paper and I can work out accurately the most complicated sums, hence with credits for book-keeping exams. A have a terrible memory for facts, dates and a right scatter brain with figures. I can't memorise my N. I. No. bank a/c No. own phone No. or postcode, no matter how many times I use them I have to look them up. The same goes for giving directions. If I have been before I can go again or take you without the aid of a map, but I can't 'see' the whole picture or remember street and road names enabling me to direct you. I find it difficult to use some new technology from written instructions, but once shown I'm fine. 21st century left Derek behind, the cash-point even swallowed his card when he tried to use it. I'm the planner, the one who makes everything fit together, from organising holidays, work bookings, to the household.

Derek could only do one thing at a time, a bit of a stick in the mud but not flapped when things aren't right, he didn't like confrontations, had no sense of direction. Ask him were he'd be next week, next year, he'd say oh I don't know. I can multi task- read paper and watch television, or be scanning, sorting and talking on the telephone. I would be bored without a challenge hence so many interests

Derek had no fears, my life has been dominated by fears, snakes by far the worse- wouldn't even touch a picture of one, the dark, heights, being confined-not necessary in small places, loneliness - not to be confused with being alone- I can enjoy my own company as long as others are around, lightening, flying - I have to grit my teeth, clench my fists and bare it - my desire to go abroad is proving greater than my fear. - irrational more relevant ones would be electric, cars and guns. But not afraid of spiders nor water. I'm also afraid of being hurt, emotionally, physically, mentally. I hurt easily - a snub, a wrong word, being laughed at. Fear of losing loved ones or being involved in an accident or struck by lightening haunts me. As a teenager I was never afraid of accidents on motor-cycles, even partaking in racing- a well known saying in our circle was "only the good die young"

I think Derek was basically introvert who turned extrovert to mask, hide behind, I have always been extremely shy, I was never very confident, I always viewed myself as rather plain

I lack confidence, I'm always wondering if people, friends really like me, these days I can cope on a one to one relationship, but in a crowd I prefer to melt into the background. I'll creep into a room full of strangers hoping I'm not noticed Derek would walk in announcing his presence to all and sundry, everyone knew when he'd arrived. But I like being the centre of attention at our family gatherings. I want to be first there, Derek hated being first person to arrive anywhere, he always wanted to make the grand entrance. I hate being late anywhere - a bus, train, appointment, I'd rather wait around than be in a rush at last minute. At a party some-one has to be first there. Derek was so laid back, one of life's characters, life and soul of parties, not short on confidence, a big head. I used to have a nasty temper, but seldom lose it nowadays, I can argue if I think I'm right and won't give up until I can prove the point, but if proven wrong will apologize, Derek would not back down, would convince you, you are wrong. Formidable, dependable my rock, but also my spark plug. He was the easiest person in the world for me to live with, because he knew me so well, if it looked like a quarrel brewing, he'd walk away, not that I always let him, little wasn't in D's vocabulary.

I look for spirit, honesty and reliability in other people, and feel an important quality is consideration for others.

I take great care of my belongings, I'm neat, methodical. Protect things i.e. fold packets biscuits, cakes down to save going soft.

Planning , designing houses, , became a way of life, a challenge, something I could do, wanted to do and was good at, and when the first one sold, it became obvious it was profitable too. I found my niche, I'd proved I was clever , I wasn't a write off. As a child I was always drawing, houses and at school I would have liked to have taken technical drawing, but in those days, girls didn't take subjects like that, it was men's work.

As the children grew up we lived a dream life in the country, we lived along-side the Chesterfield Canal. I was once asked, "how come you're living in this god forsaken place?" I looked all around at the lush fields and majestic trees and replied "just lucky I guess". We revelled in the freedom of the countryside.

We 'messed about on the river', money was always tight , we did everything on a shoestring budget, but we worked hard and played hard. Grass track cars racing, barn dances, cinema and theatre, clay shooting, ice skating, gliding, bowling, motor club, dog racing, guider, zoo's, castles, garden fest. And flower shows, theme parks, museums, photography, fishing, seaside it seems so remote as to be almost unreal now, yet at the time it was all, so incredibly hectic. We had dogs, cats, ponies, motorbikes, chickens, pigeons, chipmunks, parrot,

My greatest love is travel and it was an uphill struggle converting Derek who'd never been on holiday until he met me. I'm not cut out to be tied in one place for long, from choice I would live like I believe my ancestors lived, a gypsy, travel the highways and byways of England for ever and a day. Totally free from worry and stress.
As a child I only had two holidays and the only day visits were to Cleethorpes, but boy did I make up for it when I had my children. We've extensively visited England, we've camped, boating on the Thames, we've been to Theme Parks, Zoo's, Festivals, ah, magic.
I could write a dozen travel books and never run out of subjects.
If I could I would take (a long) time out to travel Ireland (which I believe is my spiritual home) with a horse drawn caravan, would be my first choice Then there's Venice, Italy, America, Canada, Alaska, I could go on .

Perhaps I would have made a great actress, life's a drama, in acting I loved being able to be anyone but myself, a mask.
But my role in life was destined to be, The Best Mum and Nana, I hope I managed it.

Derek when not at work, weekends, holidays, always helped with housework and loved cooking. Although his tastes in food were conservative, dinner meant, meat, potatoes, vegetables and gravy, he would make do with fish fingers and chips, or bangers and mash. Pushed he'd have a curry, but unlike me, unadventurous in food. Always flexible with mealtimes, Sunday dinner often came on Monday, …..Thursday….. Sunday could be eggs on toast for all he cared. The one thing we insist on was sitting to the table, all through raising our family we have all sat together at the table for mealtimes, the family that eats together, stays together.

Our priorities were comparable, a devoted love of family, we generally liked the same people, a love of sunshine and the outdoor life, views on current affair's, a desire to work hard for the riches of life. Every available moment was spent outdoors, even ironing was done outside in summer.

Weather permitting we'd take breakfast on the patio, and there's nothing we liked better than having a barbecue with all the family around to enjoy it. We had a family joke, if we light the 'barbie' it's smelt by each member of the family, drawing them magnetically.

Derek would have loved to dance more, he had no inhibitions and would get up and have a go, I would have loved to, but have no confidence .
When we had a meal out together, we still had plenty to say to each other, and never sat in silence, which is often the fate of married couples.
I like to be organized it maximises time, I think ahead, make lists. Crossing out gives sense of achievement.
I hate housework, there's so much more I'd rather be doing. That doesn't mean to say the house is like a tip, it's got to be done so the sooner you start the quicker you can go on to other things. Its just a matter of being organised, doing just enough to keep up appearances, somewhere between a home and showcase. The secret is to stay on top of it, I'm fairly organised person, having a place for everything and everything in its place. Lots of cupboards, shelves, hooks to put things away helps here. A quick hoover through in a morning, a flick with the duster, load the dishwasher, plump the cushions, empty waste-paper bins, make the beds (duvets were one of the best inventions), lick a cloth around the bathroom. Thanks to technology and affluence undreamed of, we now live in comparative luxury. Do one room each month thoroughly on a rota and bulk shop monthly. Only buy non-iron fabrics that go in the washing machine. Teach tidiness from an early age.

We had our ups and downs, life together has not been easy, I'm pig headed, so we locked horns many a time, we always resolved our differences in the end, we kept talking, although Derek would say I talked he listened but we stuck together and built a wholesome, contented family life.
What kept us together, a degree of mutual commitment and trust. We were comfortable with each , but not bored. We enjoyed are own space and interests , yet enjoyed time together. We agreed on most of the important issues of life, and where we did not agree we compromised. Our common interests outweighed our interesting differences.
Our mixture of love and friendship grew stronger day by day. We

made mistakes, but even the strains did not break our bond of love and affection.

I made my choices, sure I made my mistakes, but I lived my life with NO REGRETS - NO REGRETS what is both futile and unproductive is to go through life wondering what would have happened "if only I had --------- " WHAT WILL BE WILL BE.

Together we raised two beloved daughters from the ages of 13years and 15years. After having an ectopic in 1972 the chances of another pregnancy was about a million to one, so when Clair was born in 1979 our joy knew no bounds. I was afraid of something happening to spoil our happiness, no-one could be that blissful. We were together 35yrs. Having many, many happy hours and holidays with our three children, four grand children, looking forward to many more with our newest grand-children and great grand-children but sadly it was not to be.
Derek Malcolm Farmery 1951 - 2013

Those we love don't go away,
They walk beside us every day.
Unseen, unheard, but always near,
still loved, still missed and very dear

Thank God for a wonderful life.
Yesterday, Today, Tomorrow, Forever

Like all good books when one chapter ends another begins.